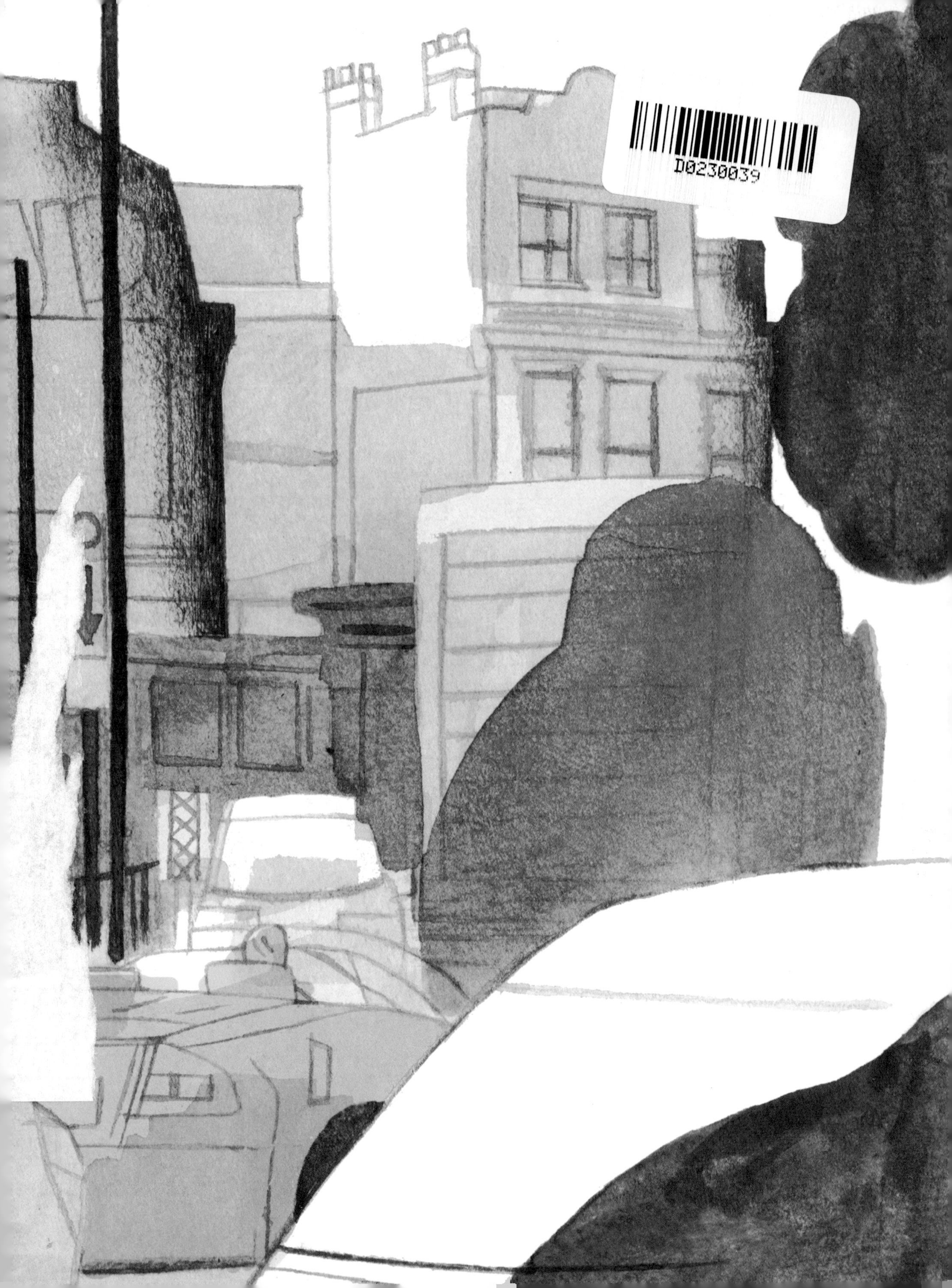

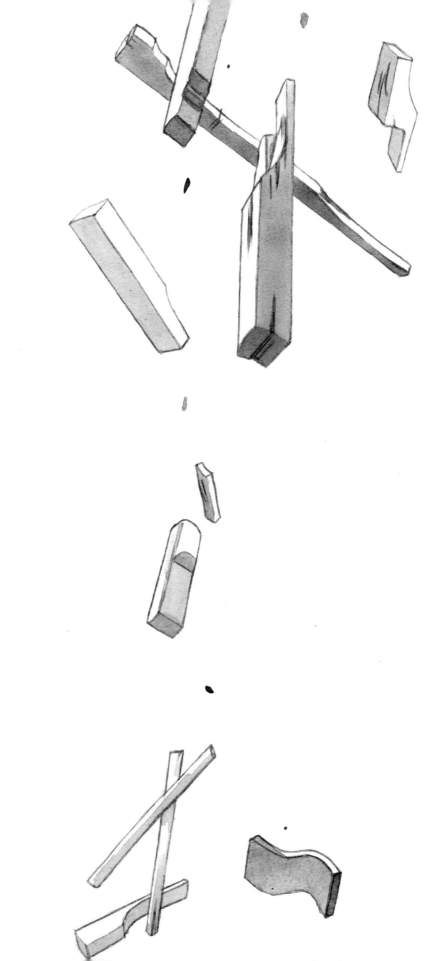

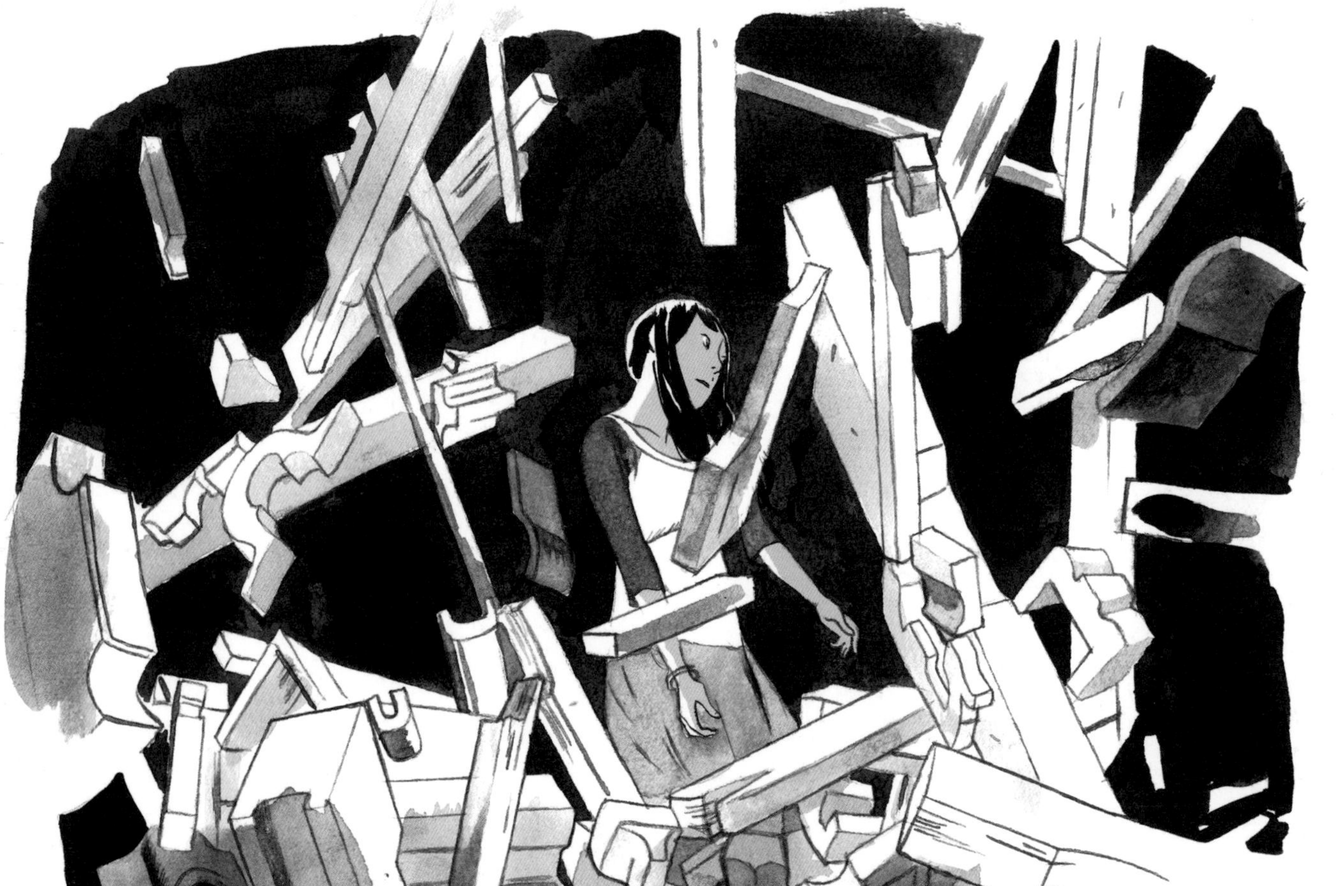

JUST SO HAPPENS

fumio obata

JONATHAN CAPE
LONDON

Published by Jonathan Cape 2014

2 4 6 8 10 9 7 5 3 1

First published in Great Britain in 2014 by Jonathan Cape Random House, 20 Vauxhall Bridge Road, London SW1V 2SA

www.vintage-books.co.uk

Addresses for companies within The Random House Group Limited can be found at: www.randomhouse.co.uk/offices.htm

The Random House Group Limited Reg. No. 954009

A CIP catalogue record for this book is available from the British Library

MIX
Paper from responsible sources
FSC® C008047

ISBN 9780224096638

The Random House Group Limited supports the Forest Stewardship Council® (FSC®),the leading international forest-certification organisation. Our books carrying the FSC label are printed on FSC® -certified paper. FSC is the only forest-certification scheme supported by the leading environmental organisations, including Greenpeace. Our paper procurement policy can be found at: www.randomhouse.co.uk/environment

Printed and bound in China by C&C Offset Printing Co., Ltd

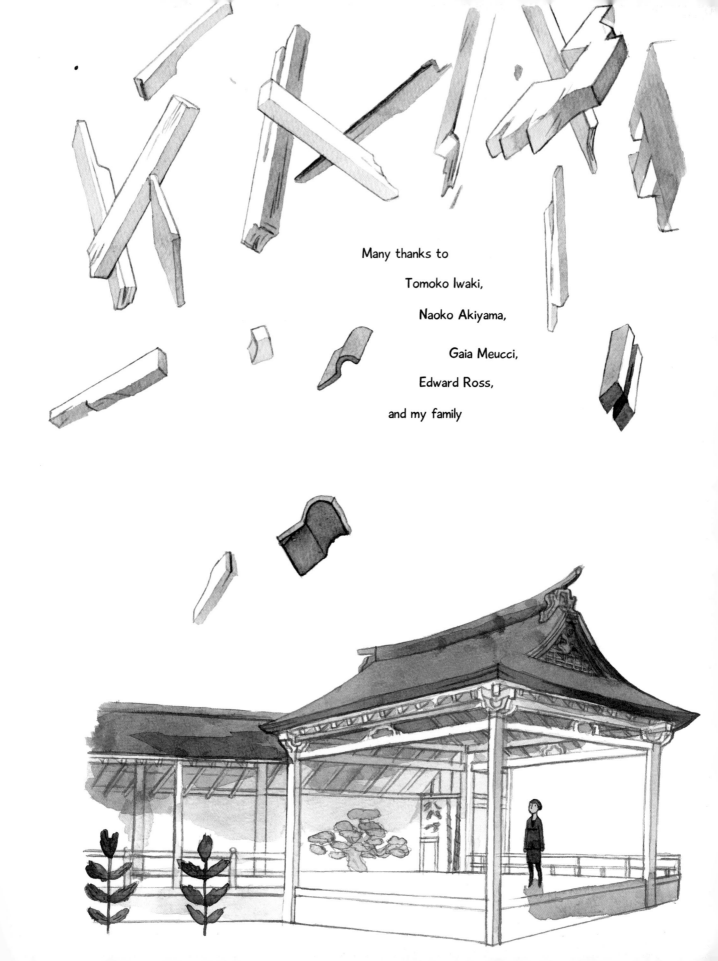

Many thanks to

Tomoko Iwaki,

Naoko Akiyama,

Gaia Meucci,

Edward Ross,

and my family

I

OK!

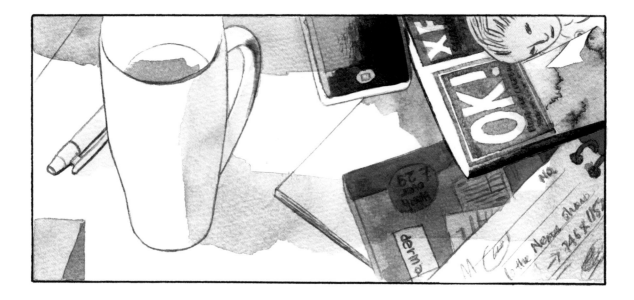

London, May 2010

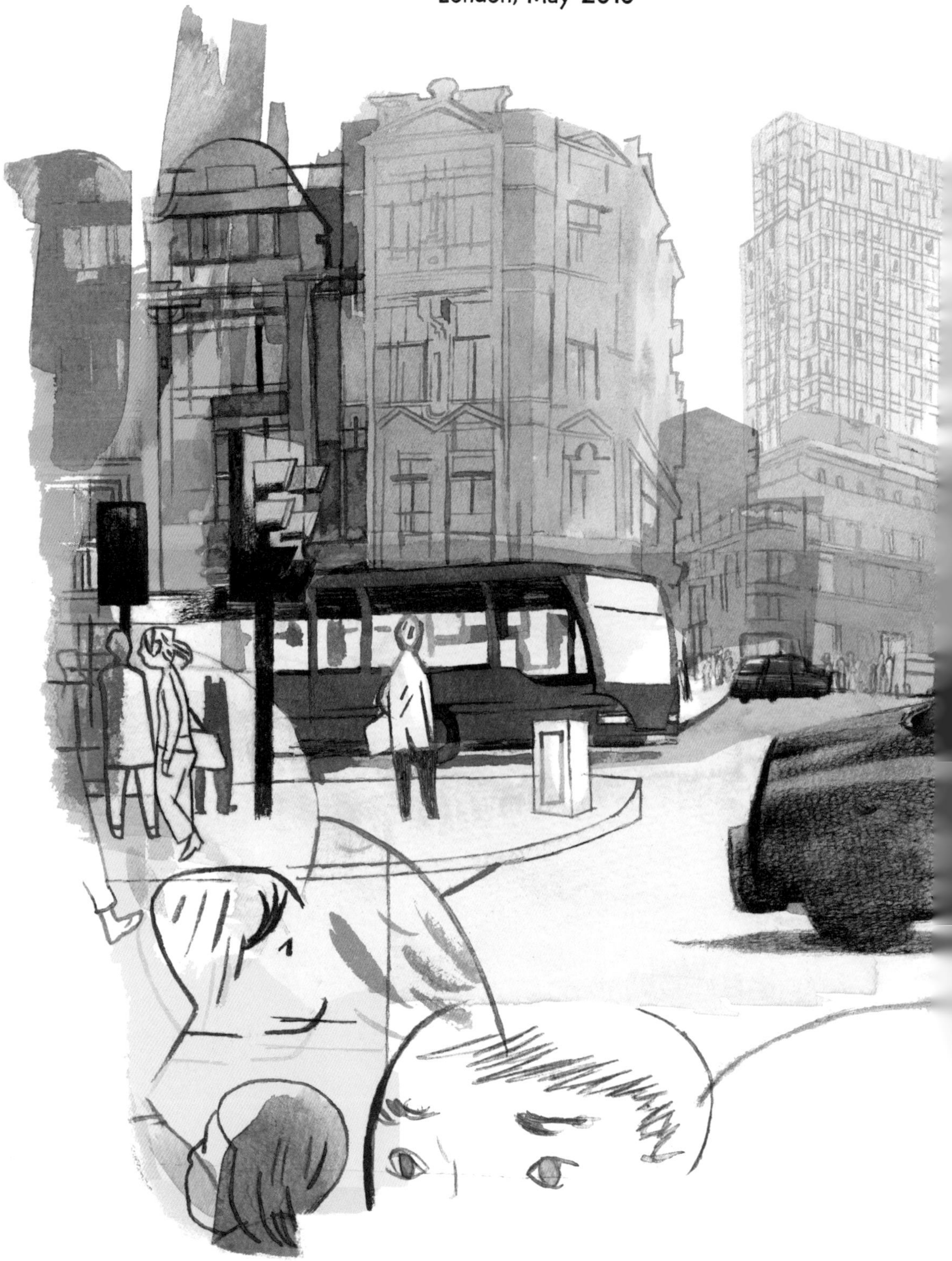

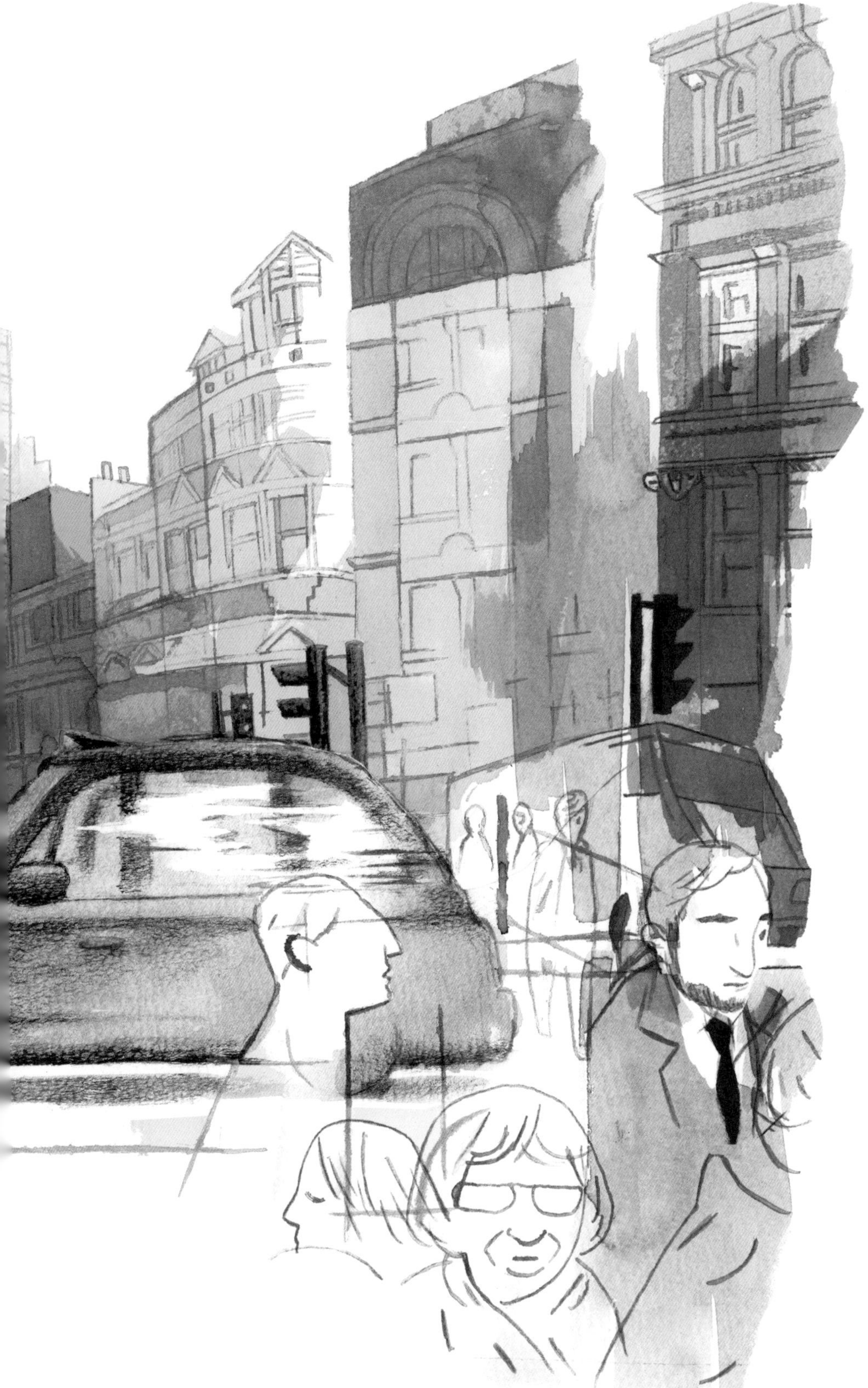

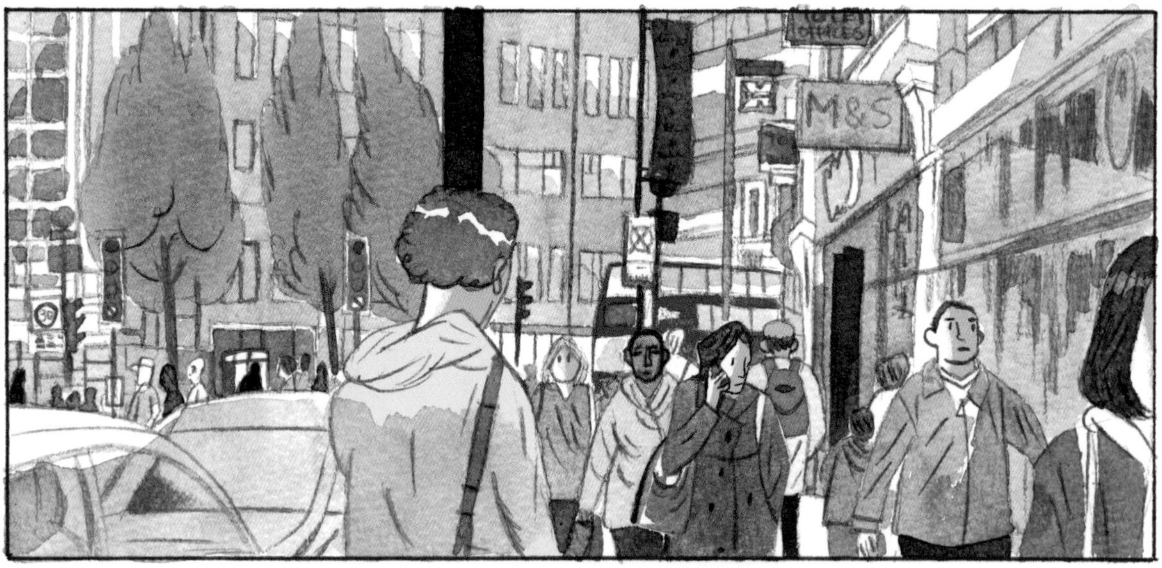
M&S

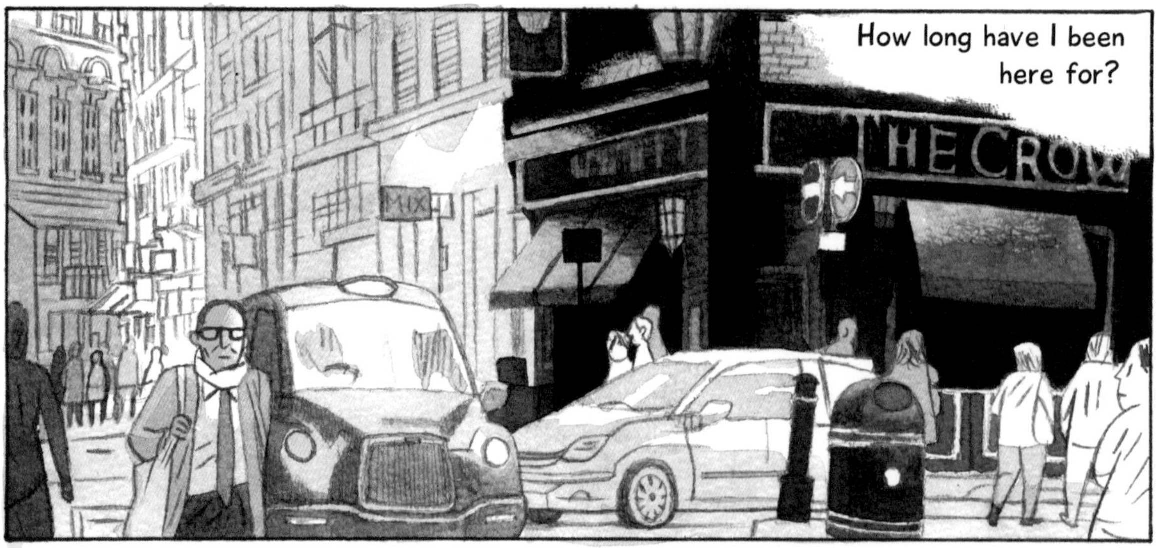
How long have I been here for?

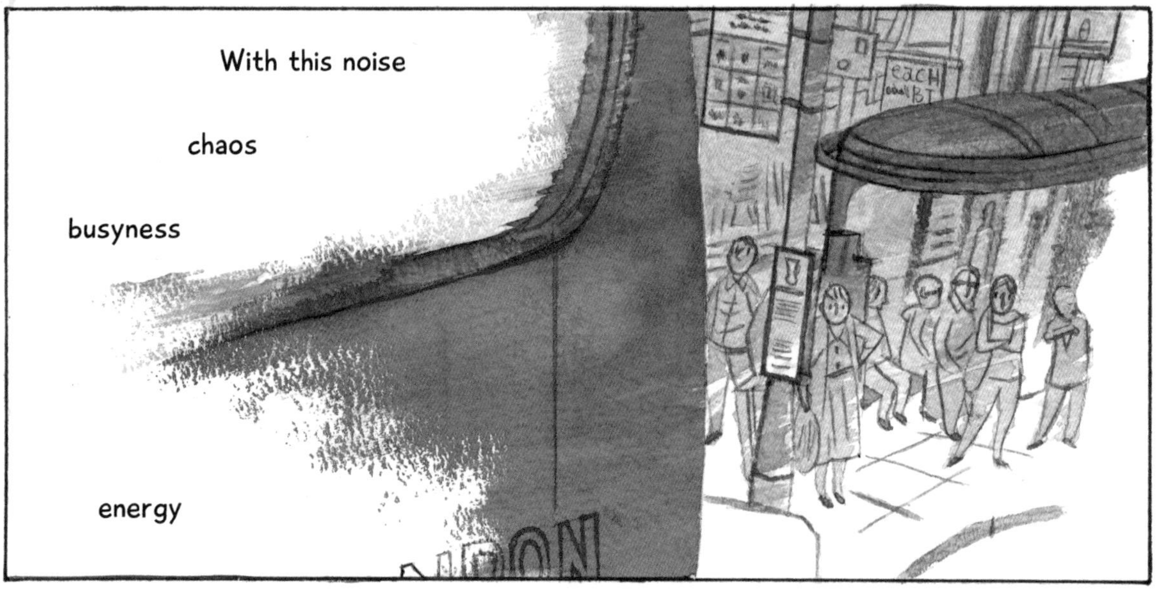
With this noise
chaos
busyness
energy

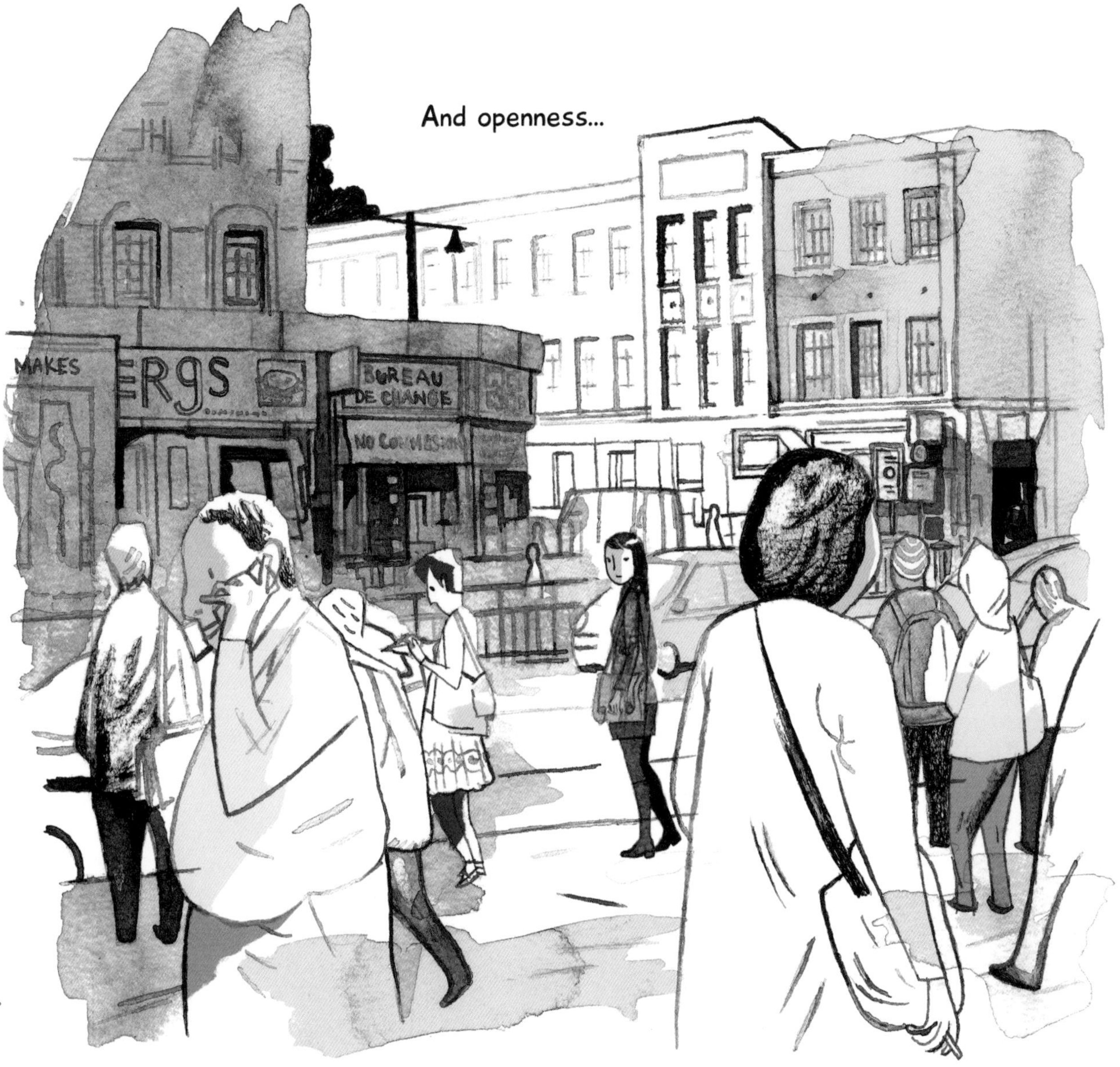
And openness...
MAKES
ERGS
BUREAU
DE CHANGE
NO COMMISSION

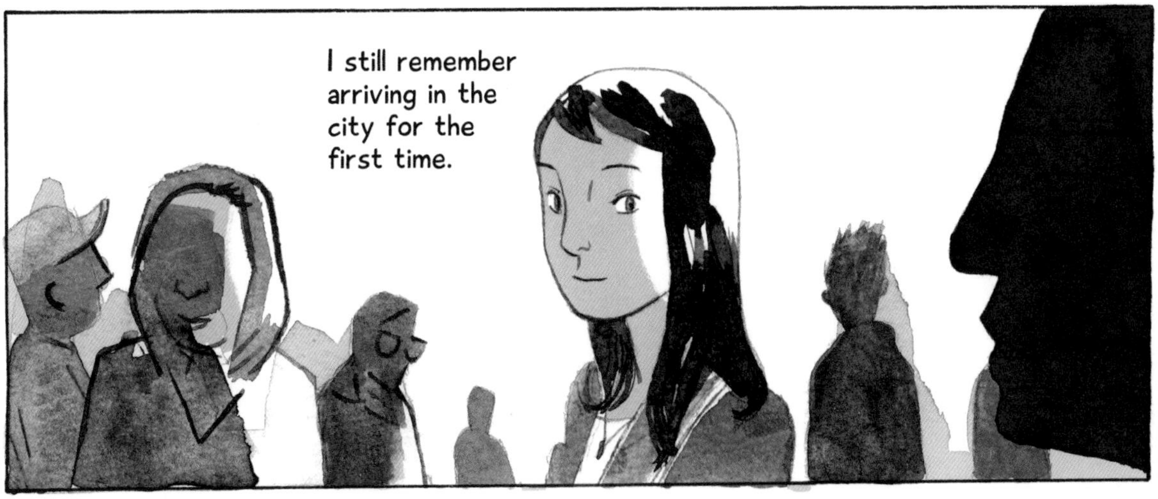
I still remember arriving in the city for the first time.

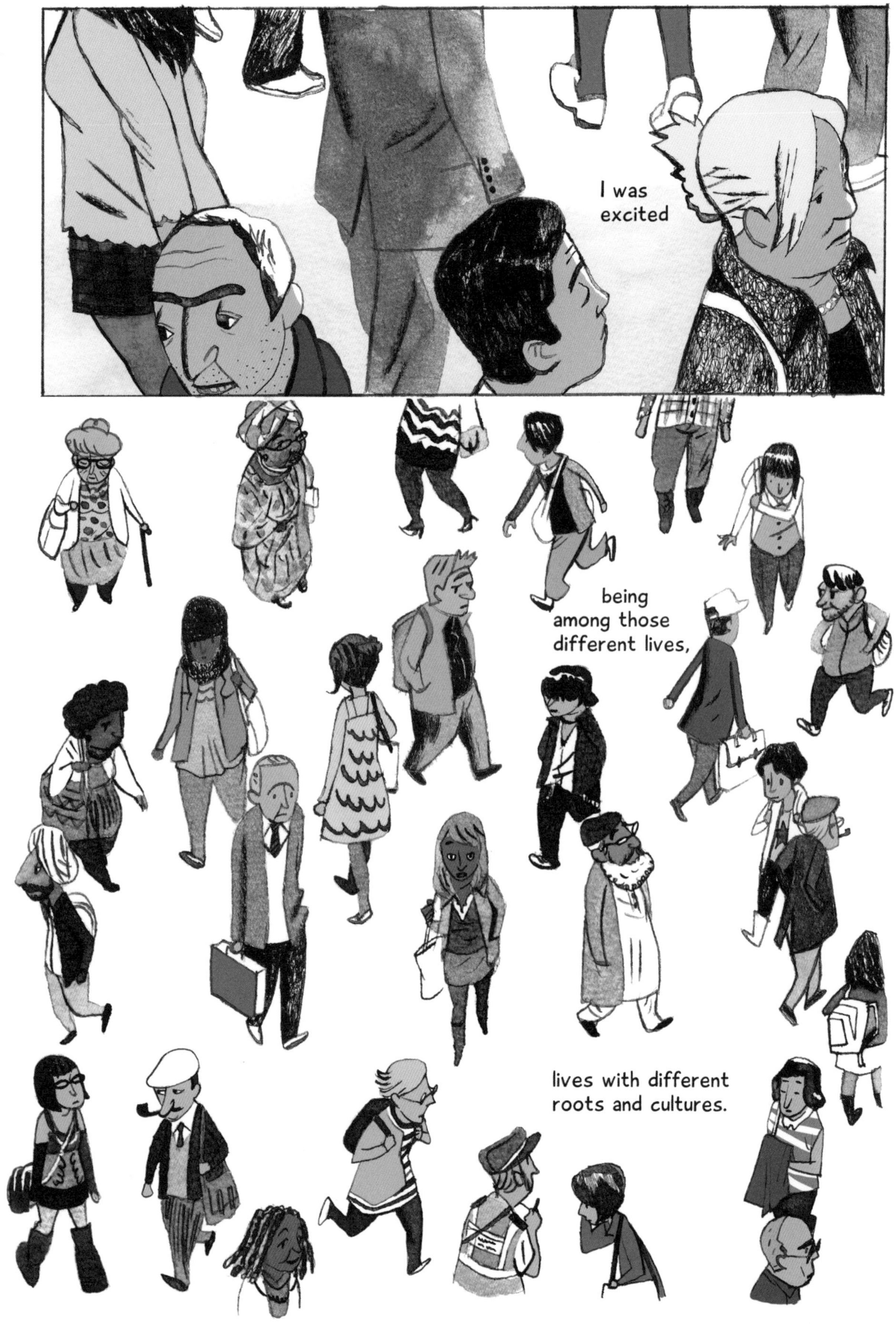
I was excited
being among those different lives,
lives with different roots and cultures.

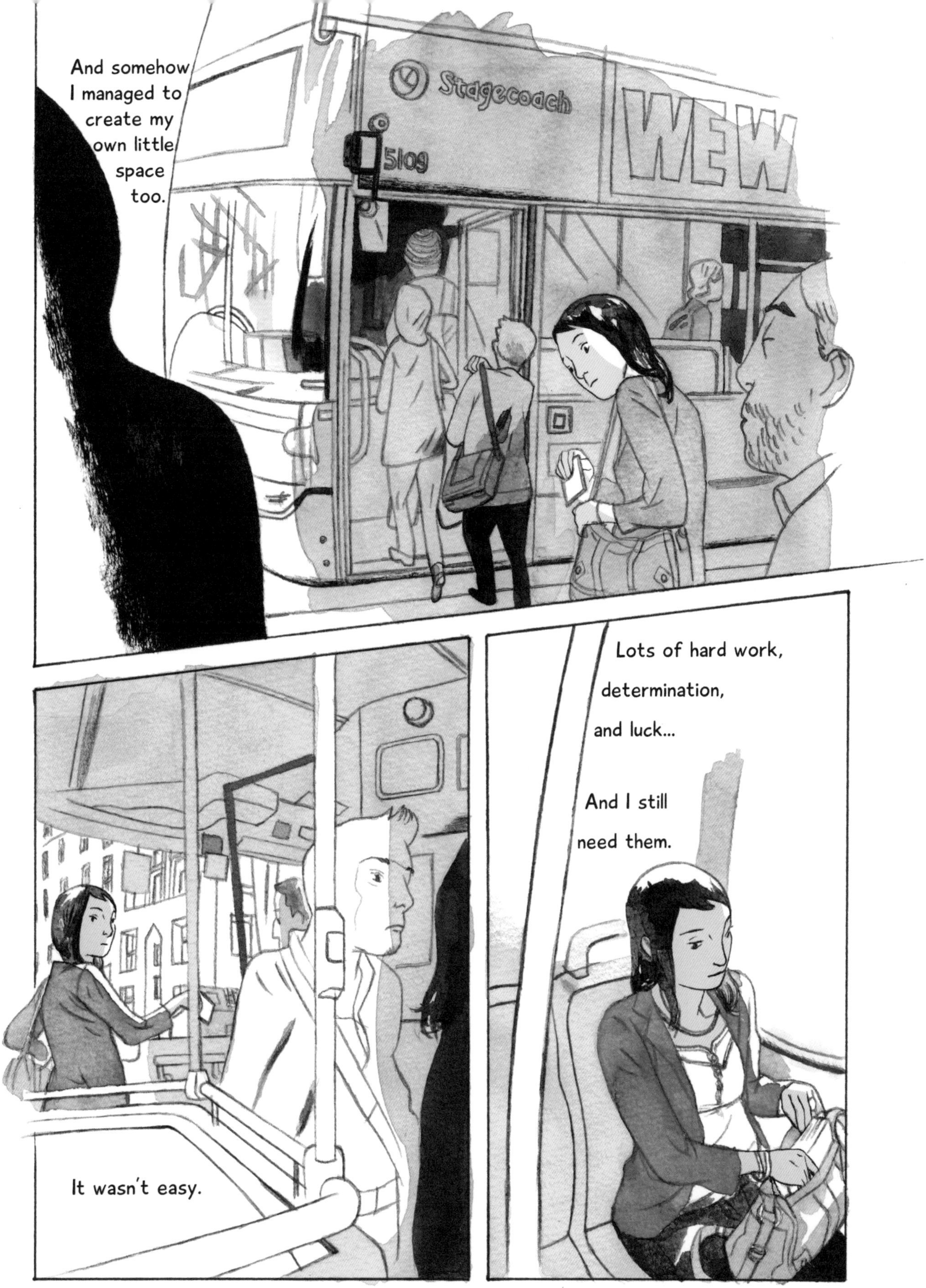
And somehow I managed to create my own little space too.
Stagecoach
5109
WEW
It wasn't easy.
Lots of hard work,
determination,
and luck...
And I still need them.

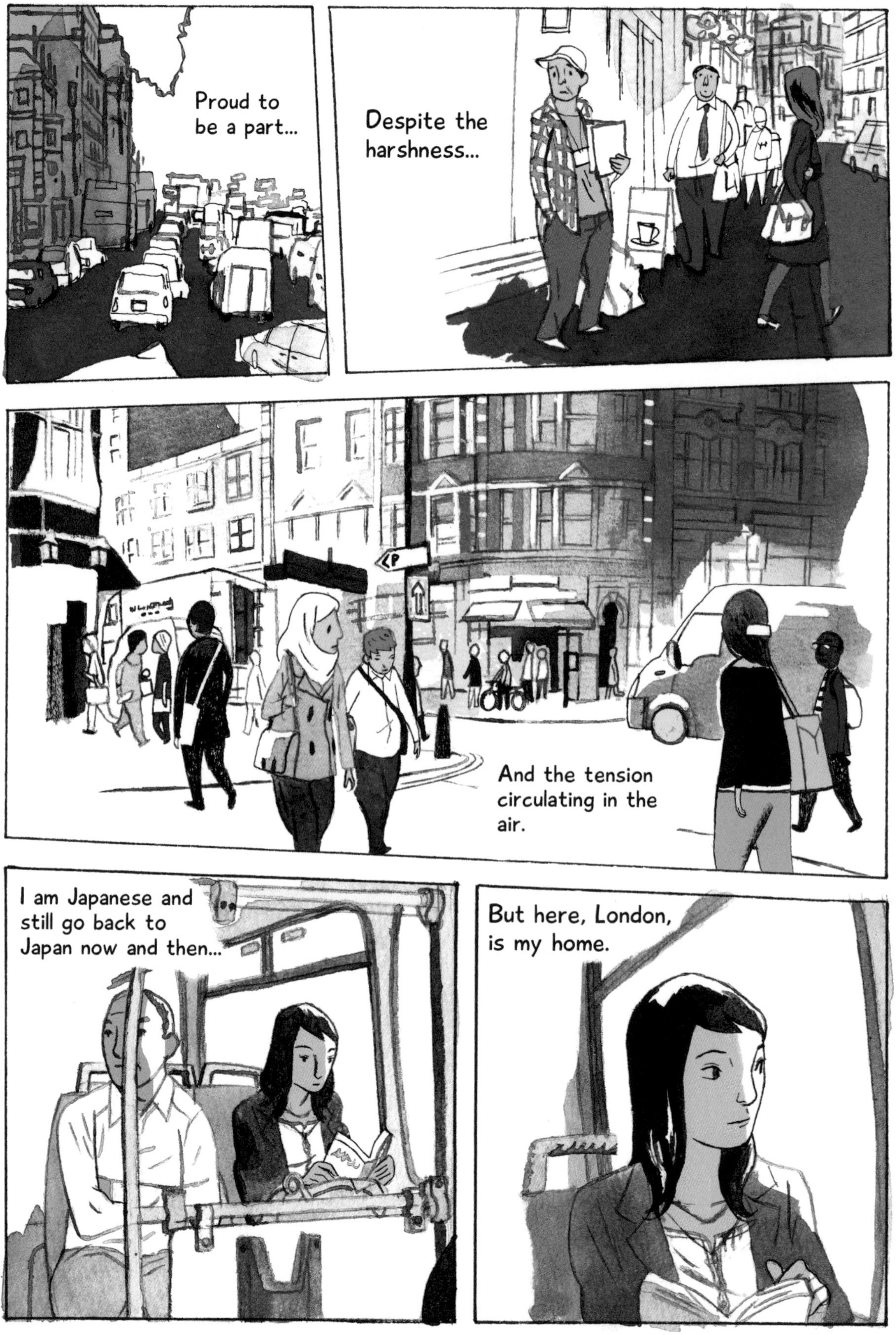
Proud to be a part...
Despite the harshness...
And the tension circulating in the air.
I am Japanese and still go back to Japan now and then...
But here, London, is my home.

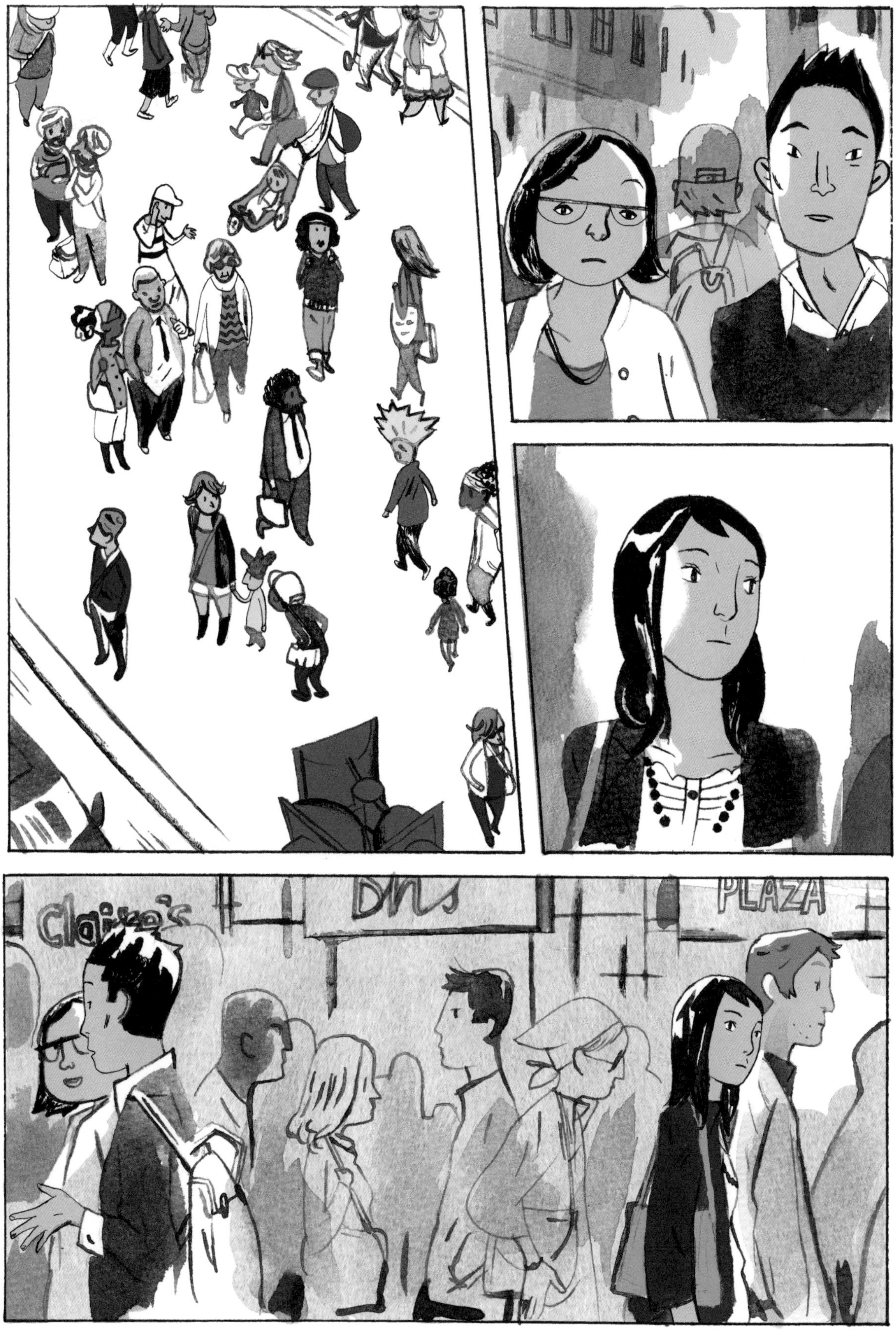

Claire's
Bhs
PLAZA

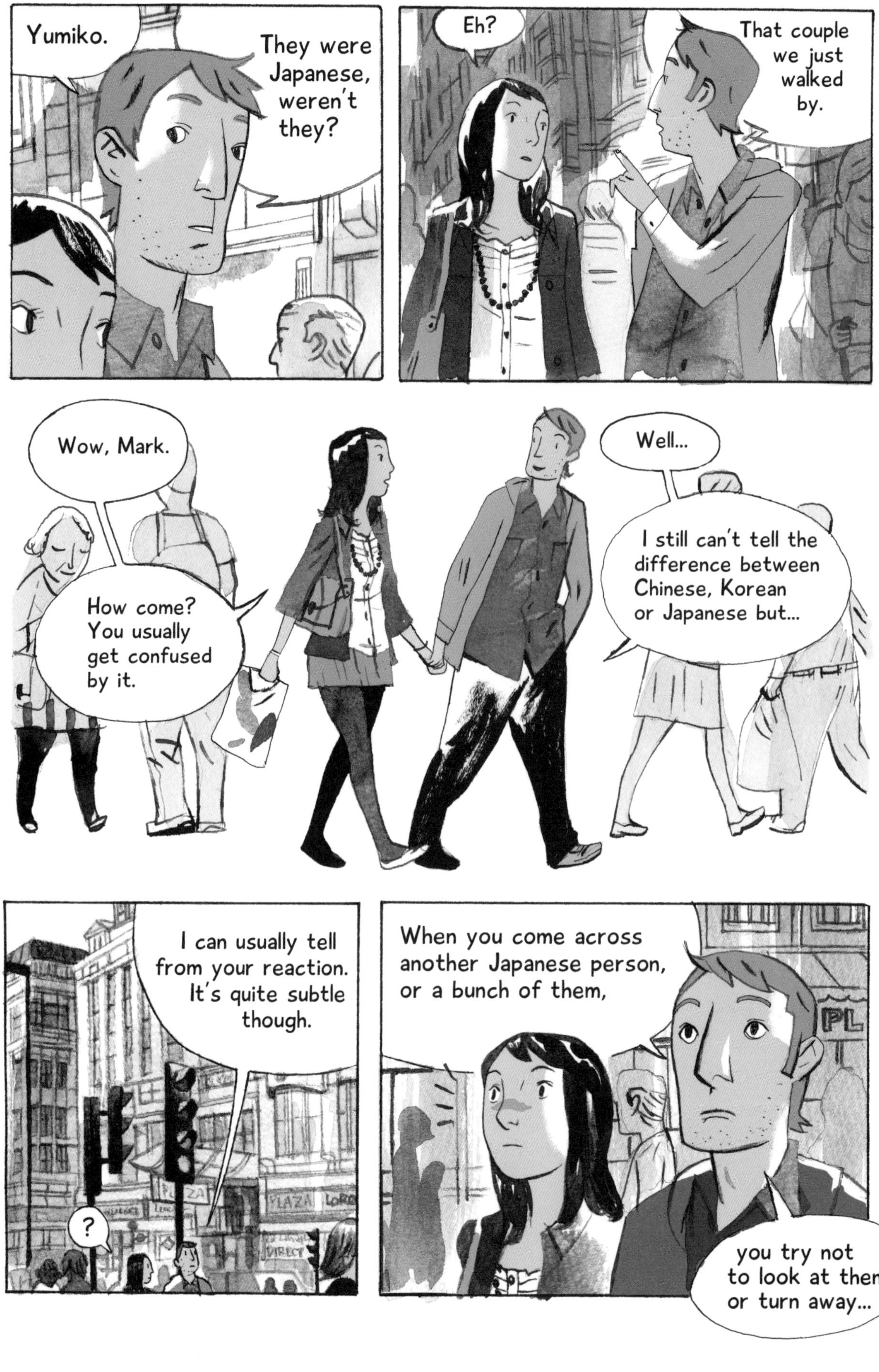
Yumiko.
They were Japanese, weren't they?
Eh?
That couple we just walked by.
Wow, Mark.
How come? You usually get confused by it.
Well...
I still can't tell the difference between Chinese, Korean or Japanese but...
I can usually tell from your reaction. It's quite subtle though.
?
When you come across another Japanese person, or a bunch of them,
you try not to look at them or turn away...

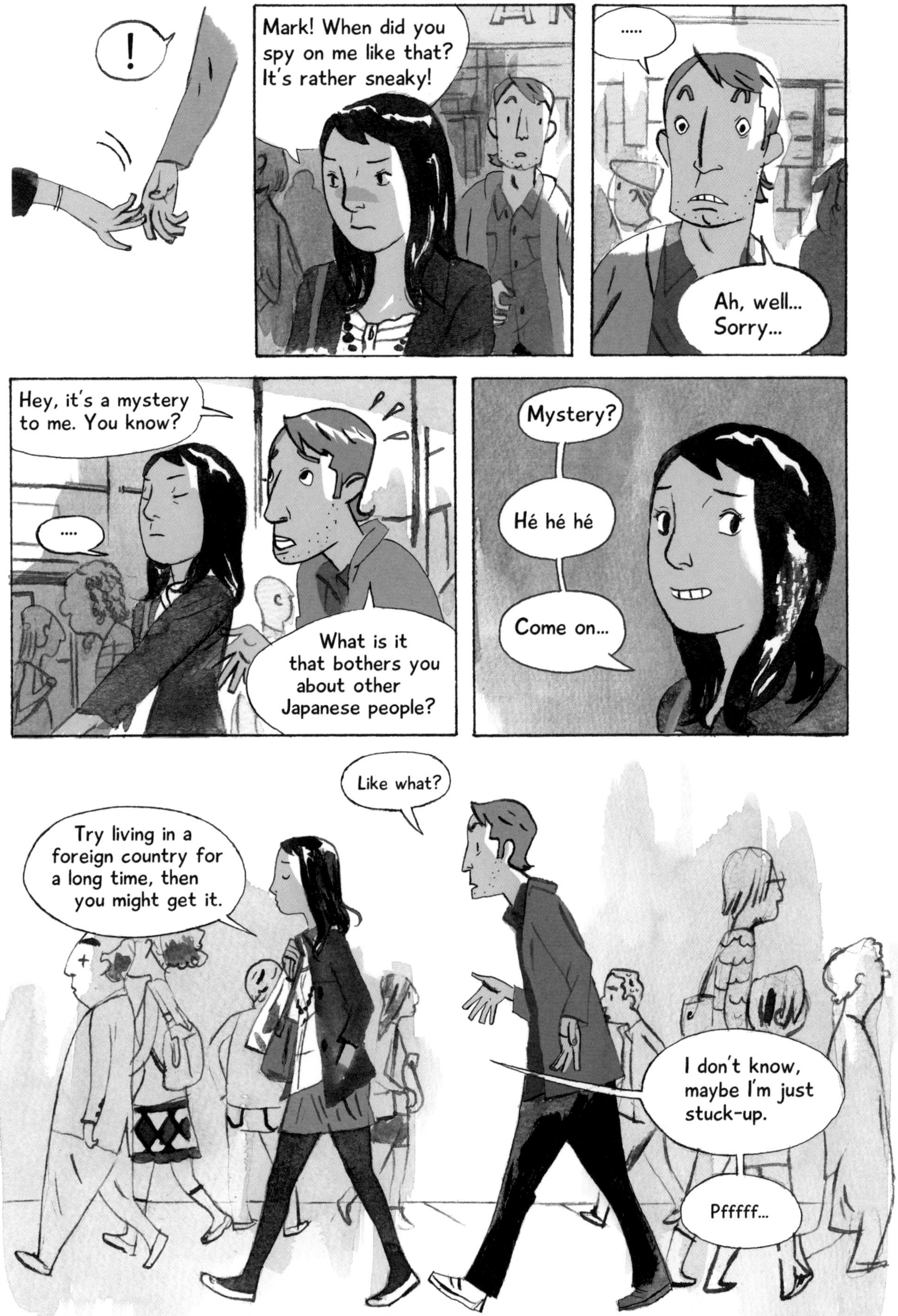
!
Mark! When did you spy on me like that? It's rather sneaky!
.....
Ah, well... Sorry...
Hey, it's a mystery to me. You know?
....
What is it that bothers you about other Japanese people?
Mystery?
Hé hé hé
Come on...
Like what?
Try living in a foreign country for a long time, then you might get it.
I don't know, maybe I'm just stuck-up.
Pfffff...

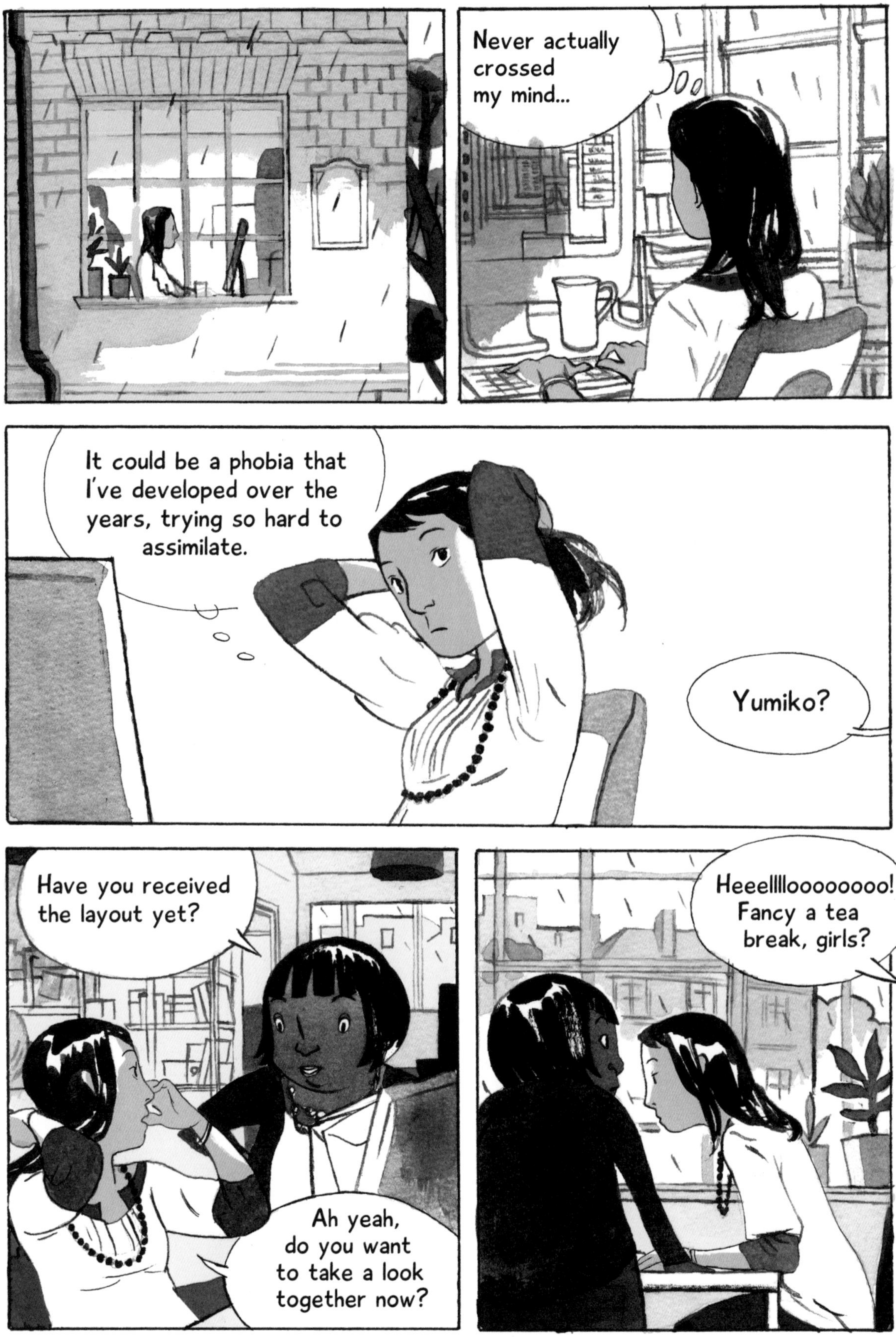

Never actually crossed my mind...
It could be a phobia that I've developed over the years, trying so hard to assimilate.
Yumiko?
Have you received the layout yet?
Ah yeah, do you want to take a look together now?
Heeellllooooooooo! Fancy a tea break, girls?

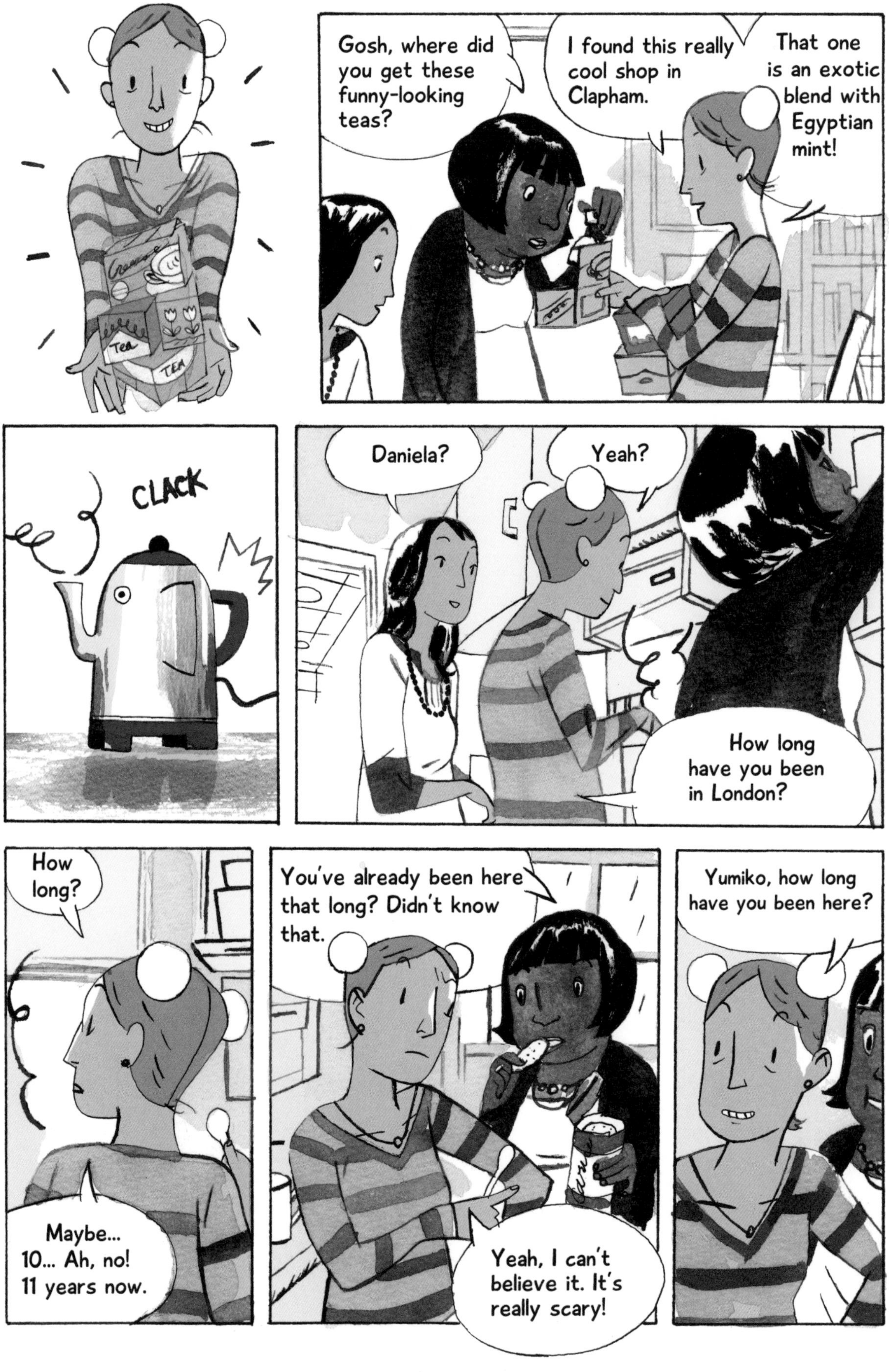
Gosh, where did you get these funny-looking teas?
I found this really cool shop in Clapham.
That one is an exotic blend with Egyptian mint!
CLACK
Daniela?
Yeah?
How long have you been in London?
How long?
Maybe... 10... Ah, no! 11 years now.
You've already been here that long? Didn't know that.
Yeah, I can't believe it. It's really scary!
Yumiko, how long have you been here?

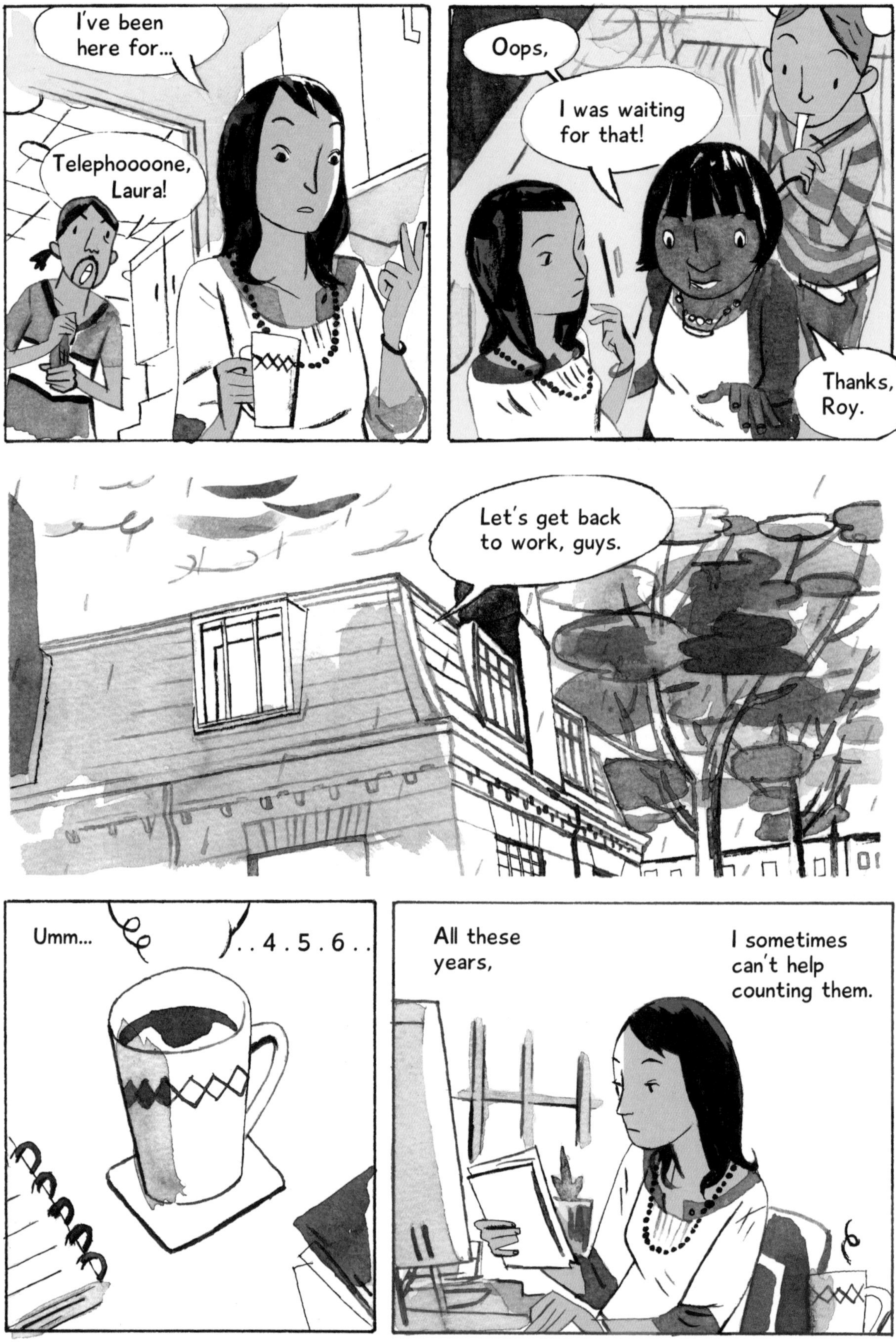
I've been here for...
Telephoooone, Laura!
Oops,
I was waiting for that!
Thanks, Roy.
Let's get back to work, guys.
Umm...
. . 4 . 5 . 6 . .
All these years,
I sometimes can't help counting them.

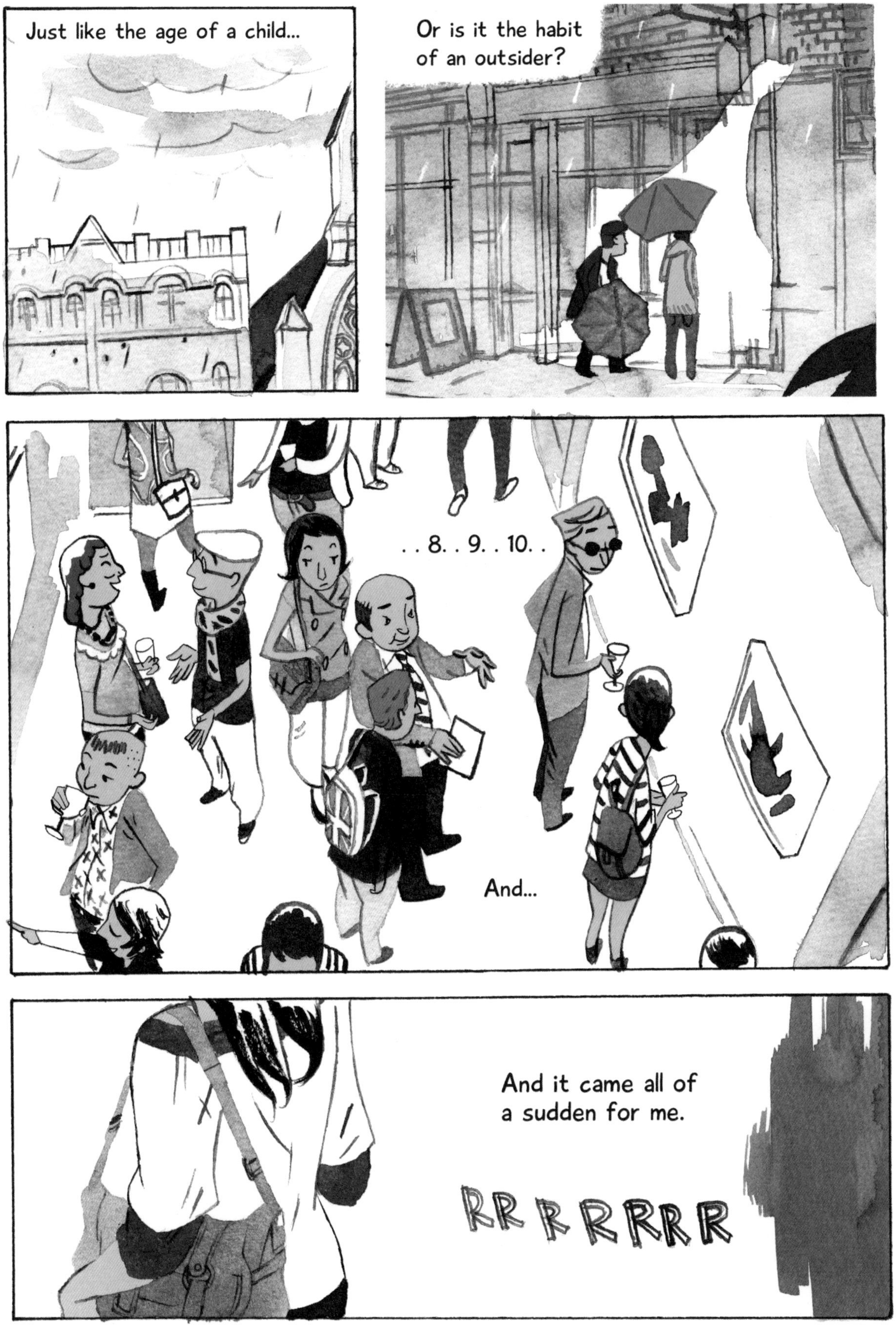
Just like the age of a child...
Or is it the habit of an outsider?
. . 8. . 9. . 10. .
And...
And it came all of a sudden for me.
RR R RRRR

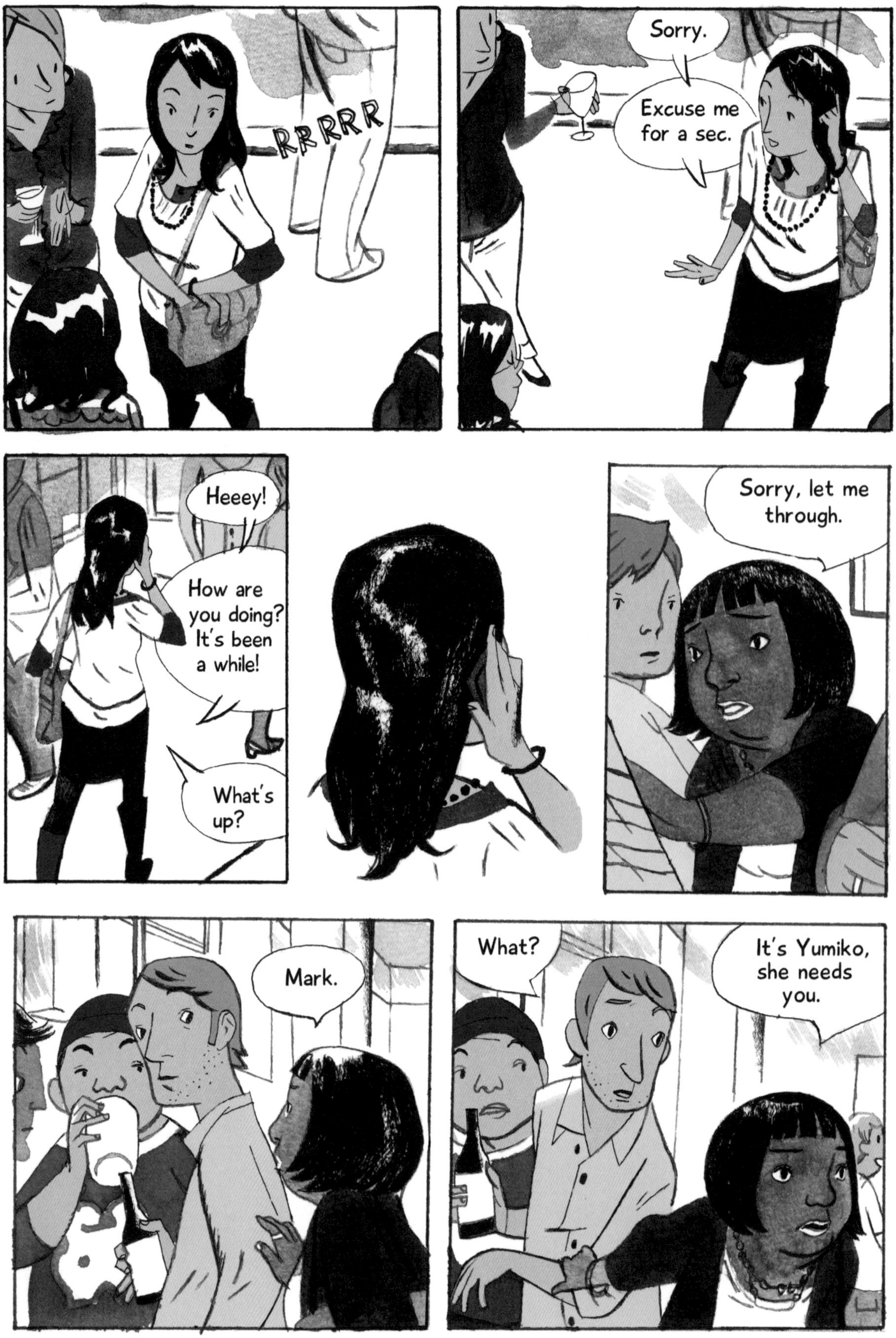
RRRRR
Sorry.
Excuse me for a sec.
Heeey!
How are you doing? It's been a while!
What's up?
Sorry, let me through.
Mark.
What?
It's Yumiko, she needs you.

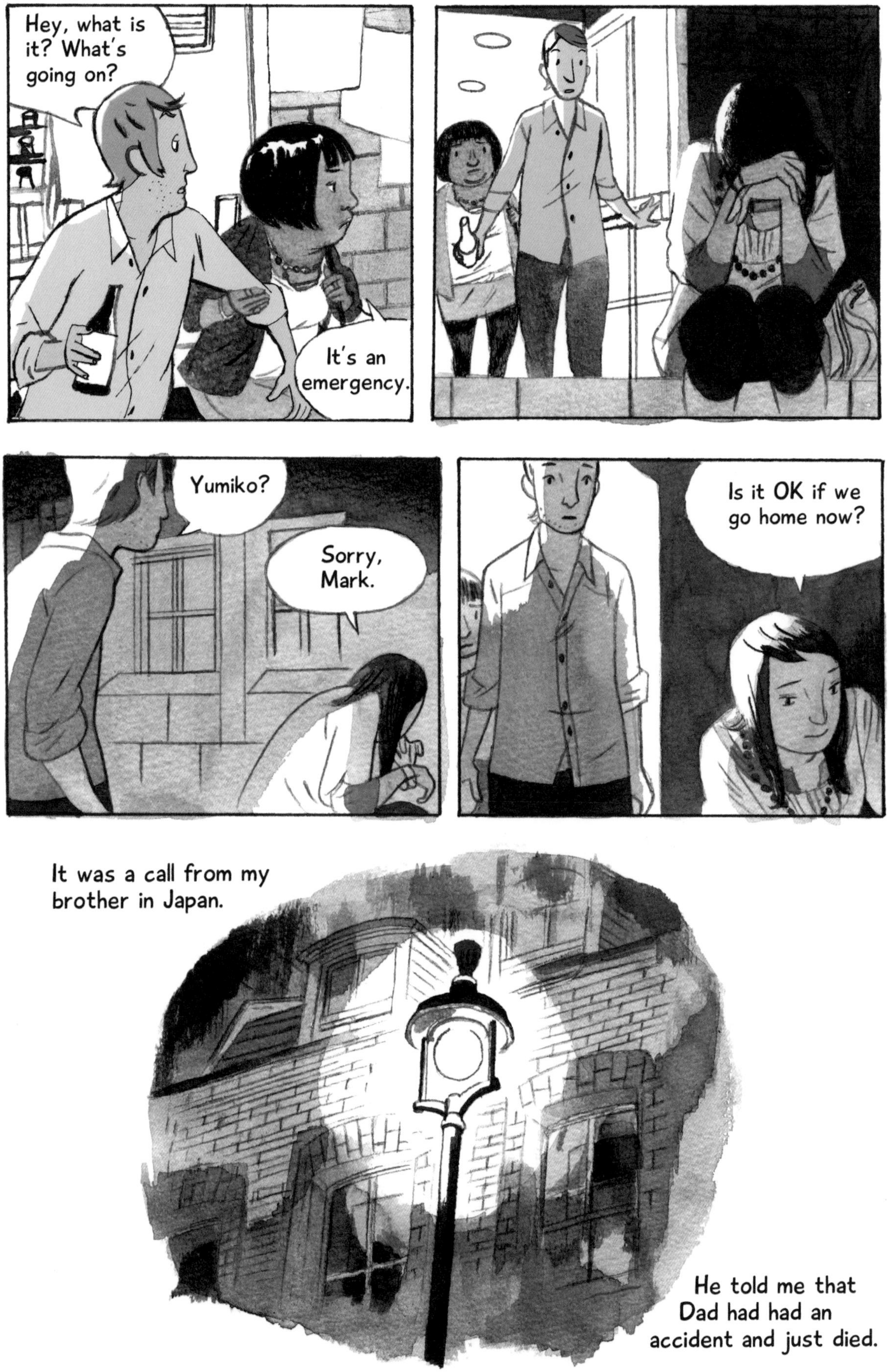
Hey, what is it? What's going on?
It's an emergency.
Yumiko?
Sorry, Mark.
Is it OK if we go home now?
It was a call from my brother in Japan.
He told me that Dad had had an accident and just died.

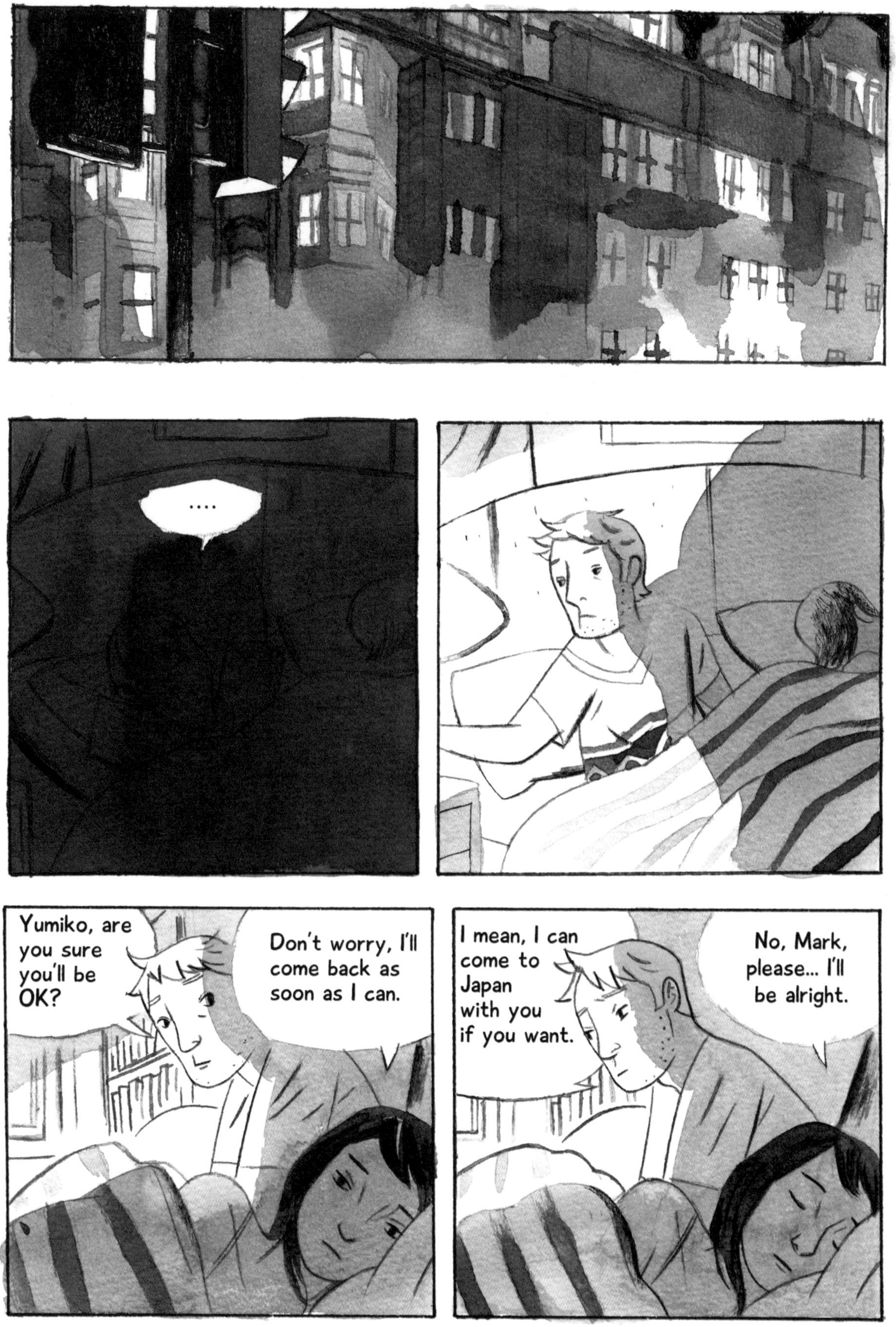
....
Yumiko, are you sure you'll be OK?
Don't worry, I'll come back as soon as I can.
I mean, I can come to Japan with you if you want.
No, Mark, please... I'll be alright.

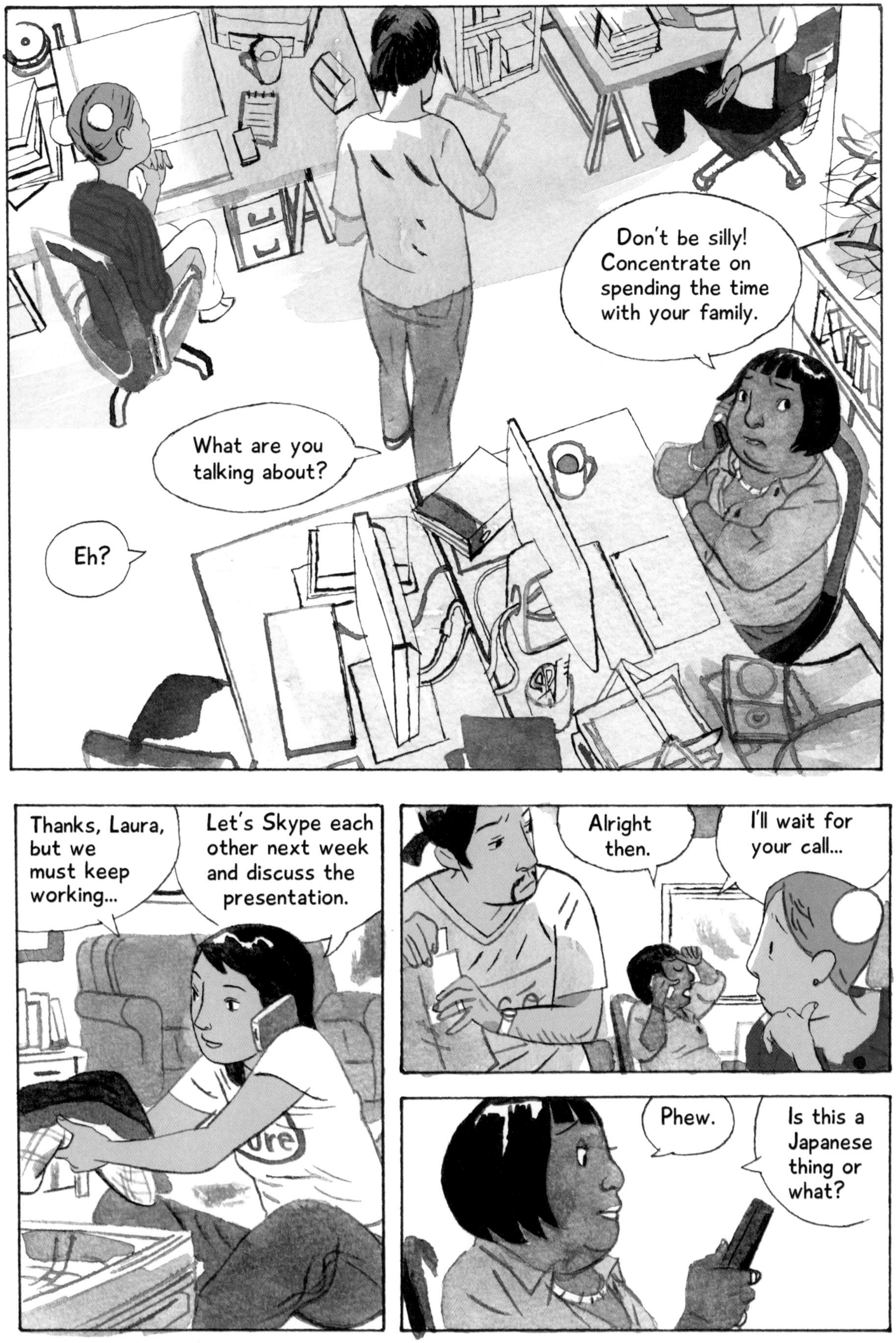

Don't be silly! Concentrate on spending the time with your family.
What are you talking about?
Eh?
Thanks, Laura, but we must keep working...
Let's Skype each other next week and discuss the presentation.
Alright then.
I'll wait for your call...
Phew.
Is this a Japanese thing or what?

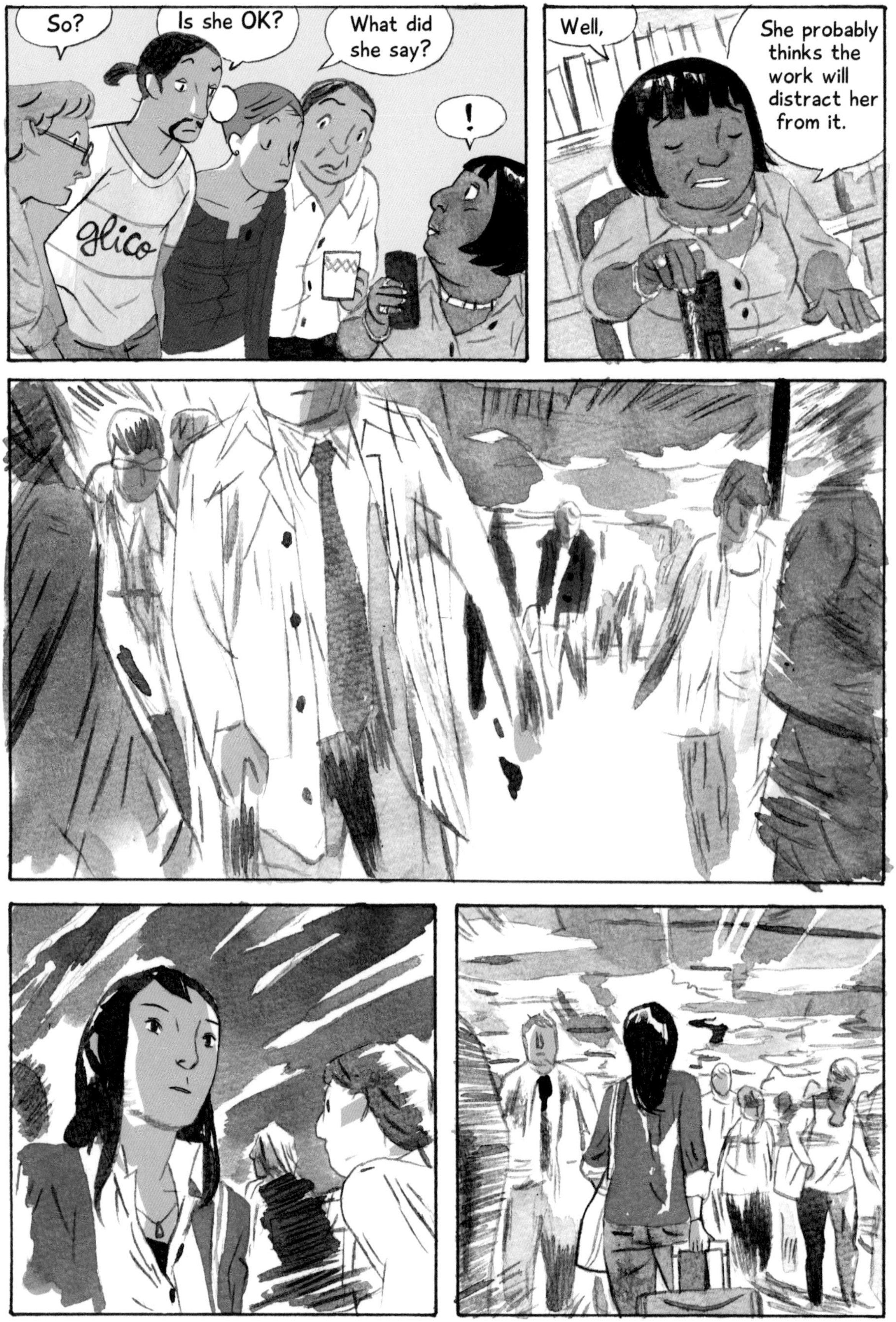
So?
Is she OK?
What did she say?
!
Well,
She probably thinks the work will distract her from it.

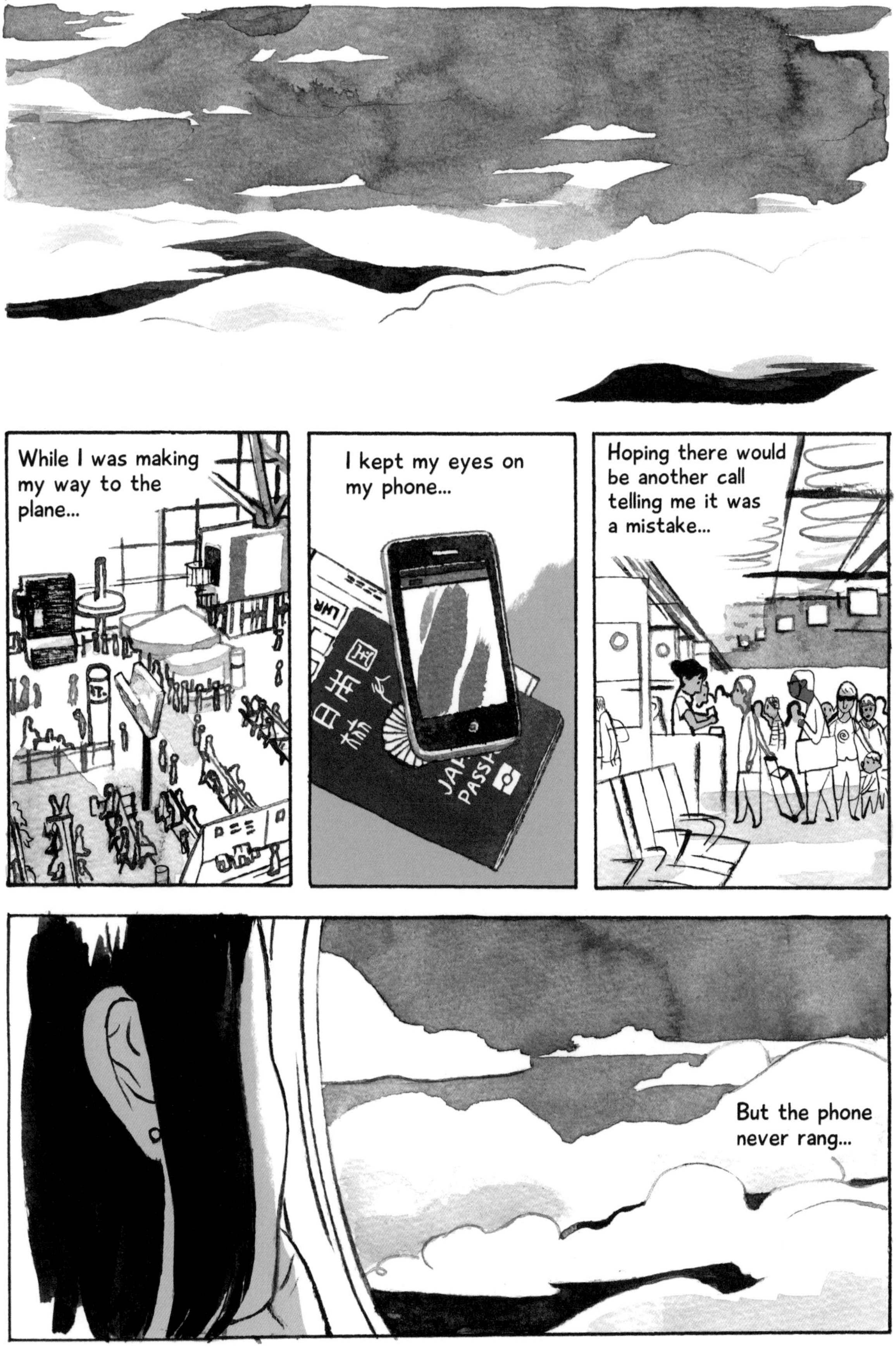
While I was making my way to the plane...
I kept my eyes on my phone...
Hoping there would be another call telling me it was a mistake...
But the phone never rang...

Another trip back home...
but this time it's
different...

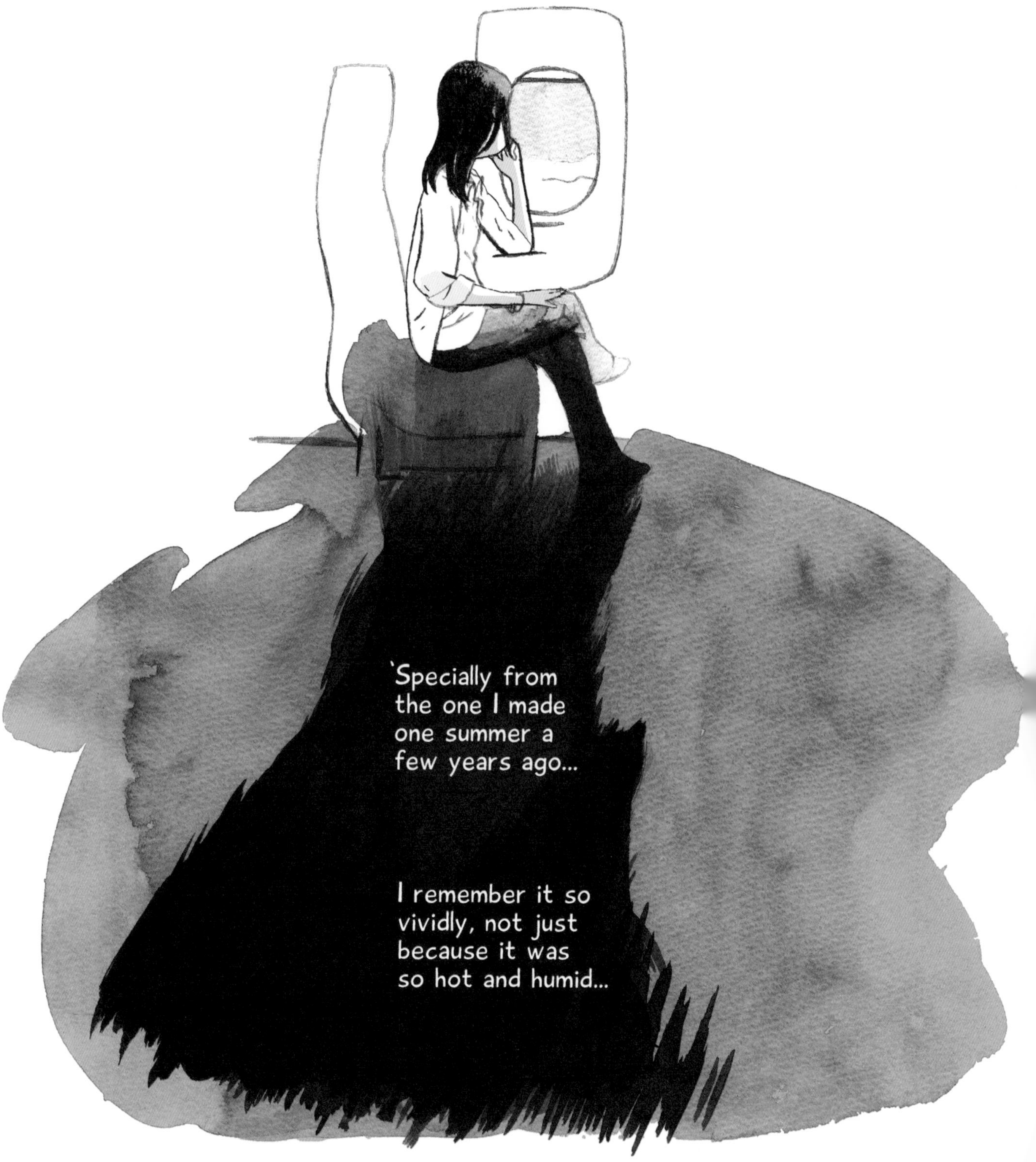
`Specially from the one I made one summer a few years ago...
I remember it so vividly, not just because it was so hot and humid...

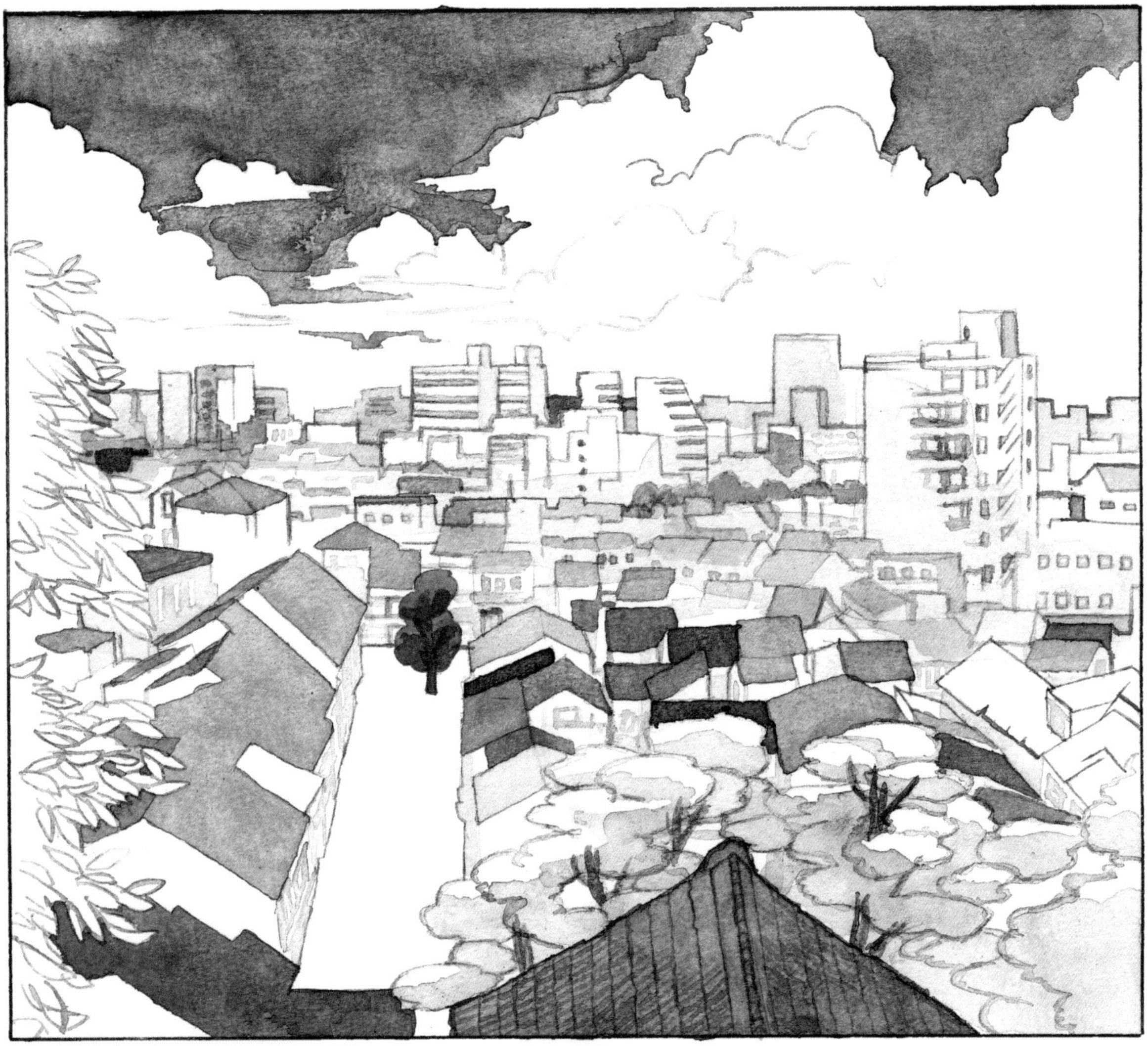
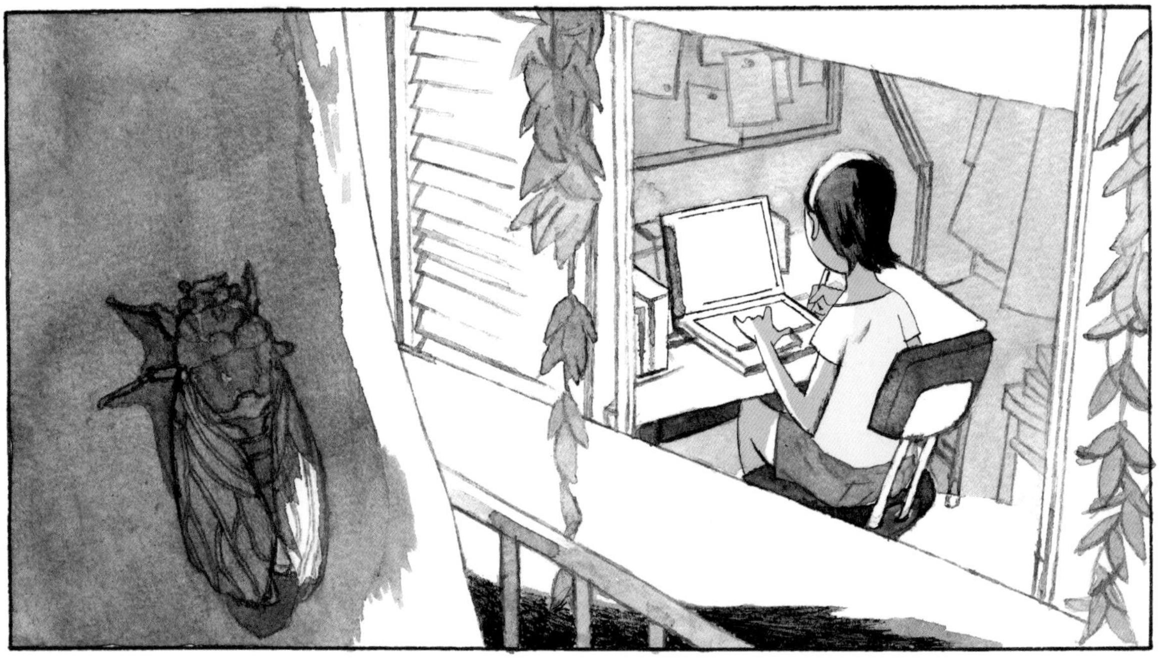

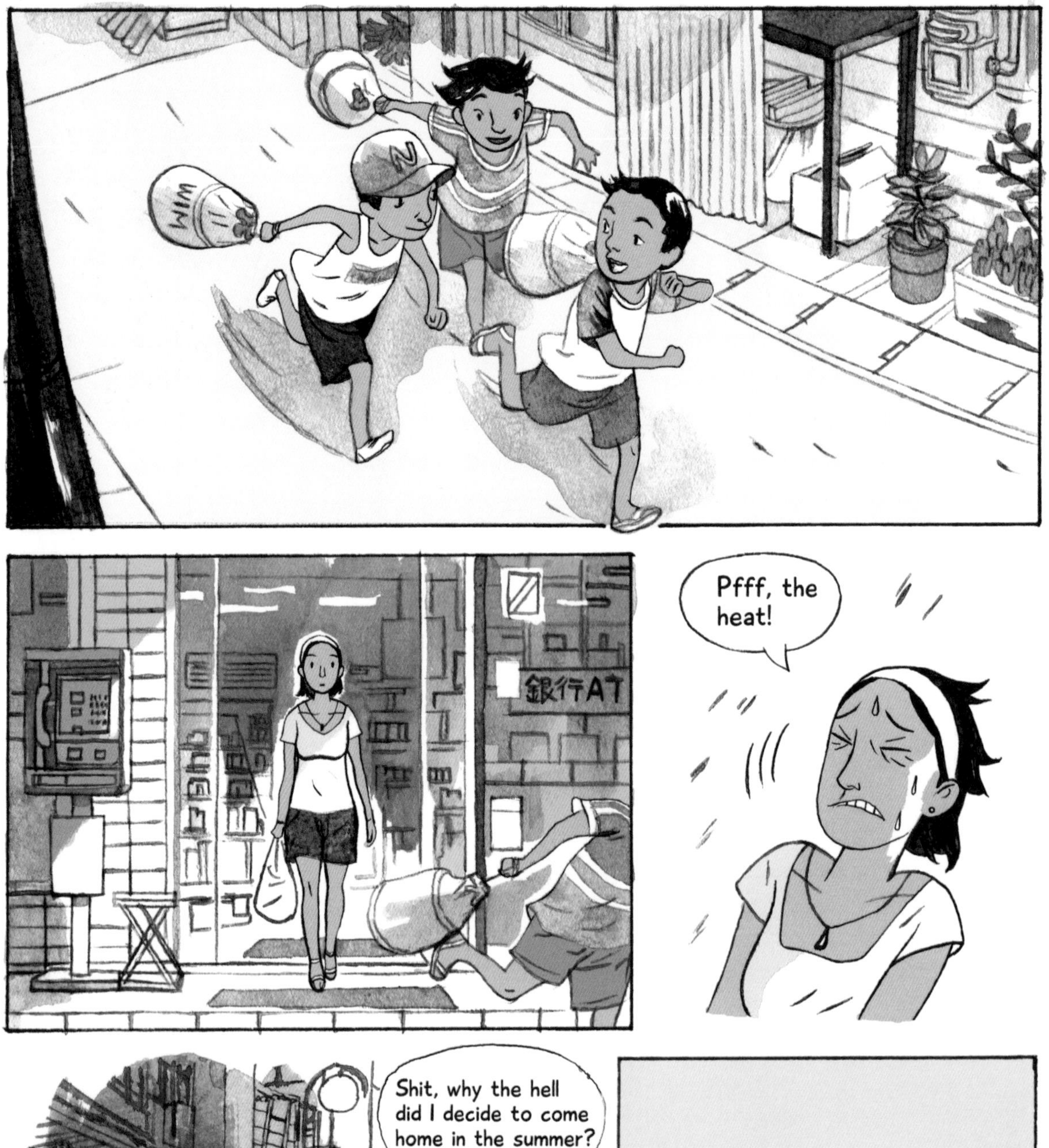
銀行AT
Pfff, the heat!
Shit, why the hell did I decide to come home in the summer?

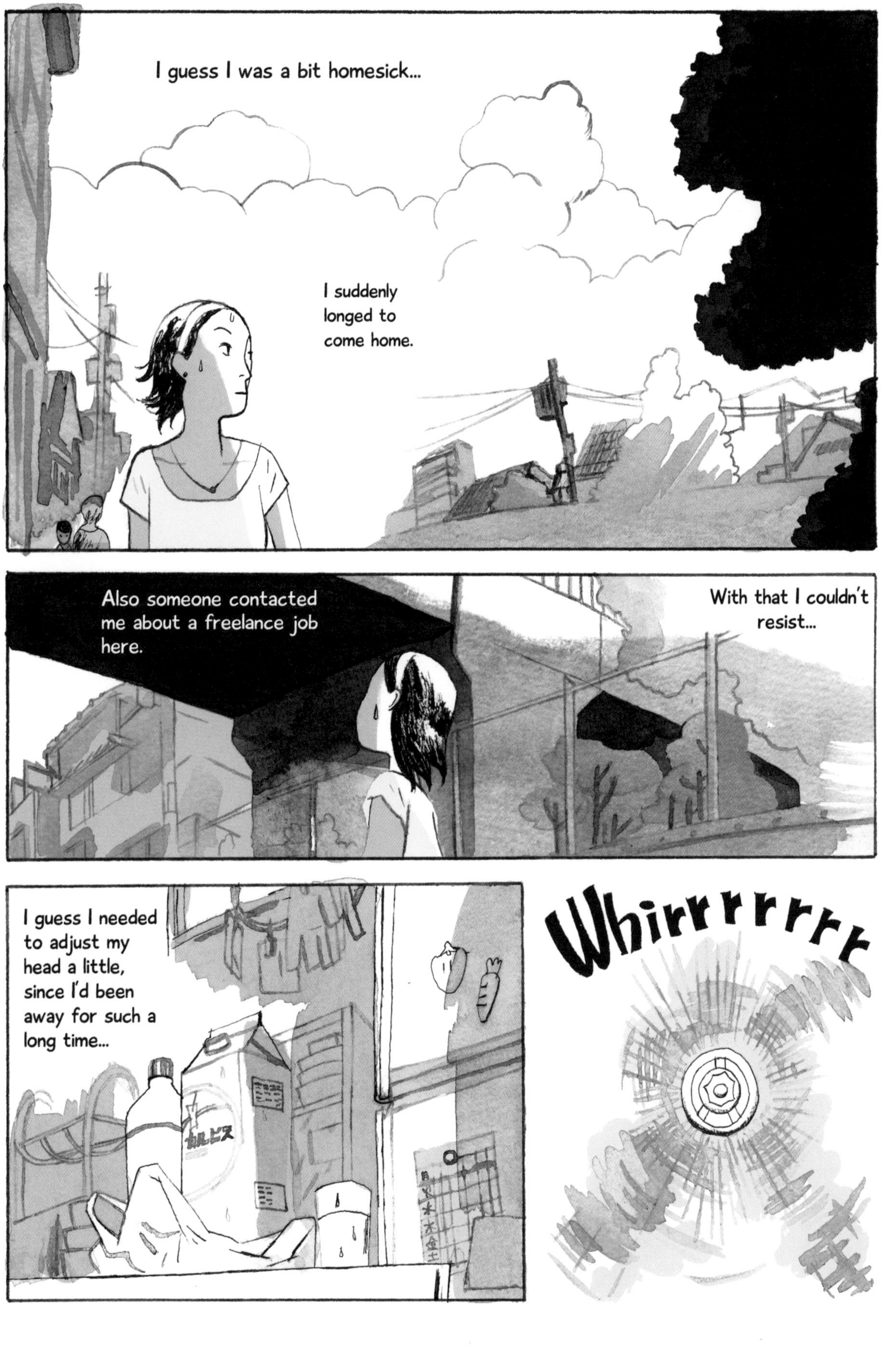
I guess I was a bit homesick...
I suddenly longed to come home.
Also someone contacted me about a freelance job here.
With that I couldn't resist...
I guess I needed to adjust my head a little, since I'd been away for such a long time...
Whirrrrrrt

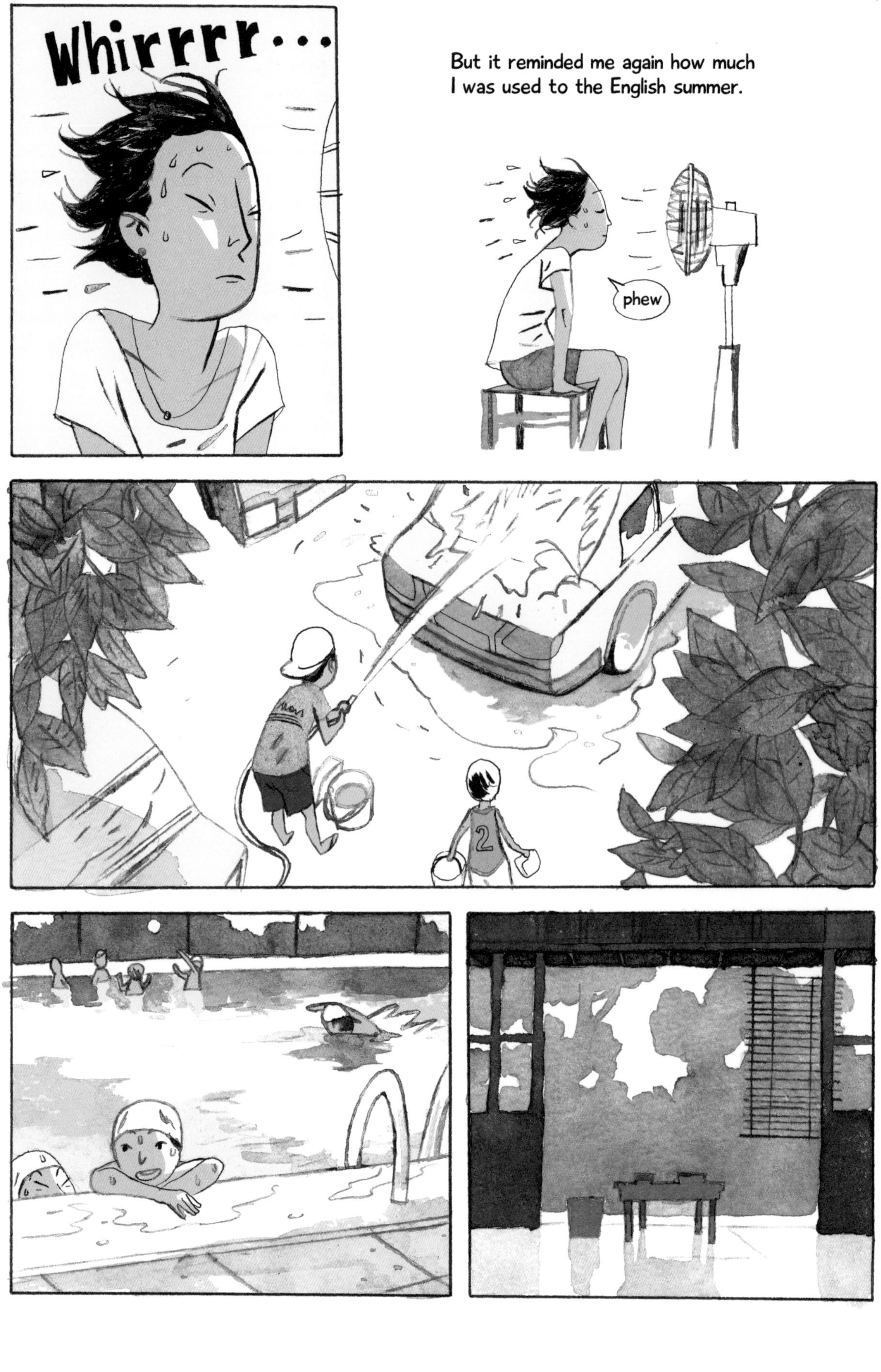
Whirrrr...
But it reminded me again how much I was used to the English summer.
phew

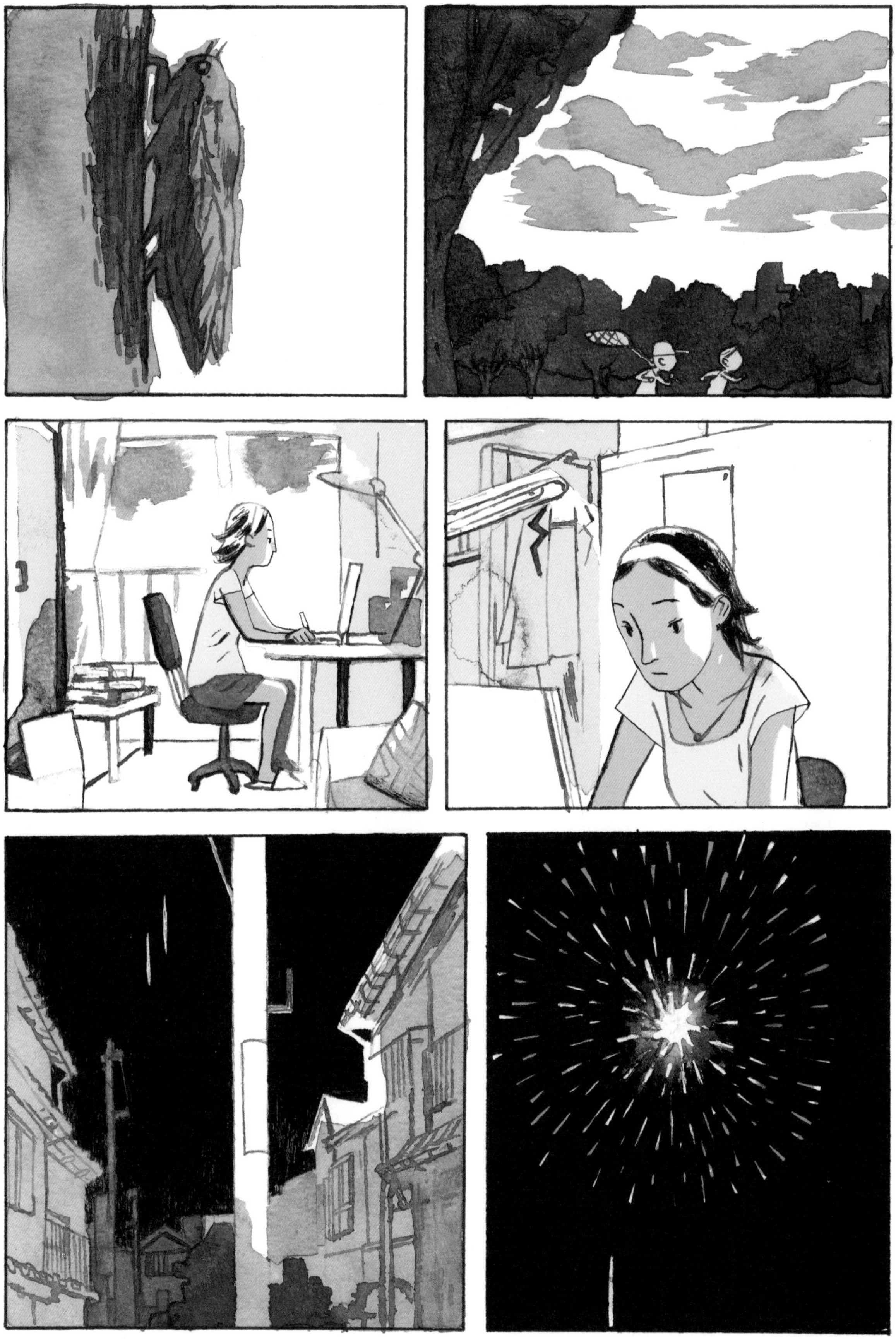

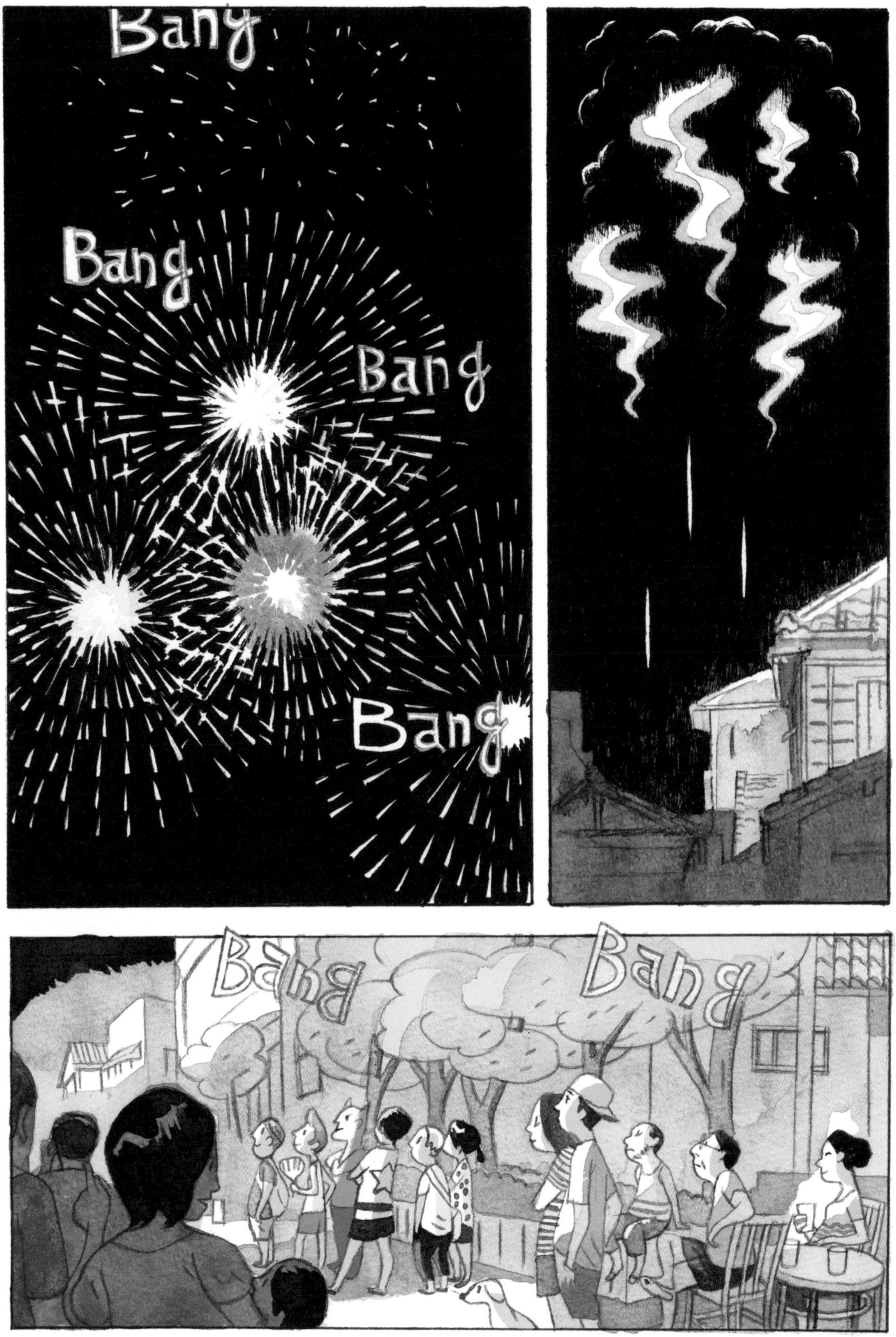
Bang
Bang
Bang
Bang
Bang
Bang

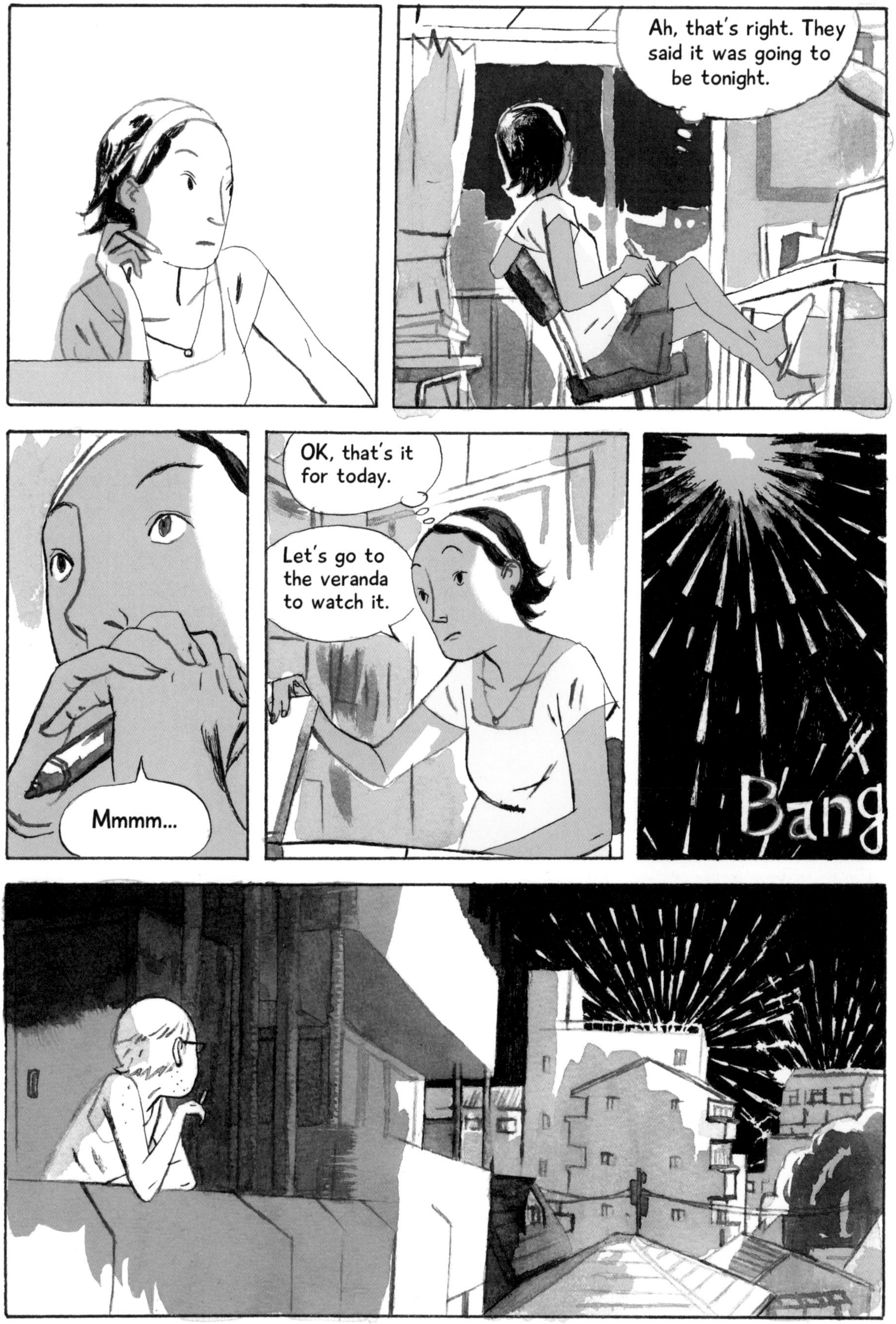
Ah, that's right. They said it was going to be tonight.
Mmmm...
OK, that's it for today.
Let's go to the veranda to watch it.
Bang

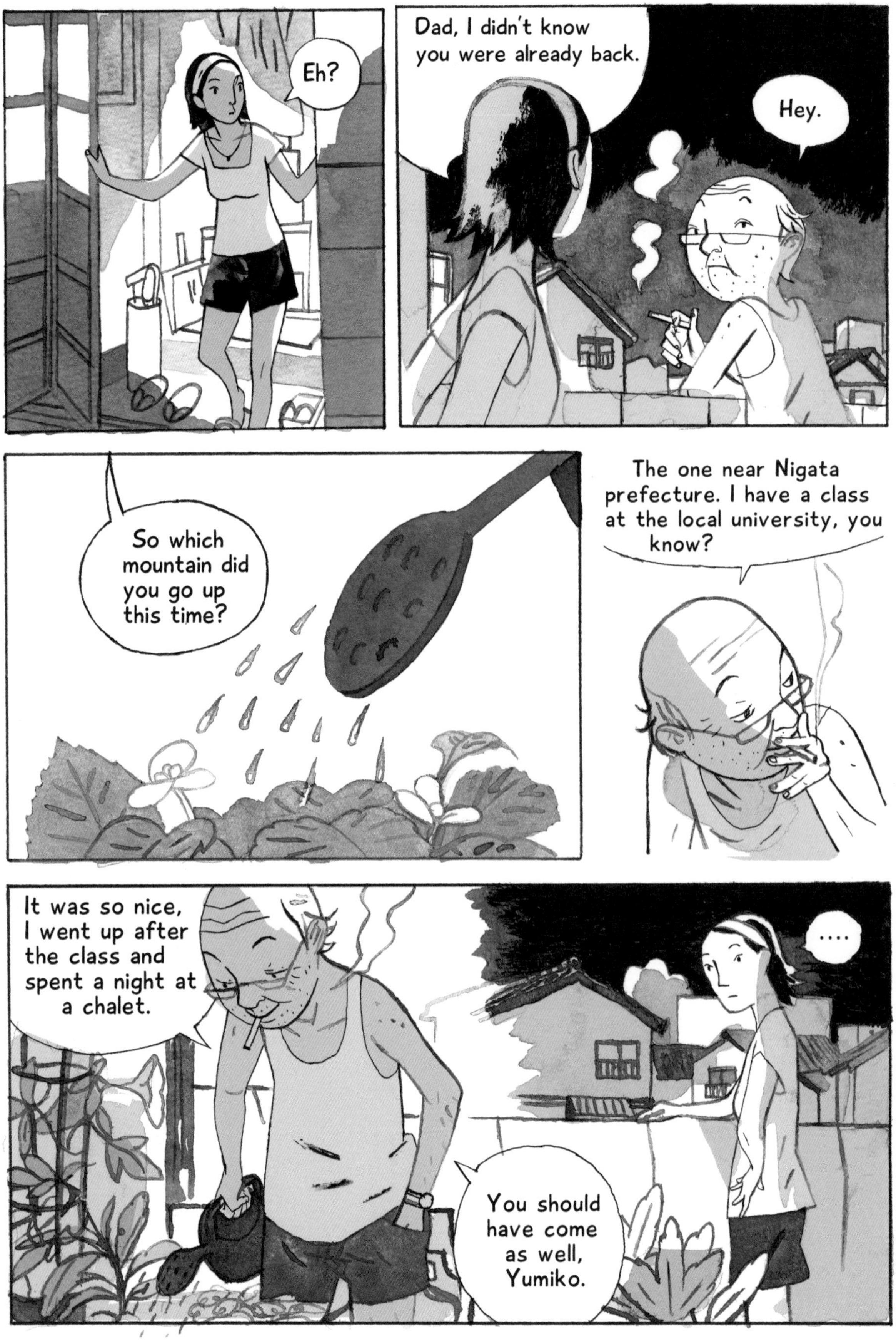
Eh?
Dad, I didn't know you were already back.
Hey.
So which mountain did you go up this time?
The one near Nigata prefecture. I have a class at the local university, you know?
It was so nice, I went up after the class and spent a night at a chalet.
....
You should have come as well, Yumiko.

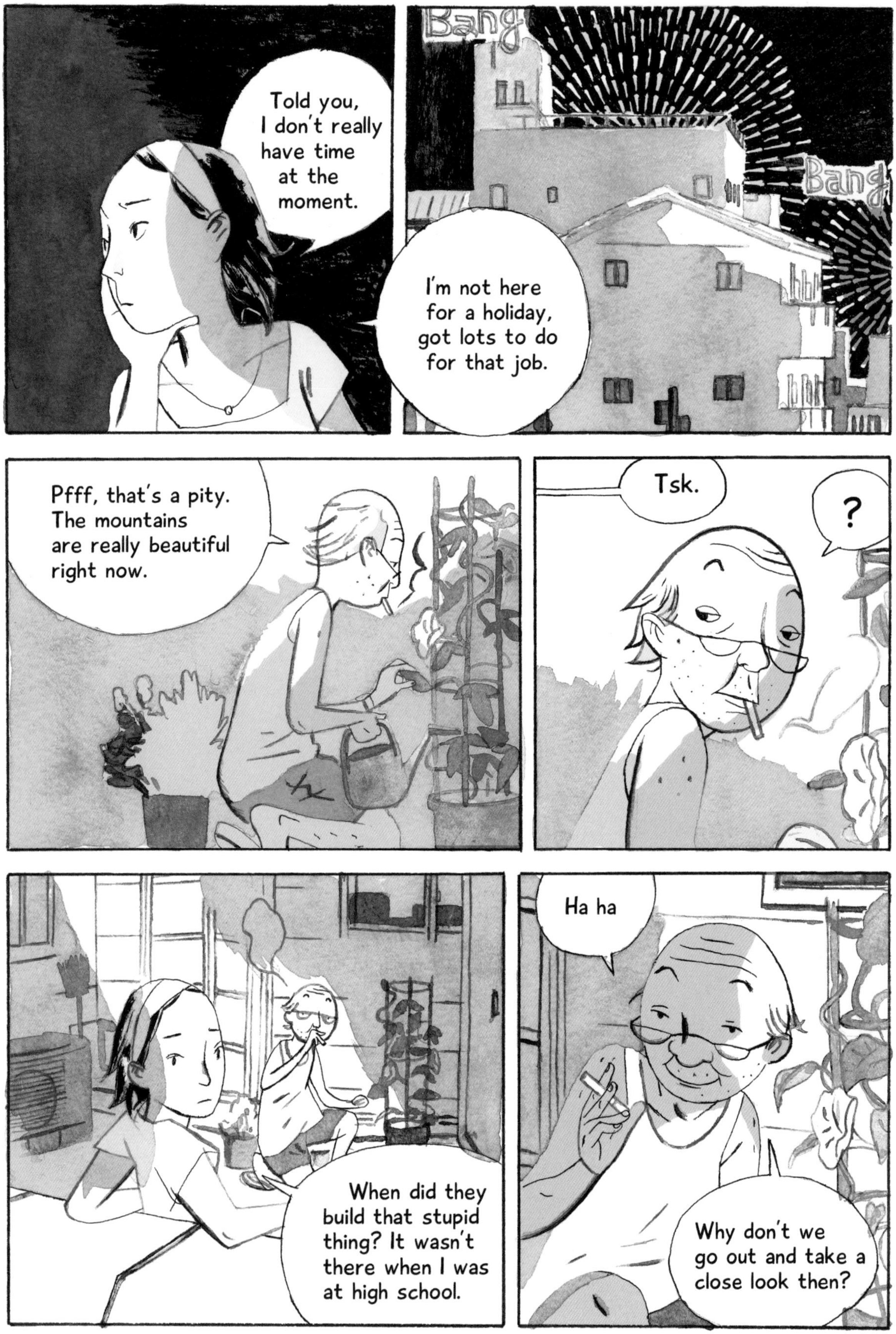
Told you, I don't really have time at the moment.
Bang
Bang
I'm not here for a holiday, got lots to do for that job.
Pfff, that's a pity. The mountains are really beautiful right now.
Tsk.
?
When did they build that stupid thing? It wasn't there when I was at high school.
Ha ha
Why don't we go out and take a close look then?

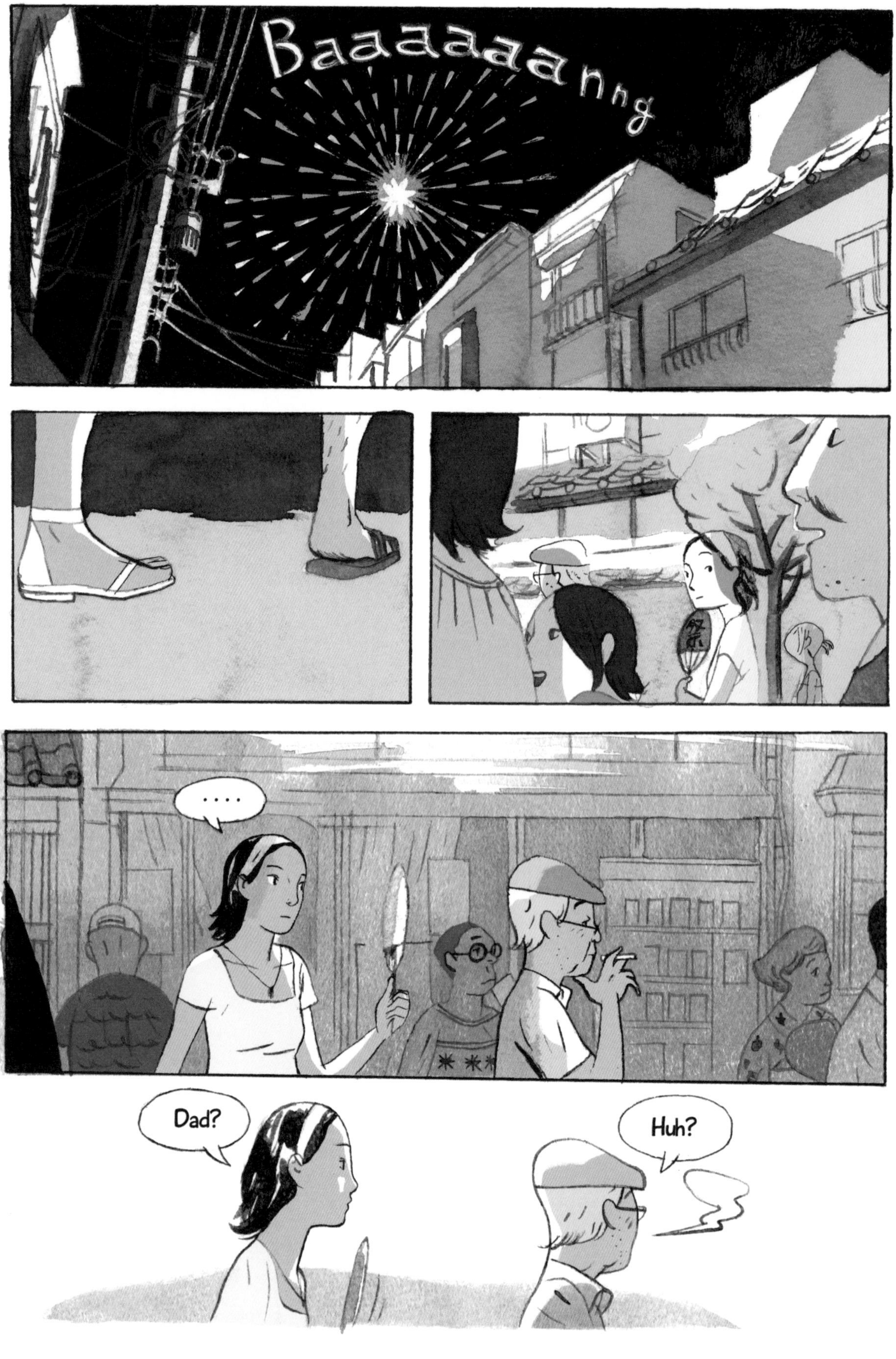
Baaaaaaanng
....
Dad?
Huh?

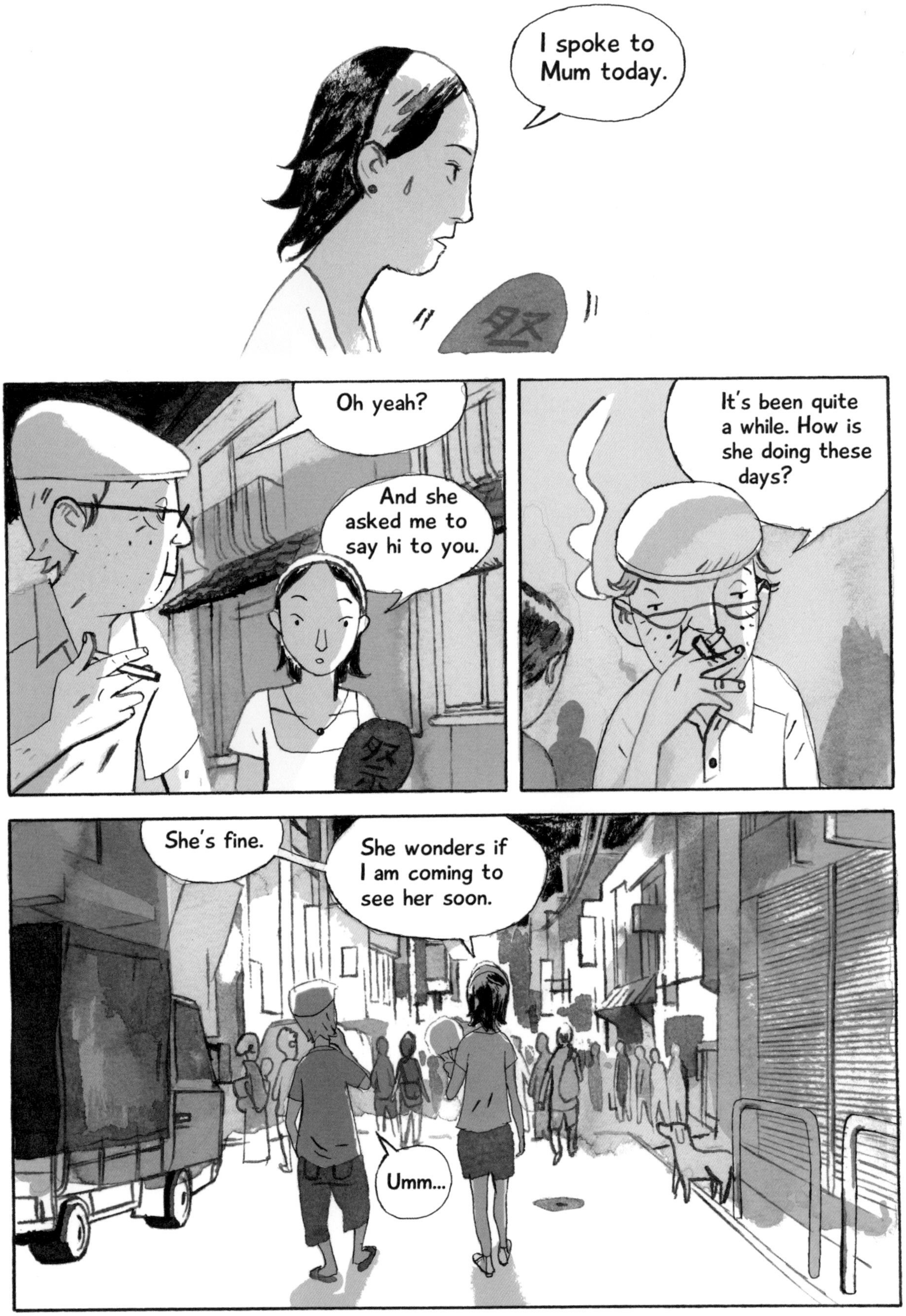
I spoke to Mum today.
Oh yeah?
And she asked me to say hi to you.
It's been quite a while. How is she doing these days?
She's fine.
She wonders if I am coming to see her soon.
Umm...

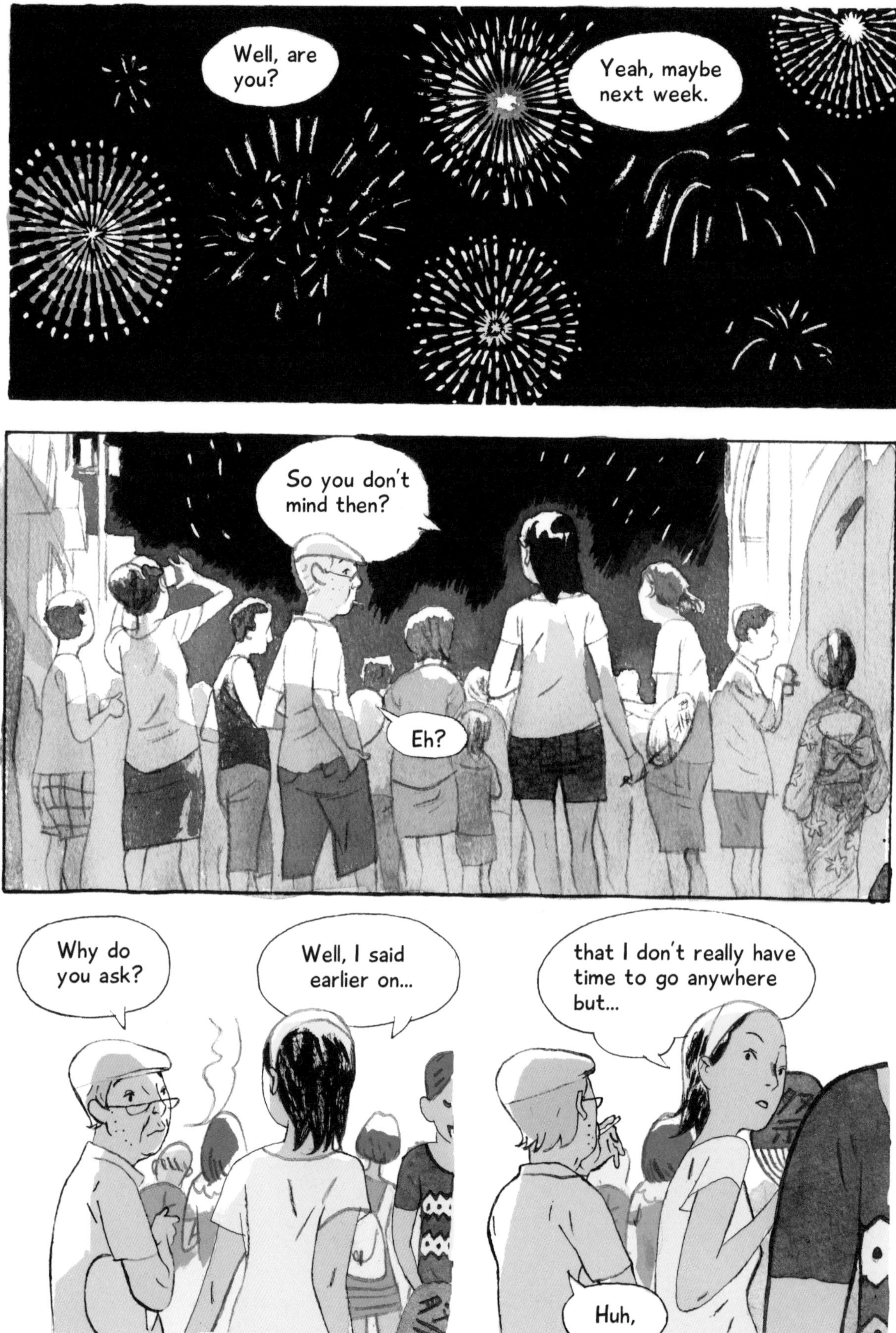
Well, are you?
Yeah, maybe next week.
So you don't mind then?
Eh?
Why do you ask?
Well, I said earlier on...
that I don't really have time to go anywhere but...
Huh,

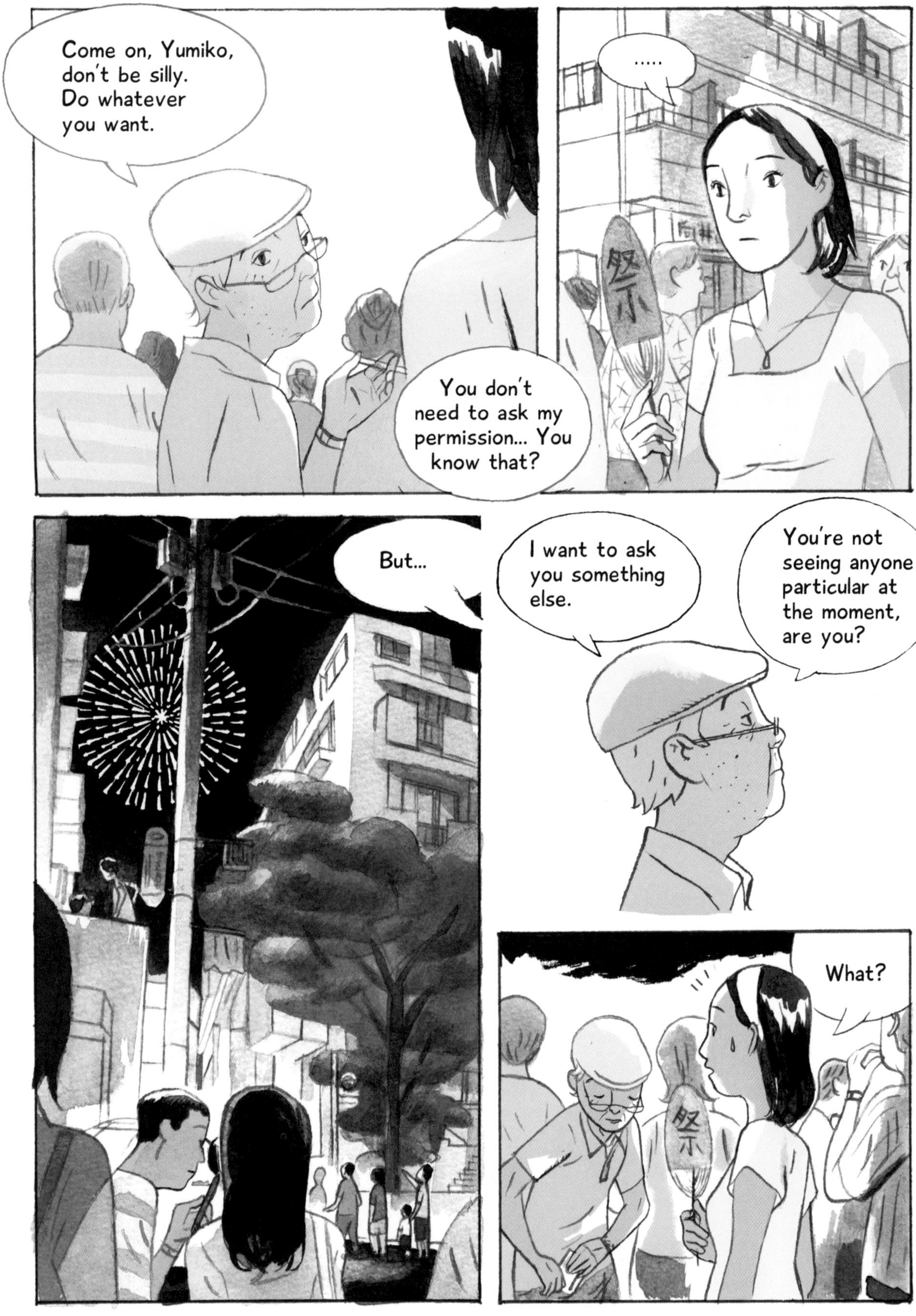
Come on, Yumiko, don't be silly. Do whatever you want.
.....
You don't need to ask my permission... You know that?
But...
I want to ask you something else.
You're not seeing anyone particular at the moment, are you?
What?

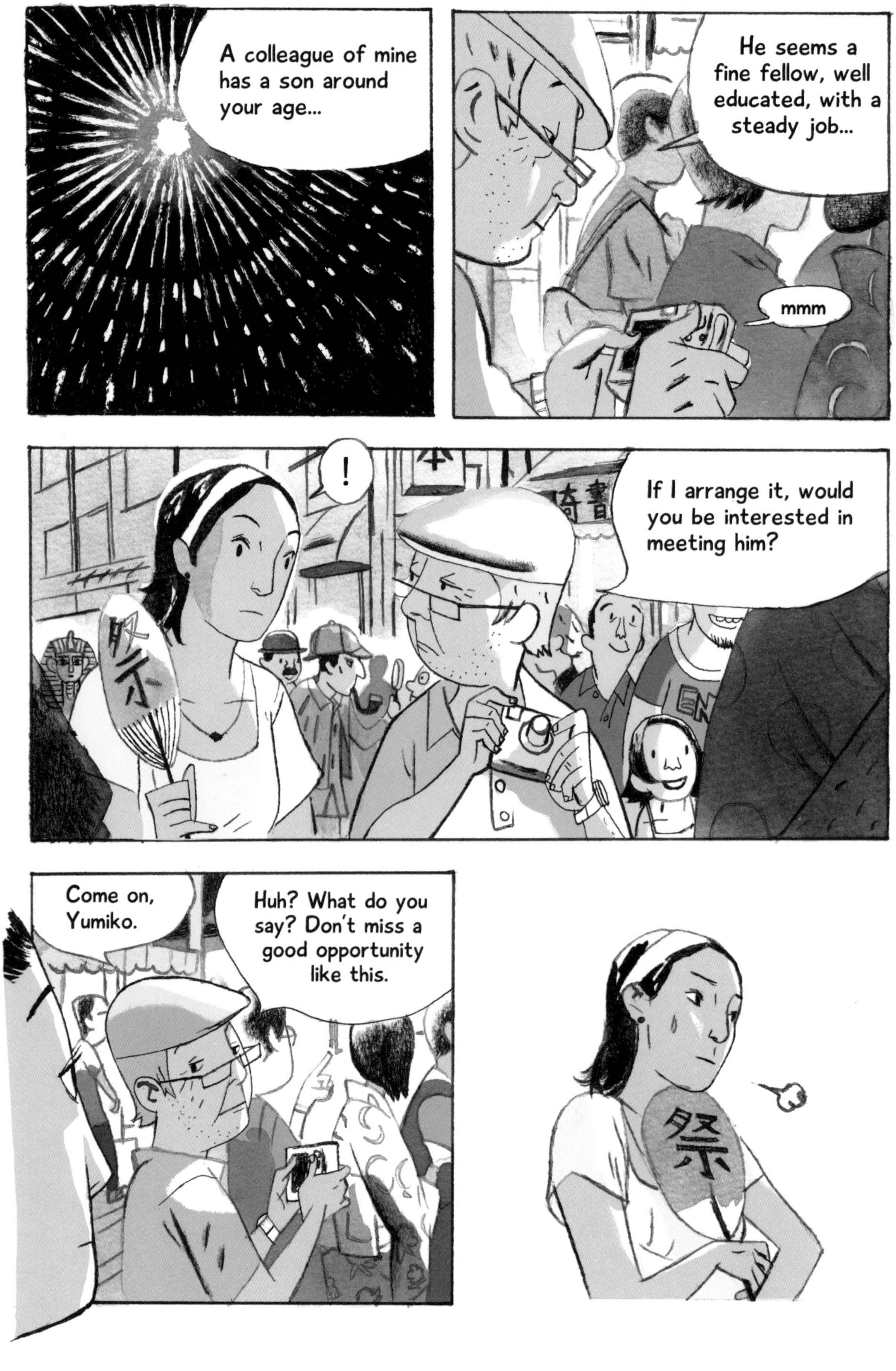
A colleague of mine has a son around your age...
He seems a fine fellow, well educated, with a steady job...
mmm
!
If I arrange it, would you be interested in meeting him?
Come on, Yumiko.
Huh? What do you say? Don't miss a good opportunity like this.

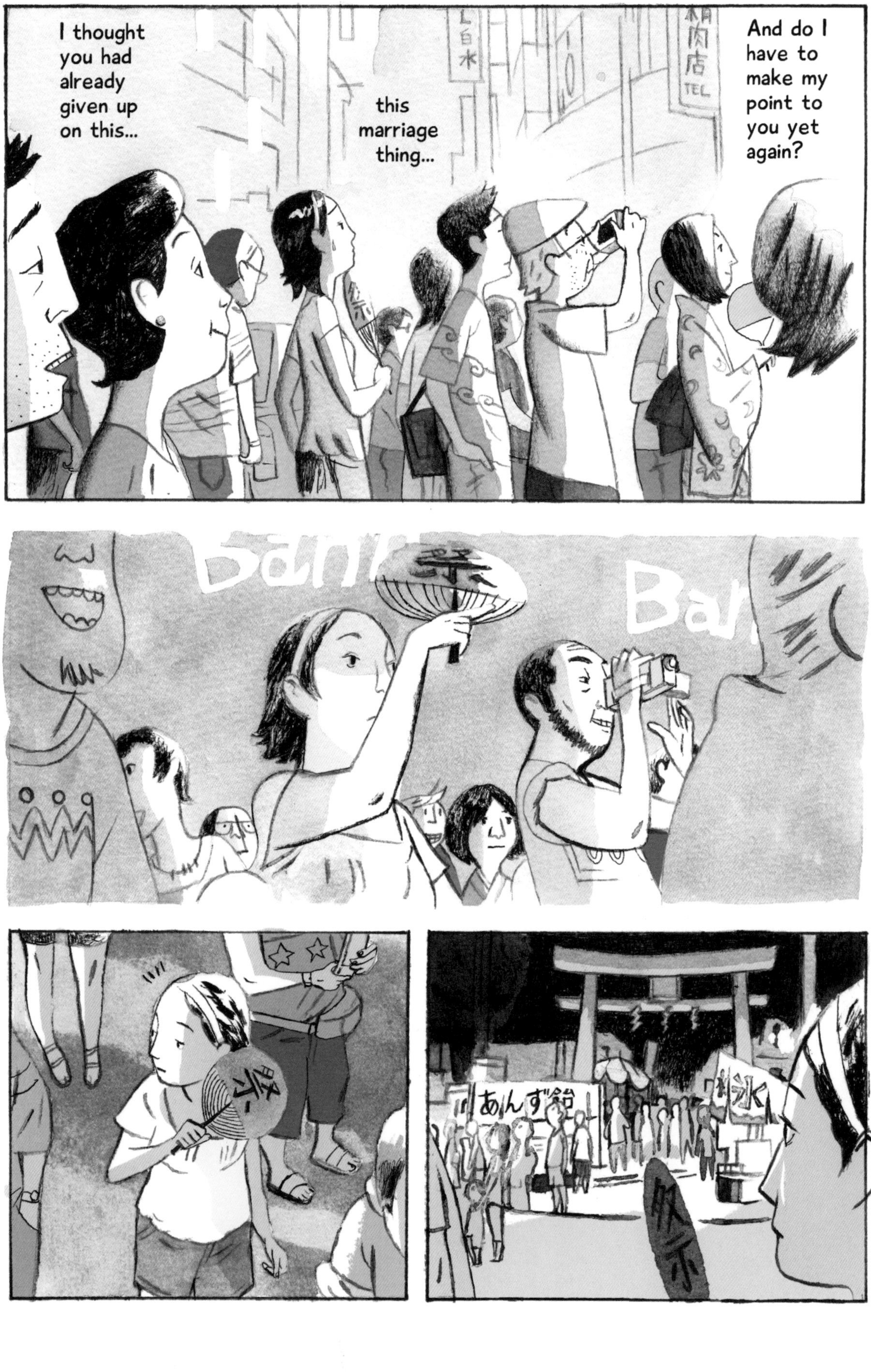
I thought you had already given up on this...
this marriage thing...
And do I have to make my point to you yet again?

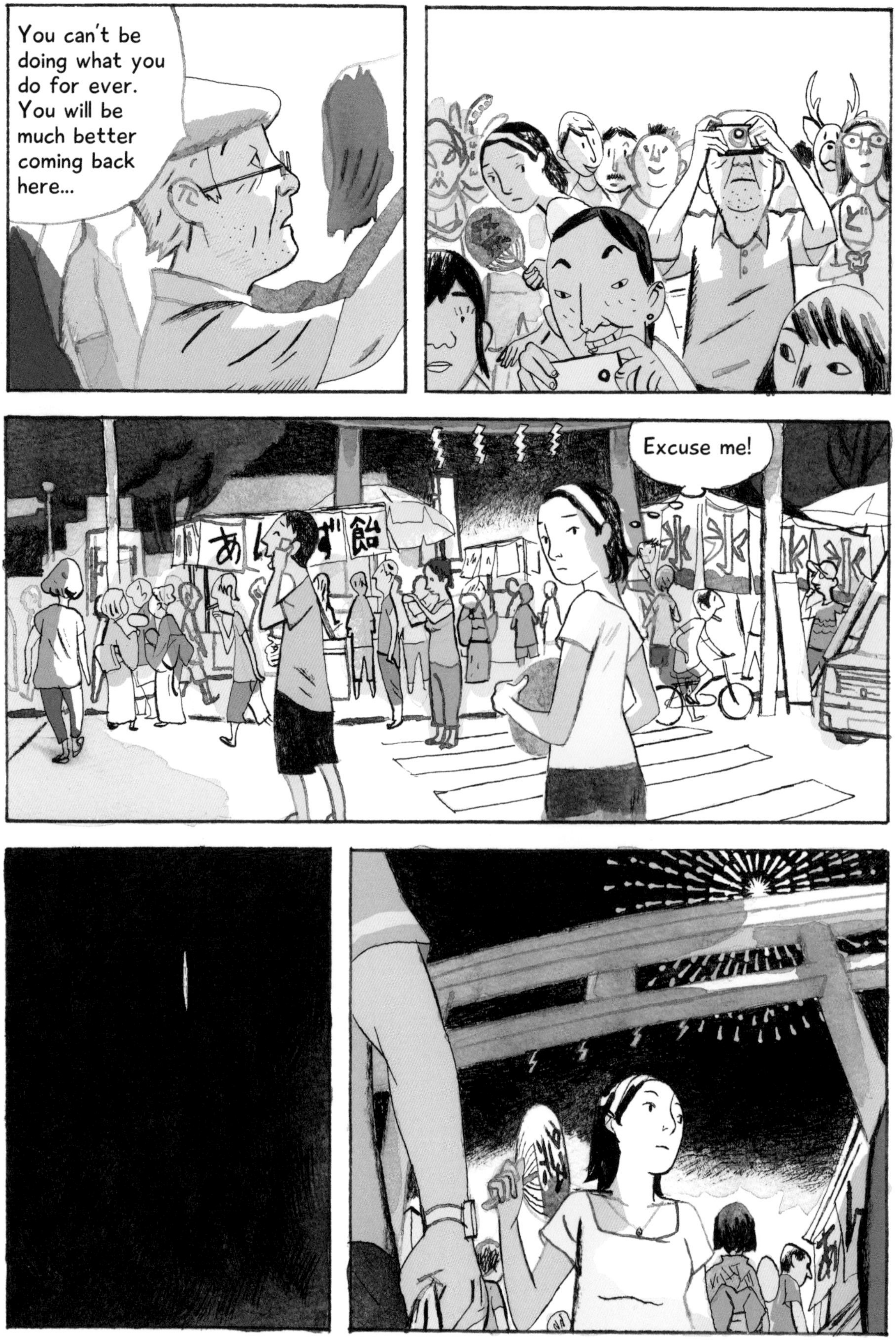
You can't be doing what you do for ever. You will be much better coming back here...
Excuse me!

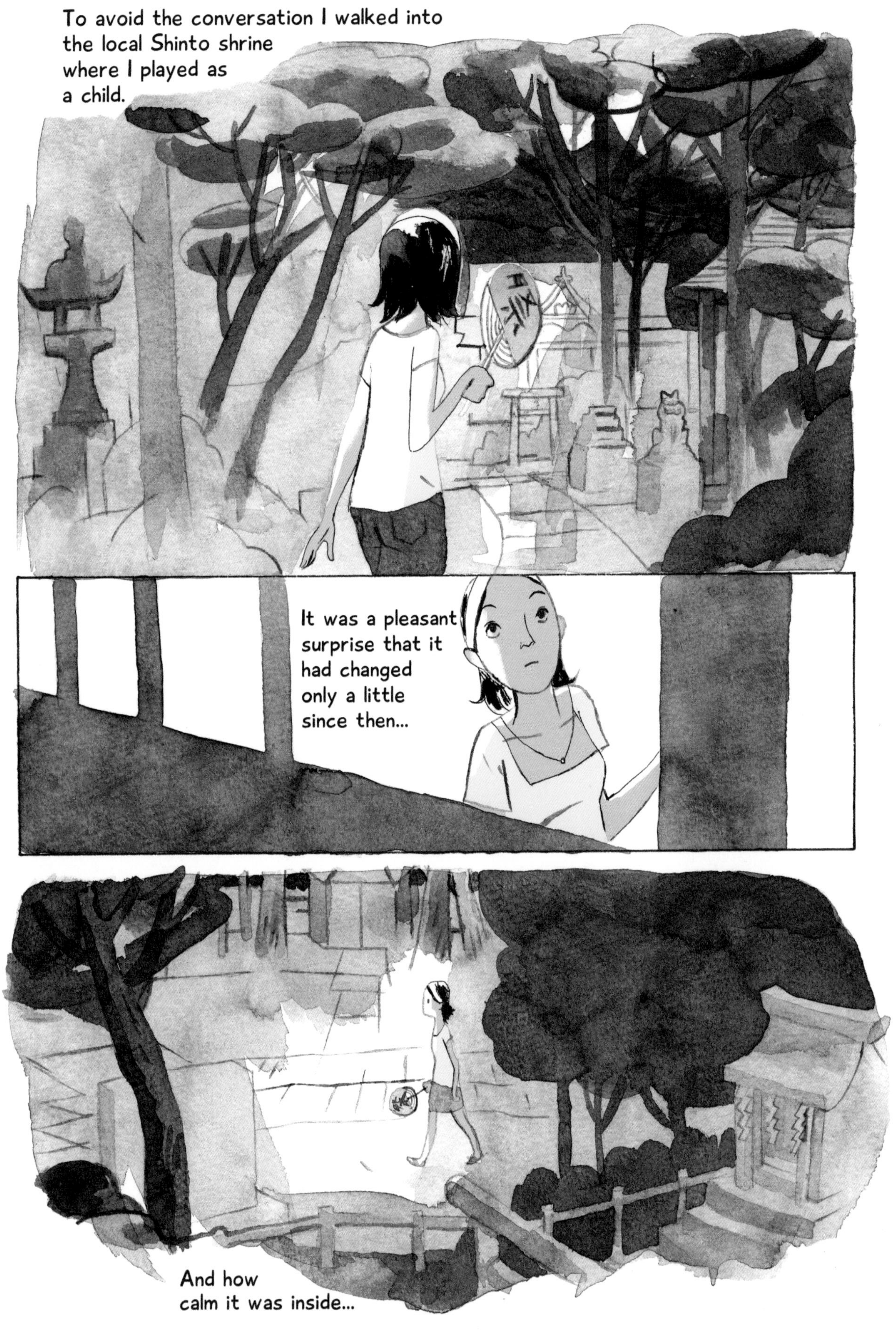
To avoid the conversation I walked into the local Shinto shrine where I played as a child.
It was a pleasant surprise that it had changed only a little since then...
And how calm it was inside...

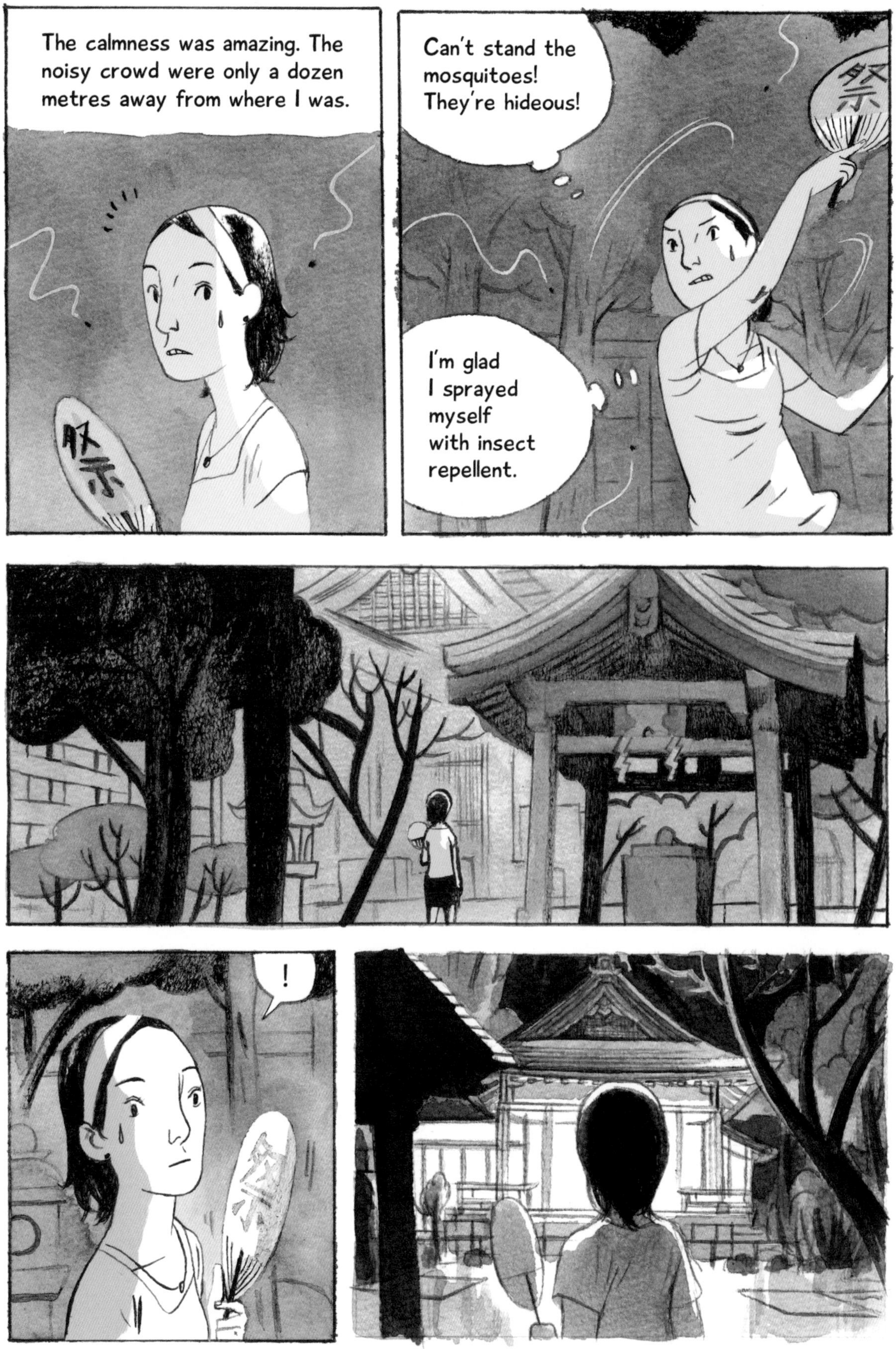
The calmness was amazing. The noisy crowd were only a dozen metres away from where I was.
Can't stand the mosquitoes! They're hideous!
I'm glad I sprayed myself with insect repellent.
!

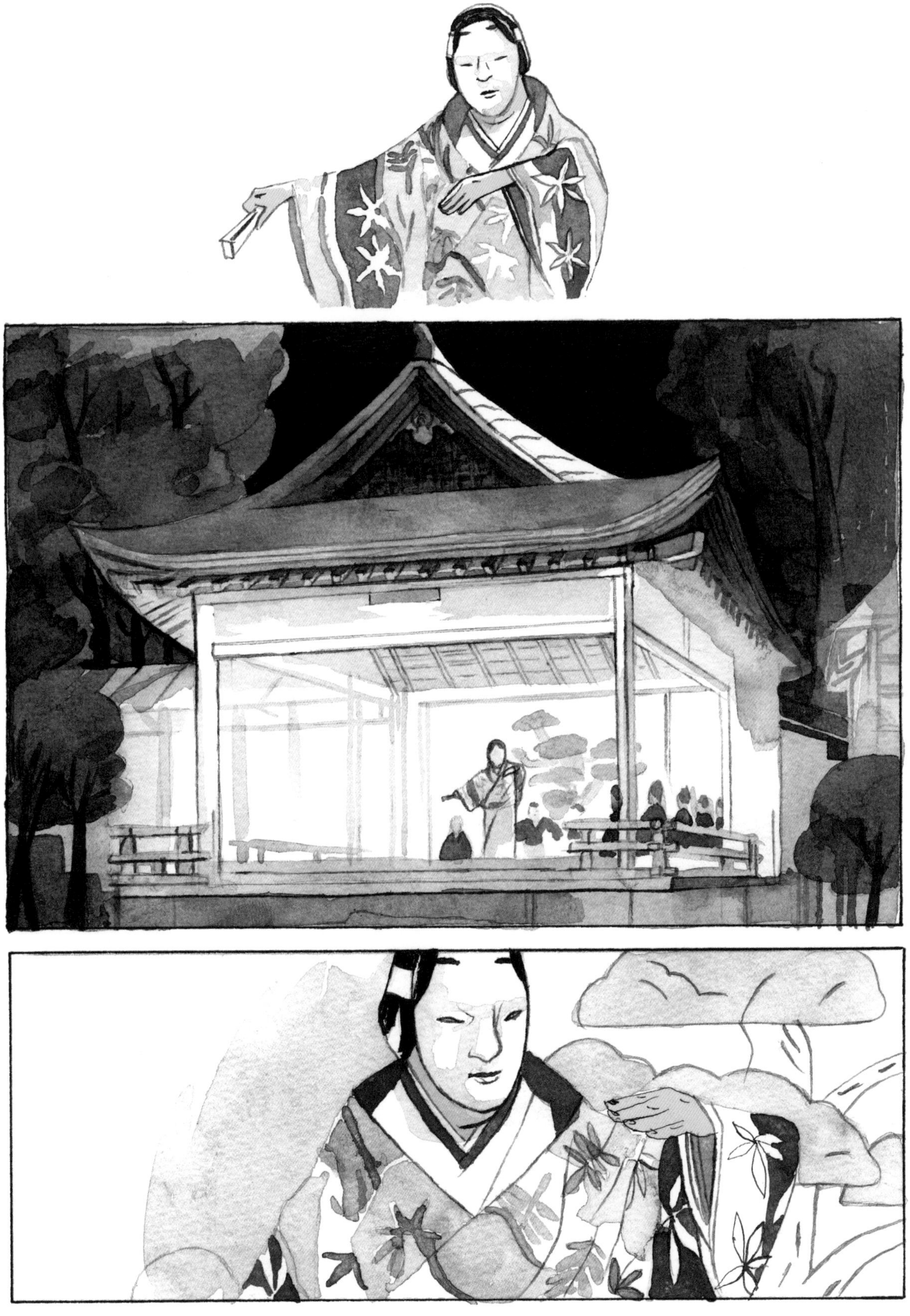

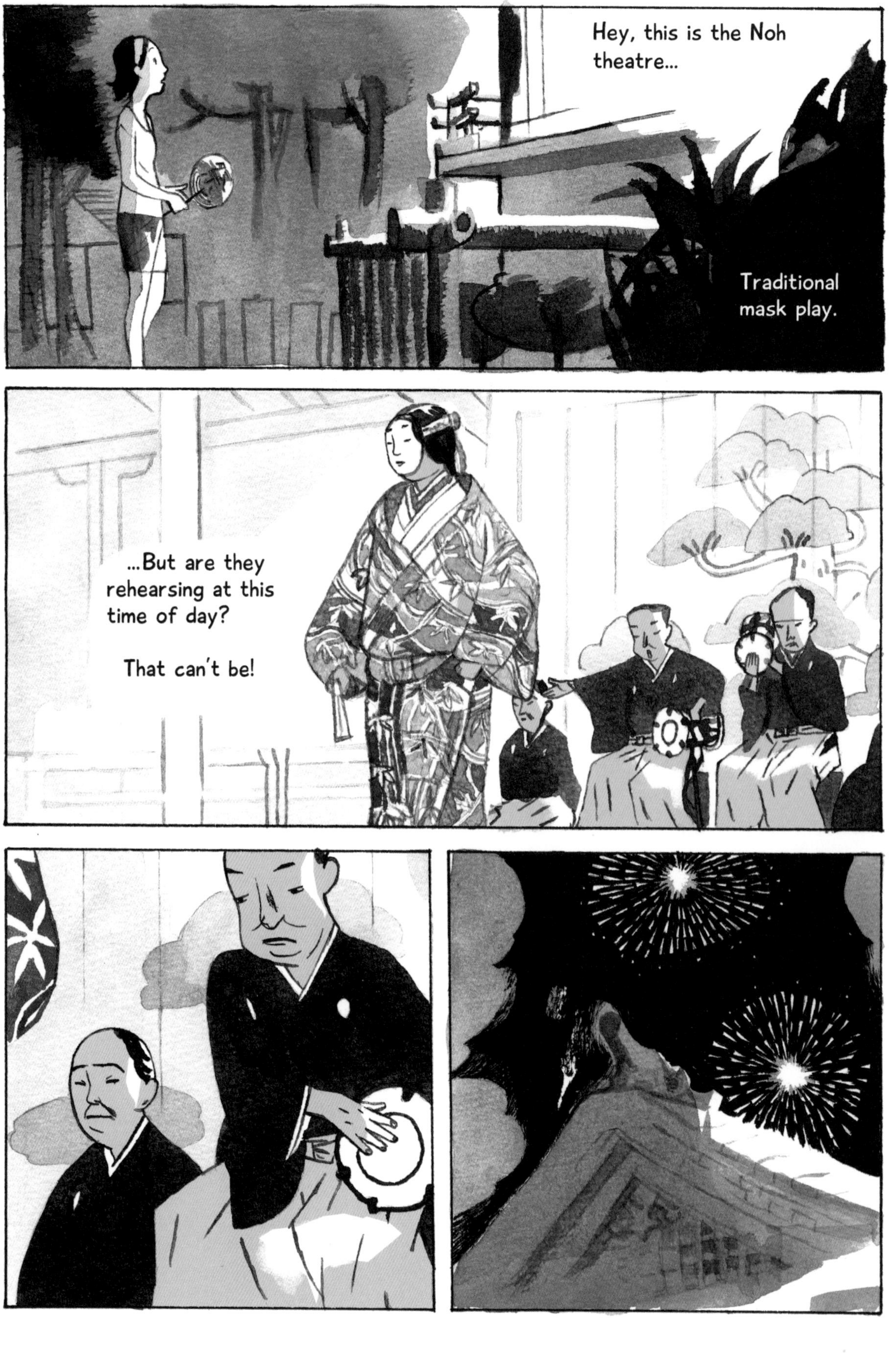
Hey, this is the Noh theatre...
Traditional mask play.
...But are they rehearsing at this time of day?
That can't be!

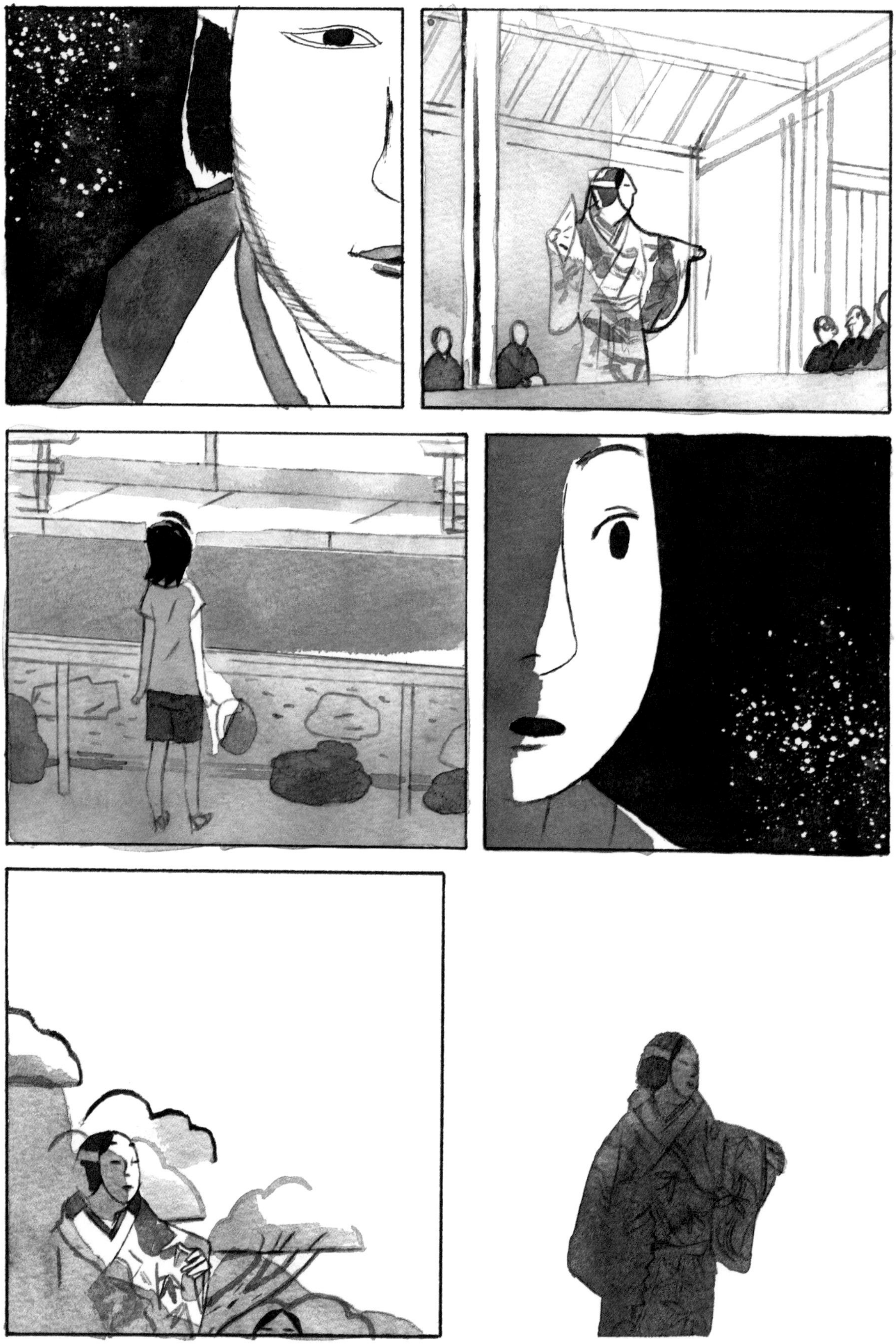

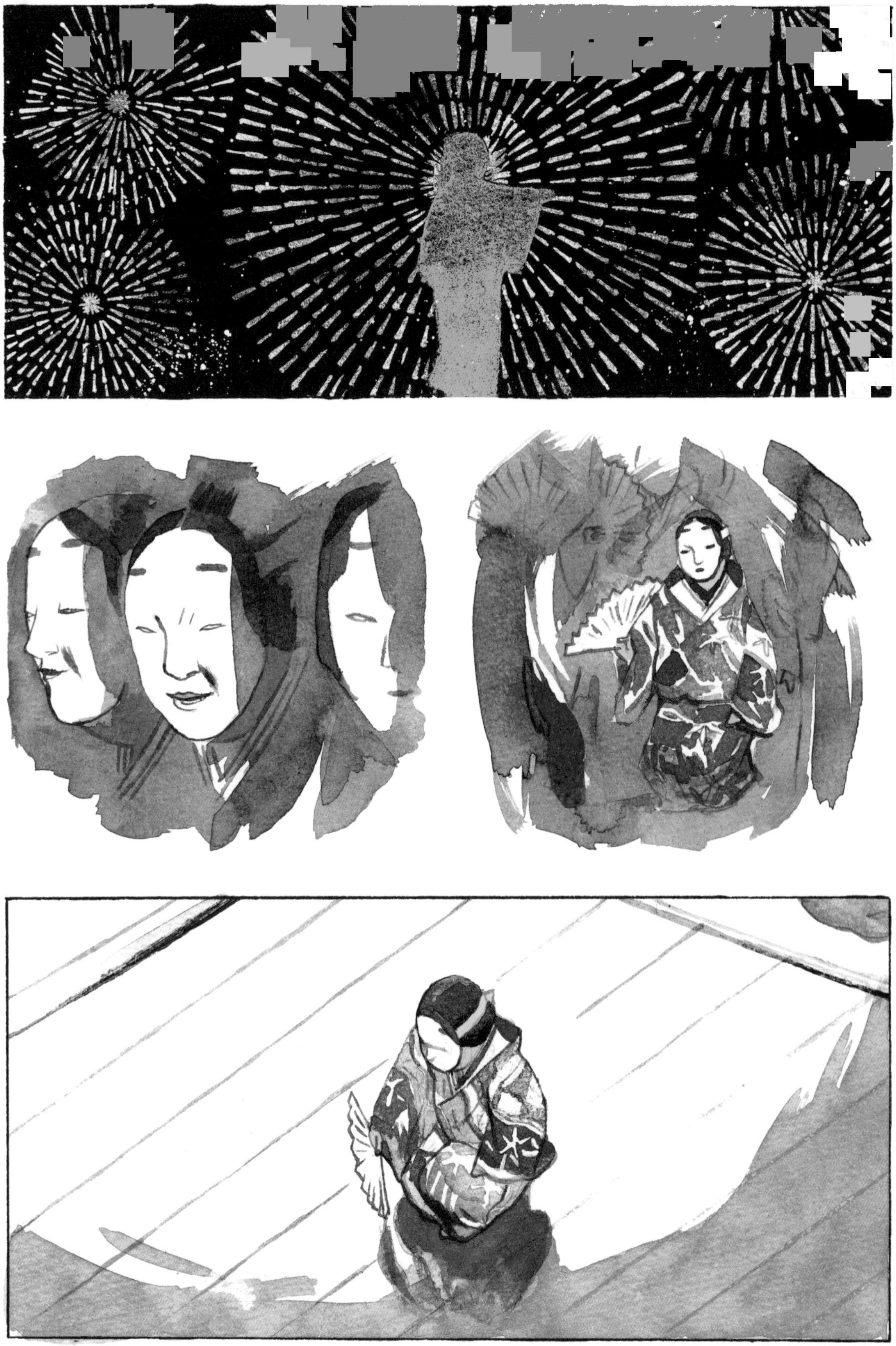

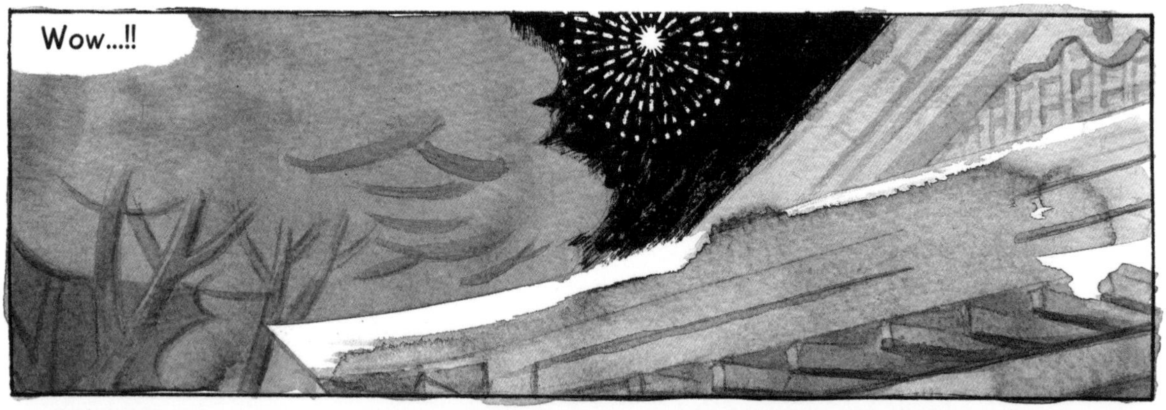
Wow...!!

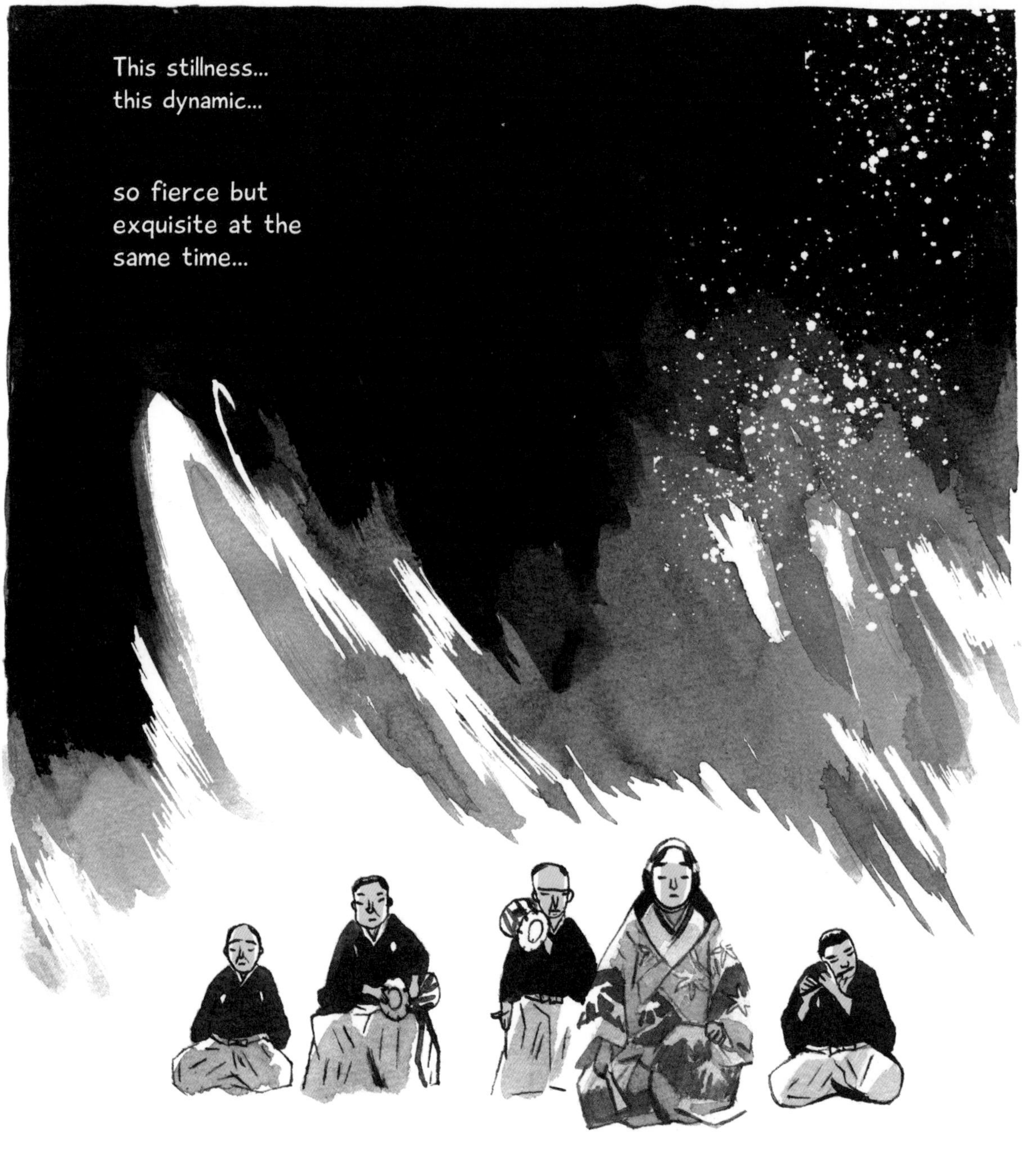
This stillness...
this dynamic...
so fierce but
exquisite at the
same time...

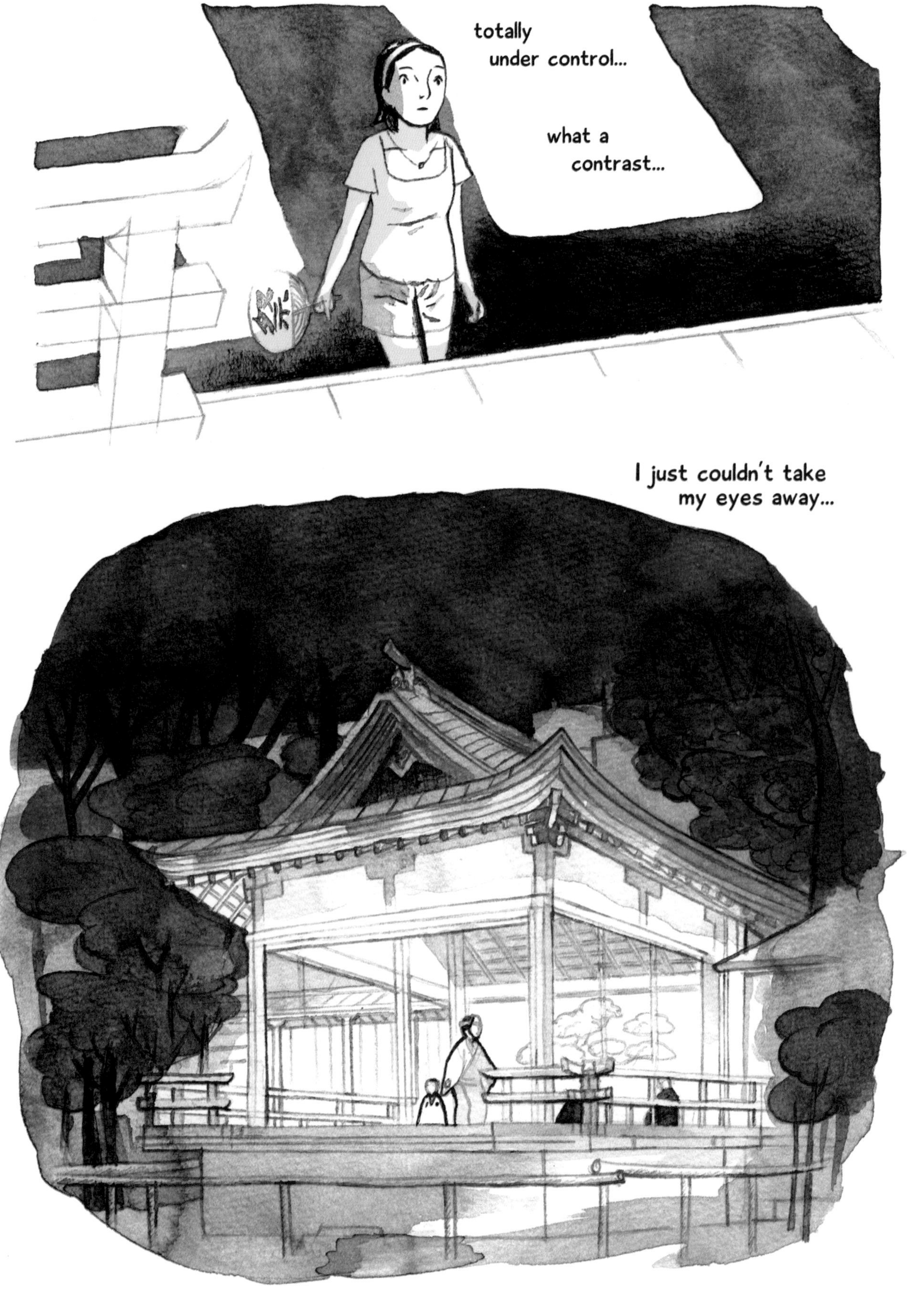
totally under control...
what a contrast...
I just couldn't take my eyes away...

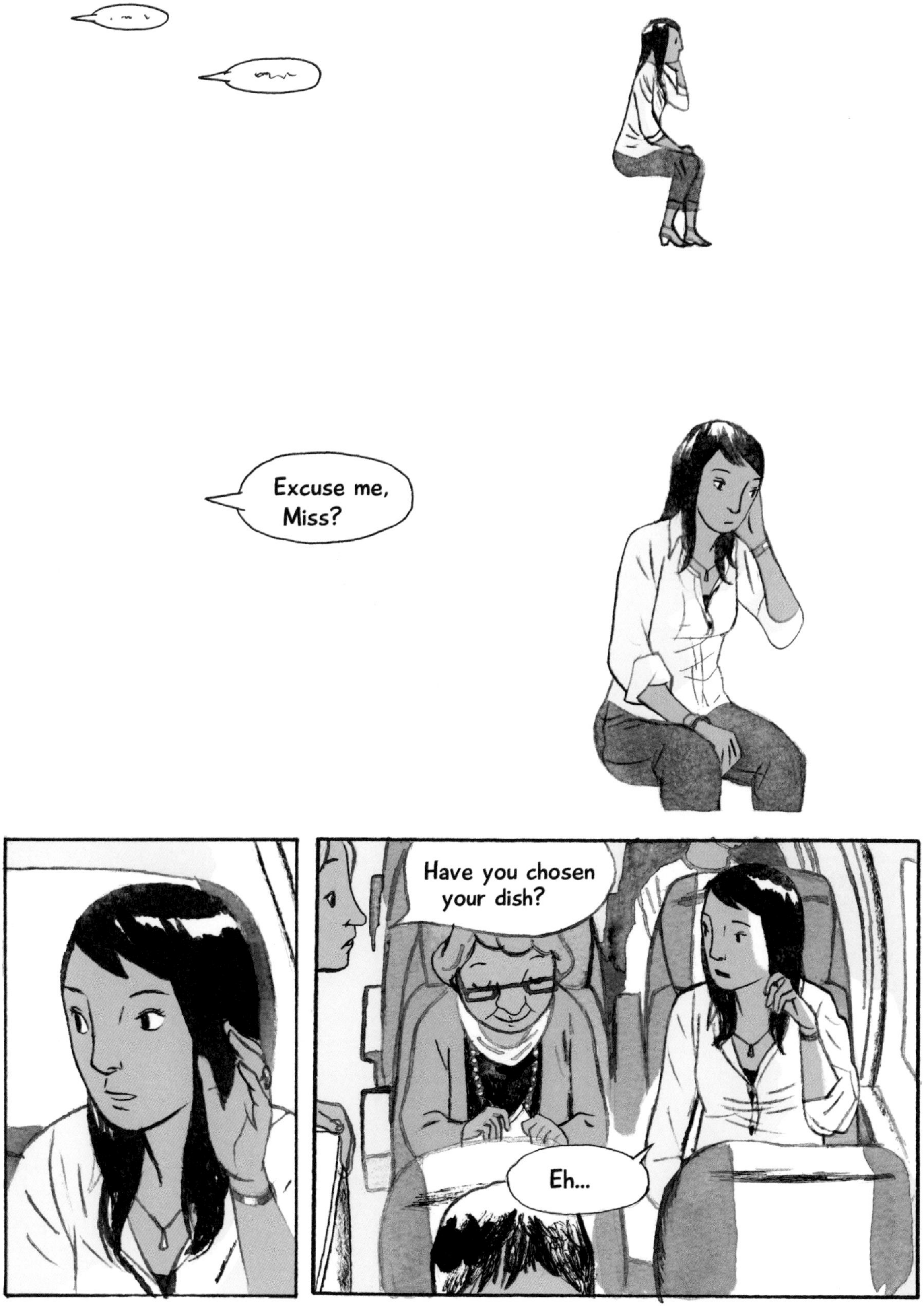
Excuse me, Miss?
Have you chosen your dish?
Eh...

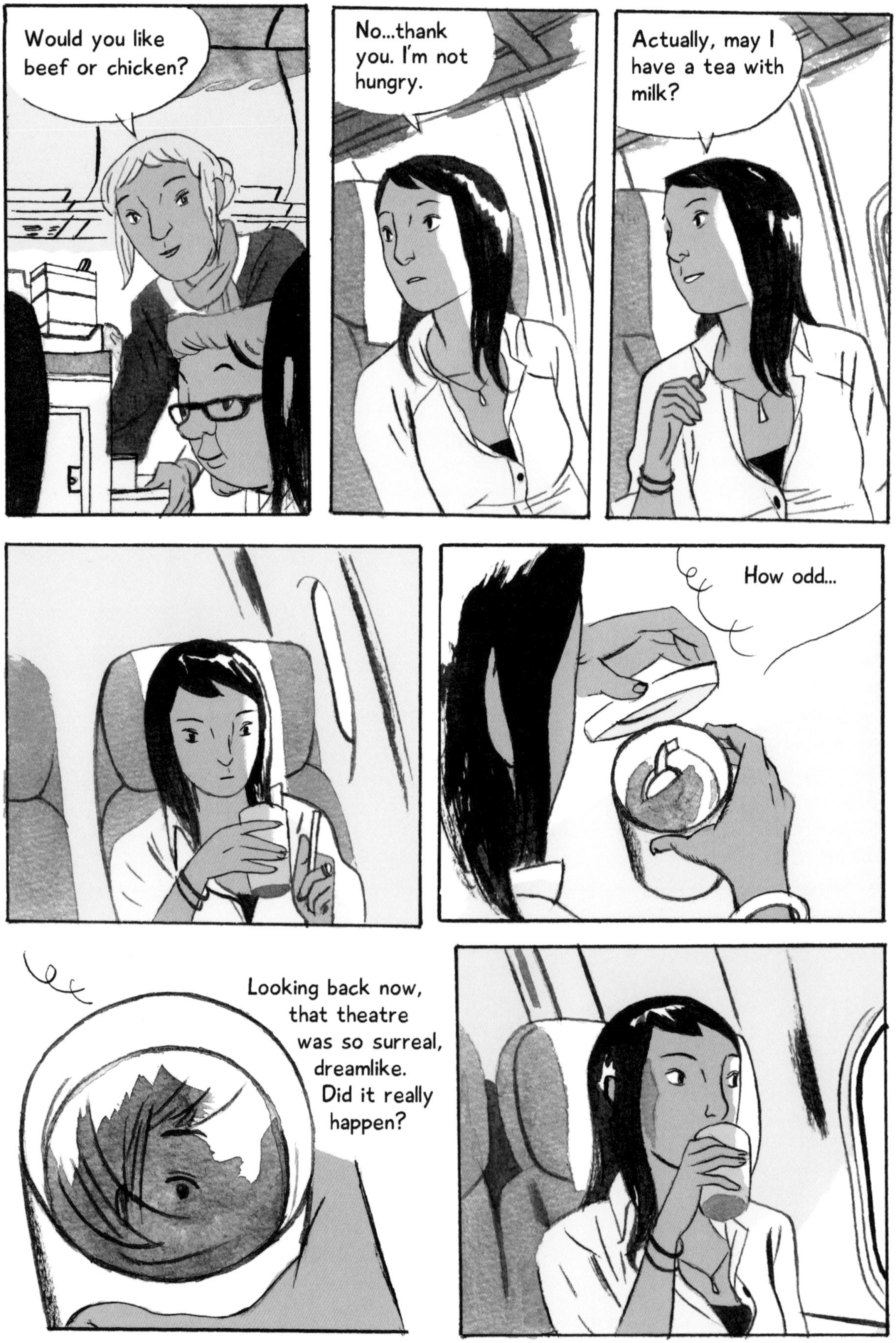
Would you like beef or chicken?
No...thank you. I'm not hungry.
Actually, may I have a tea with milk?
How odd...
Looking back now, that theatre was so surreal, dreamlike. Did it really happen?

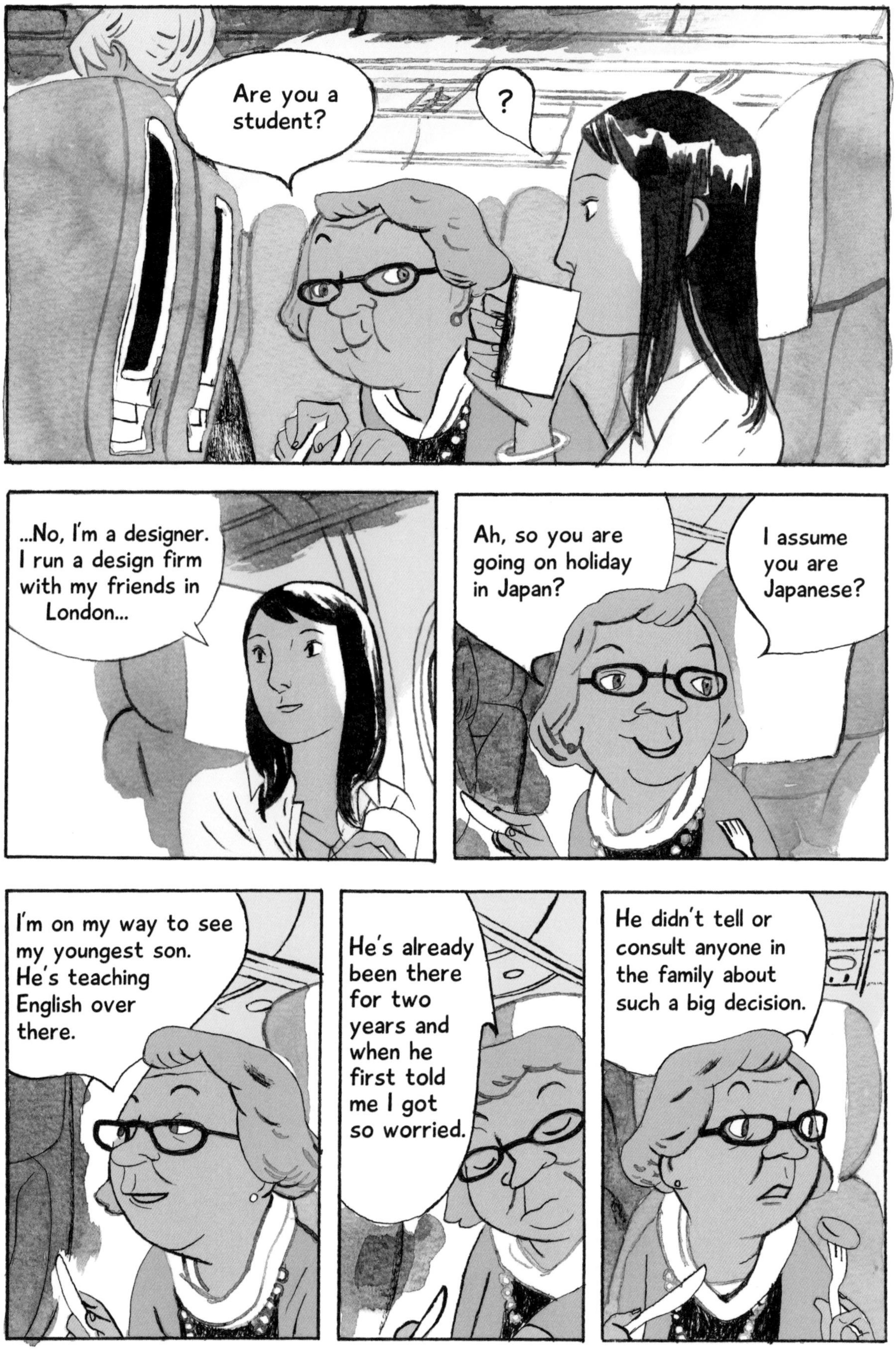
Are you a student?
?
...No, I'm a designer. I run a design firm with my friends in London...
I assume you are Japanese?
Ah, so you are going on holiday in Japan?
I'm on my way to see my youngest son. He's teaching English over there.
He's already been there for two years and when he first told me I got so worried.
He didn't tell or consult anyone in the family about such a big decision.

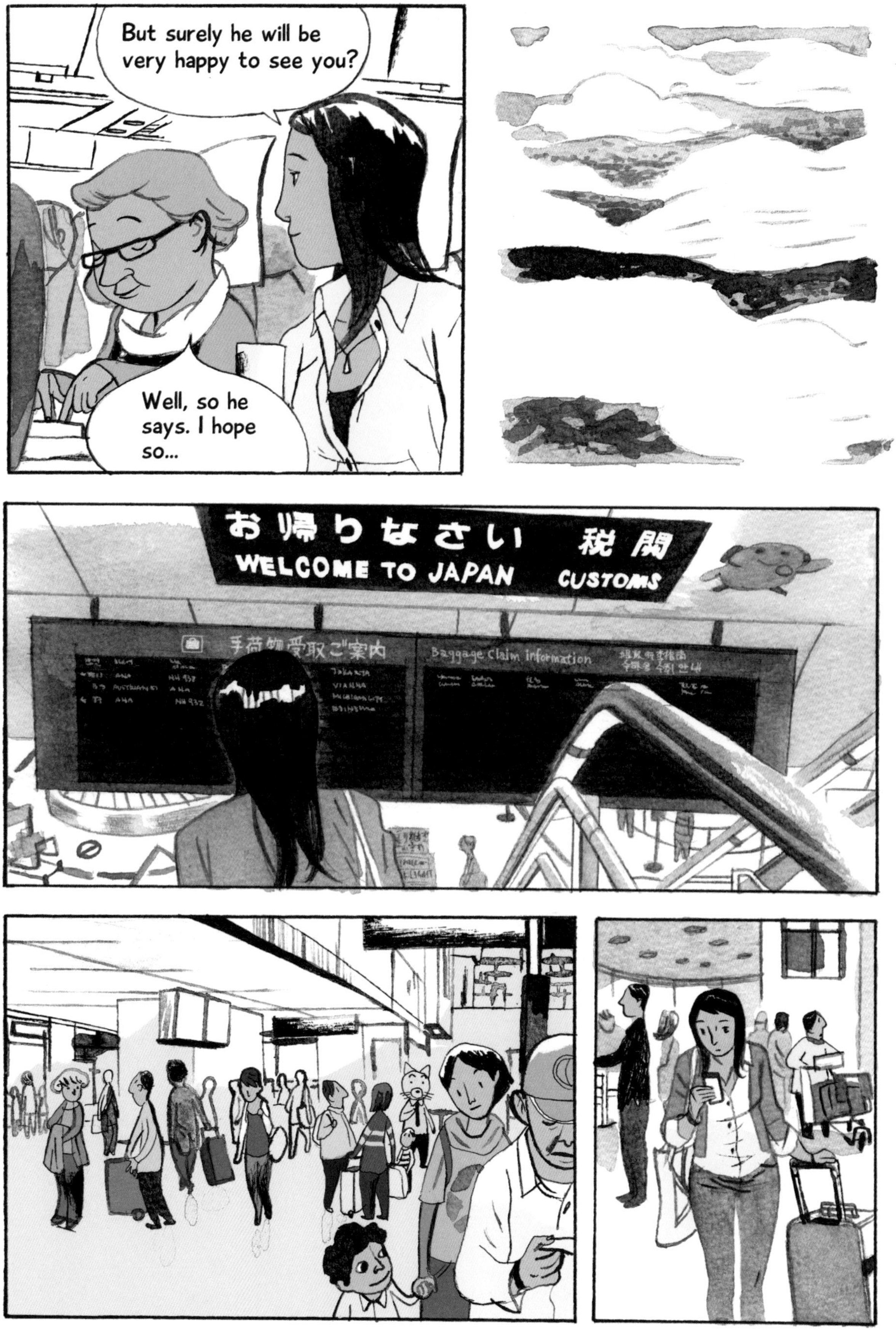

But surely he will be very happy to see you?
Well, so he says. I hope so...
お帰りなさい
税関
WELCOME TO JAPAN
CUSTOMS
手荷物受取ご案内
Baggage Claim information

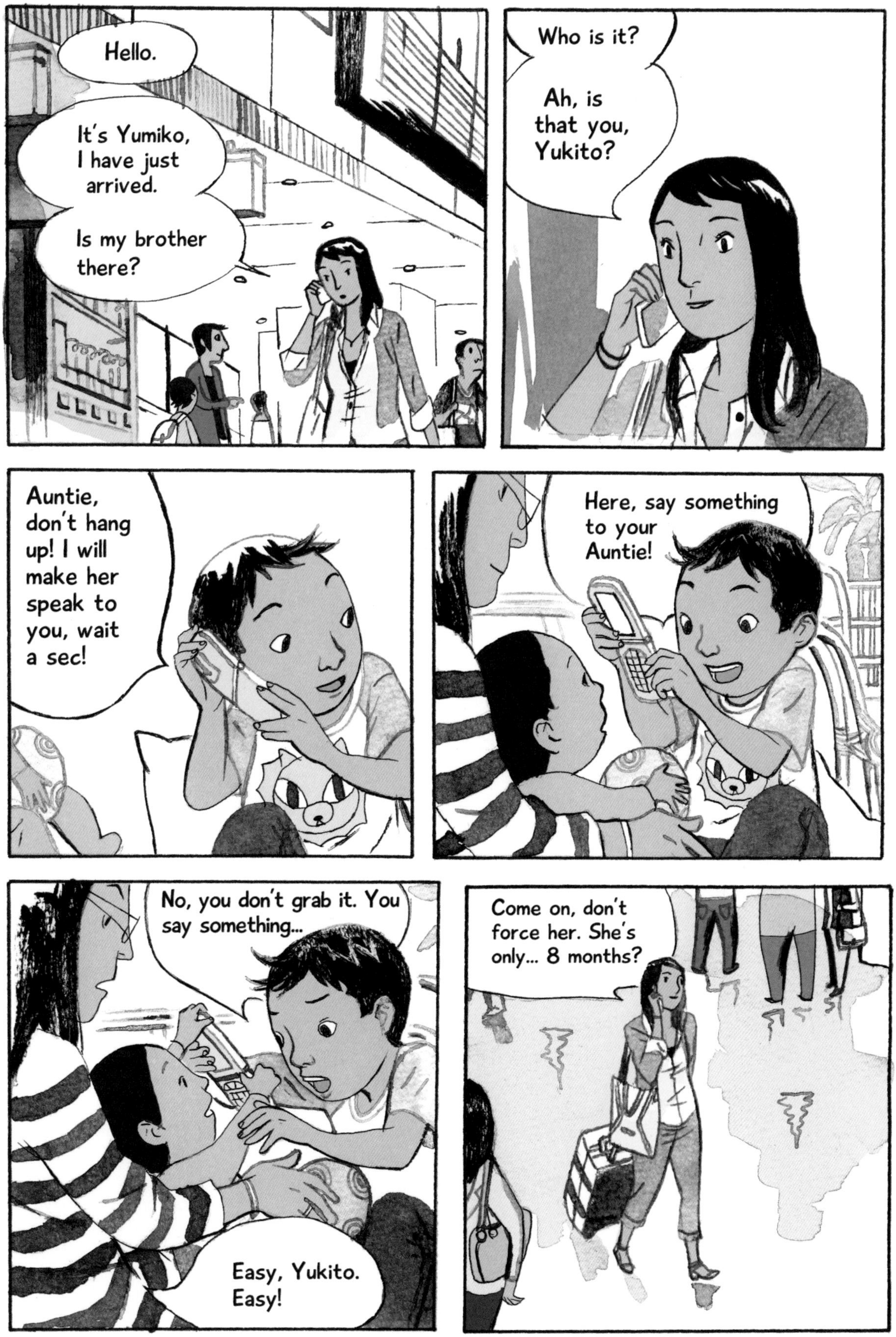
Hello.
It's Yumiko, I have just arrived.
Is my brother there?
Who is it?
Ah, is that you, Yukito?
Auntie, don't hang up! I will make her speak to you, wait a sec!
Here, say something to your Auntie!
No, you don't grab it. You say something...
Easy, Yukito. Easy!
Come on, don't force her. She's only... 8 months?

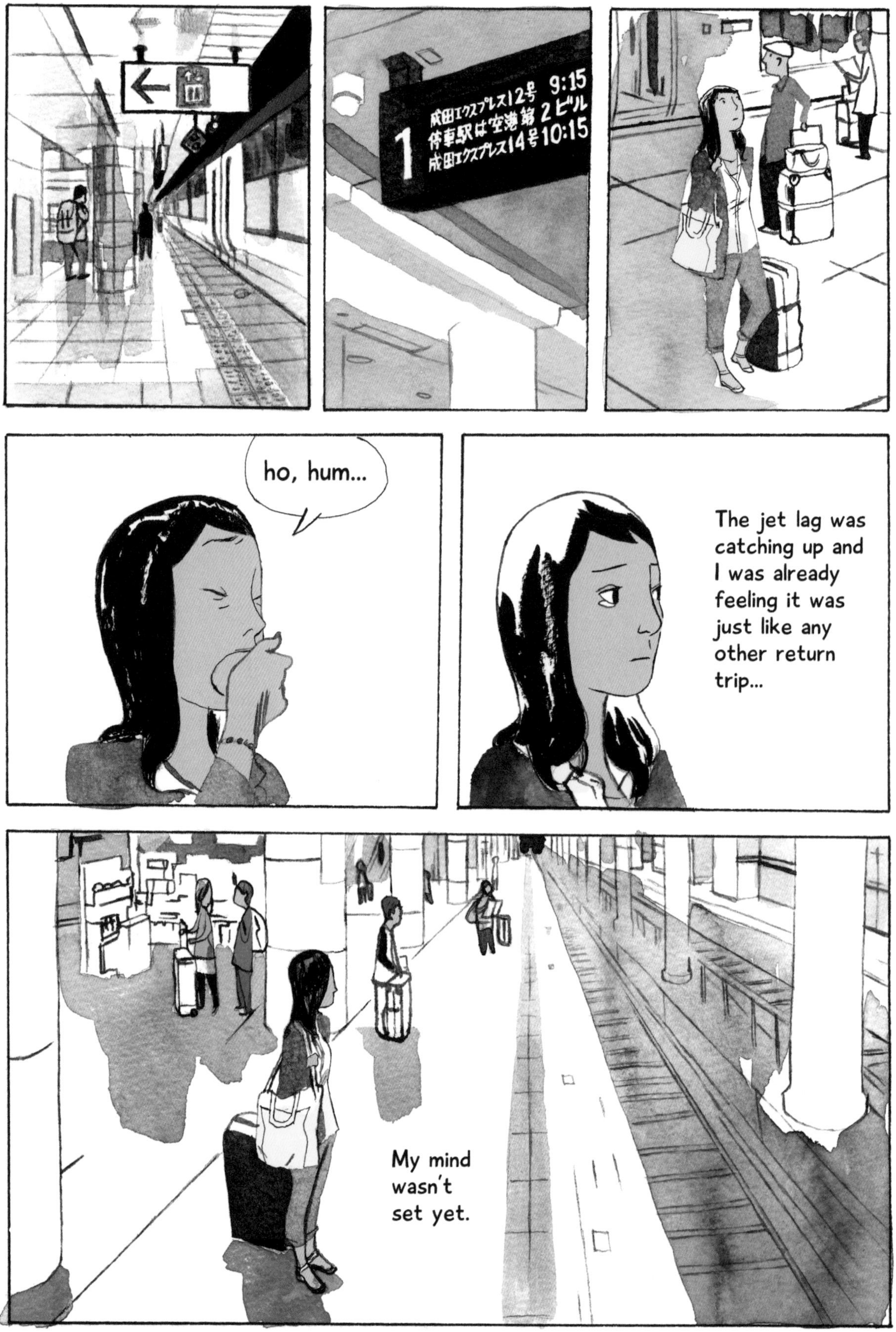
1
成田エクスプレス12号 9:15
停車駅は空港第2ビル
成田エクスプレス14号 10:15
ho, hum...
The jet lag was catching up and I was already feeling it was just like any other return trip...
My mind wasn't set yet.

II

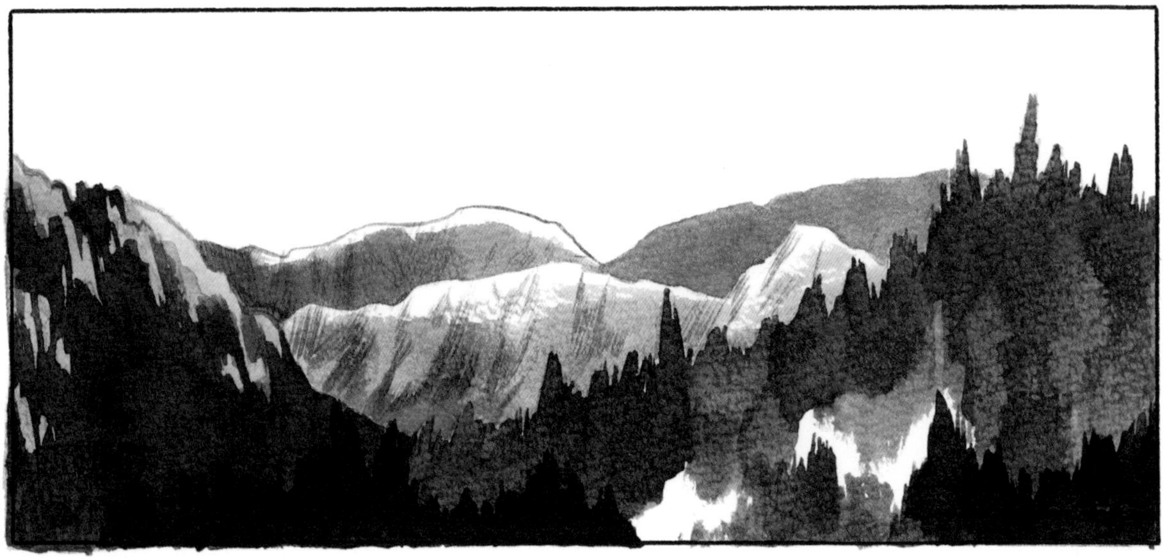

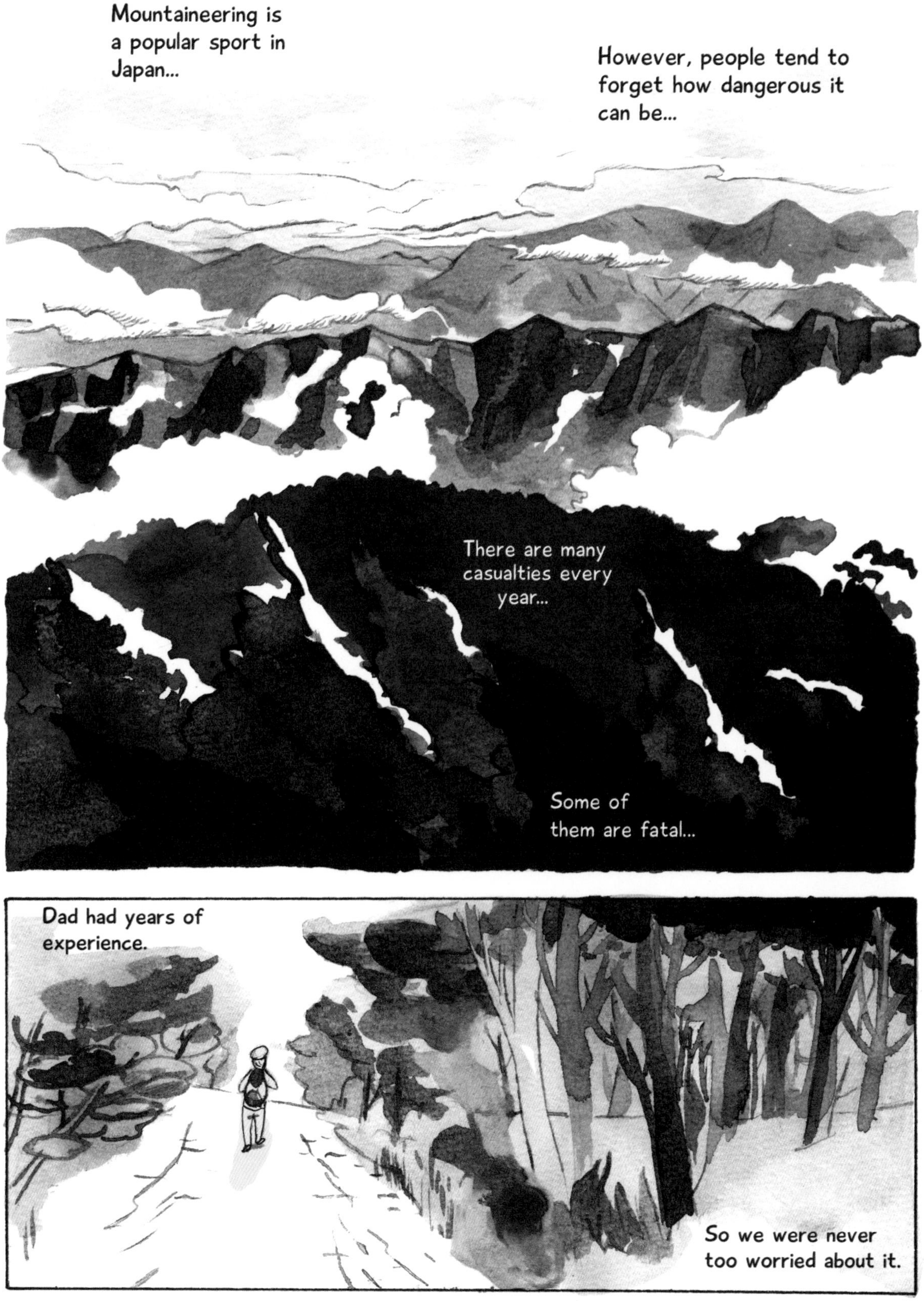
Mountaineering is a popular sport in Japan...
However, people tend to forget how dangerous it can be...
There are many casualties every year...
Some of them are fatal...
Dad had years of experience.
So we were never too worried about it.

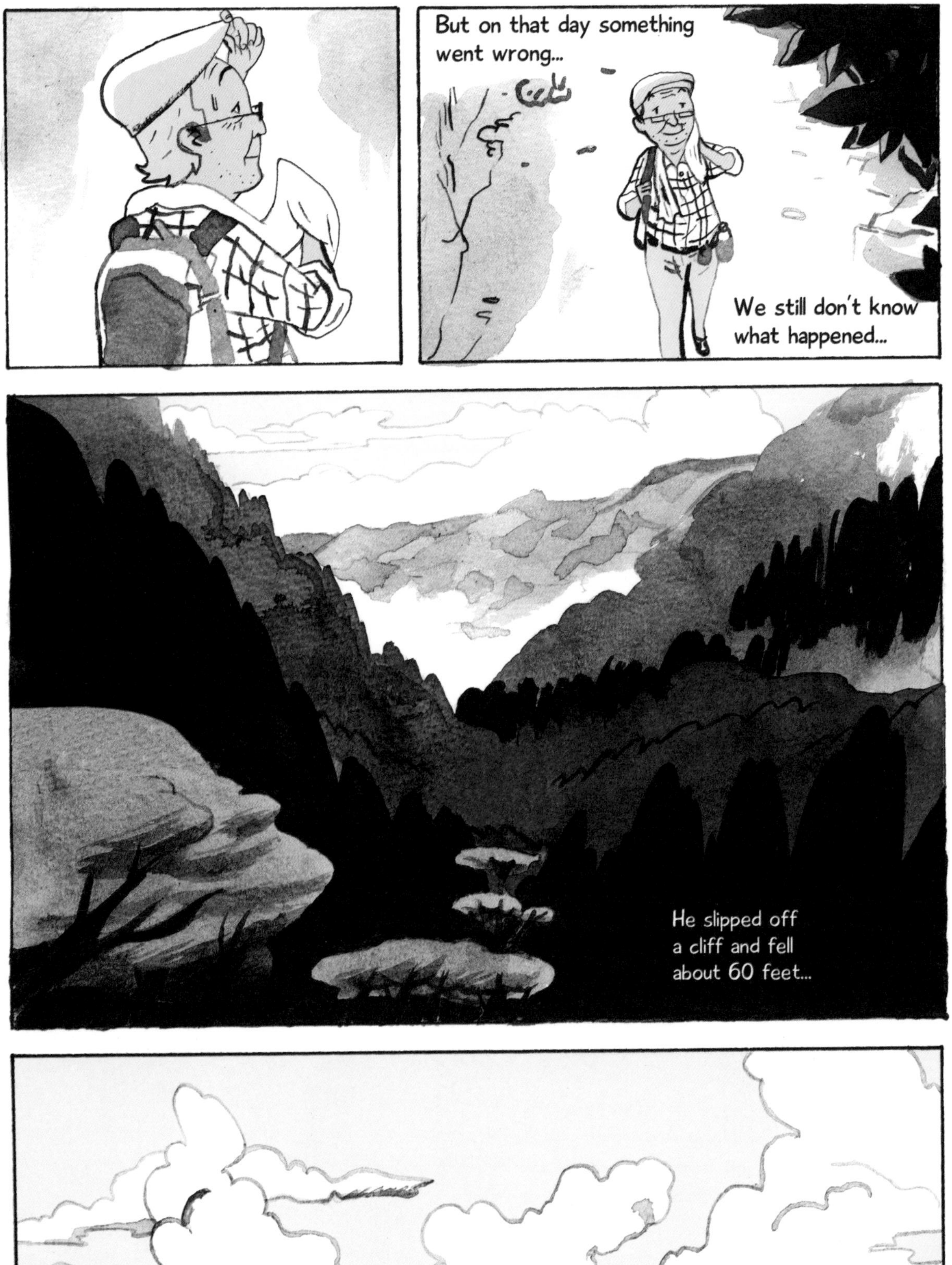
But on that day something went wrong...
We still don't know what happened...
He slipped off a cliff and fell about 60 feet...

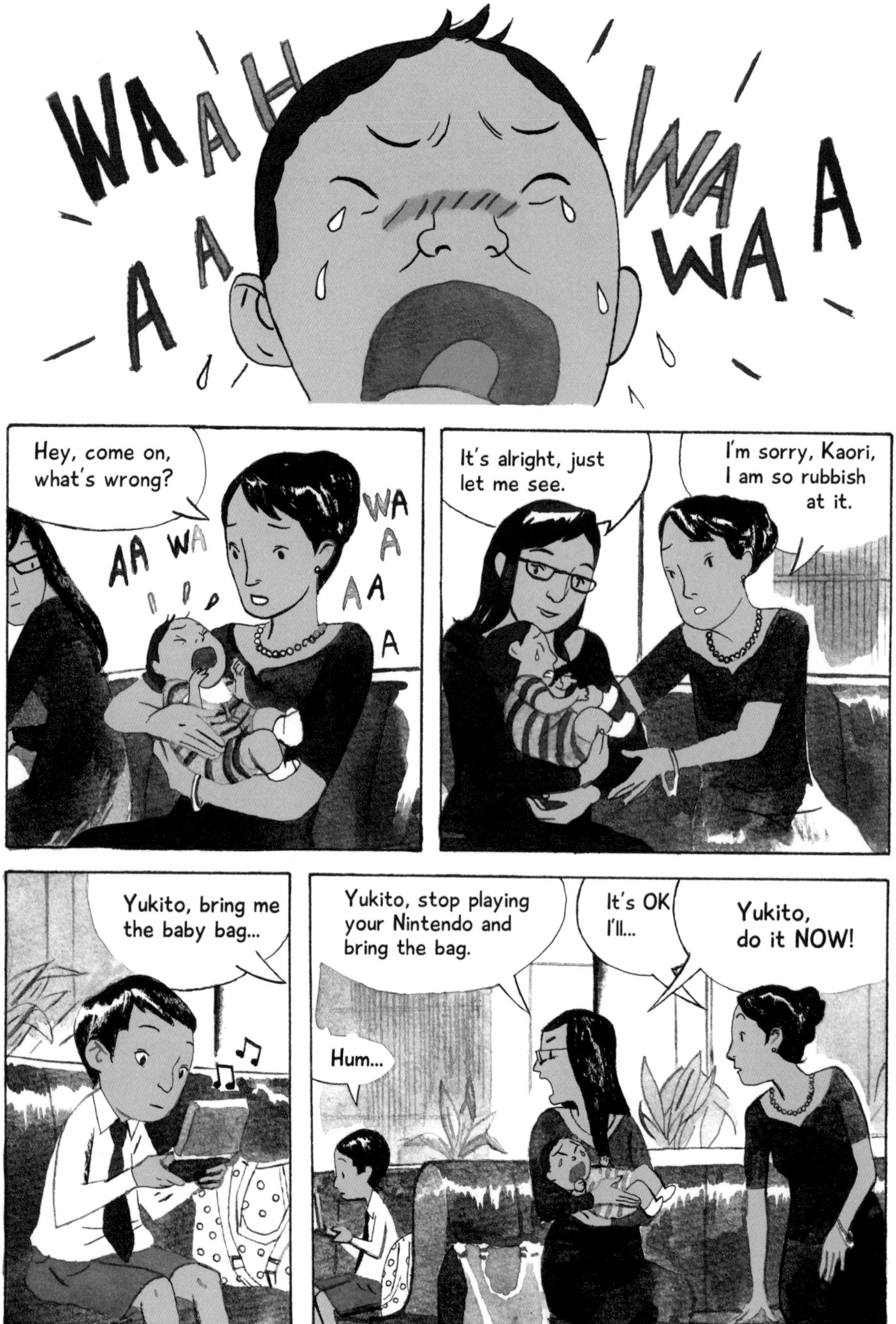
WAAH
AA
WAWA
WAA
Hey, come on, what's wrong?
AA WA
WA A AA A
It's alright, just let me see.
I'm sorry, Kaori, I am so rubbish at it.
Yukito, bring me the baby bag...
Yukito, stop playing your Nintendo and bring the bag.
Hum...
It's OK I'll...
Yukito, do it NOW!

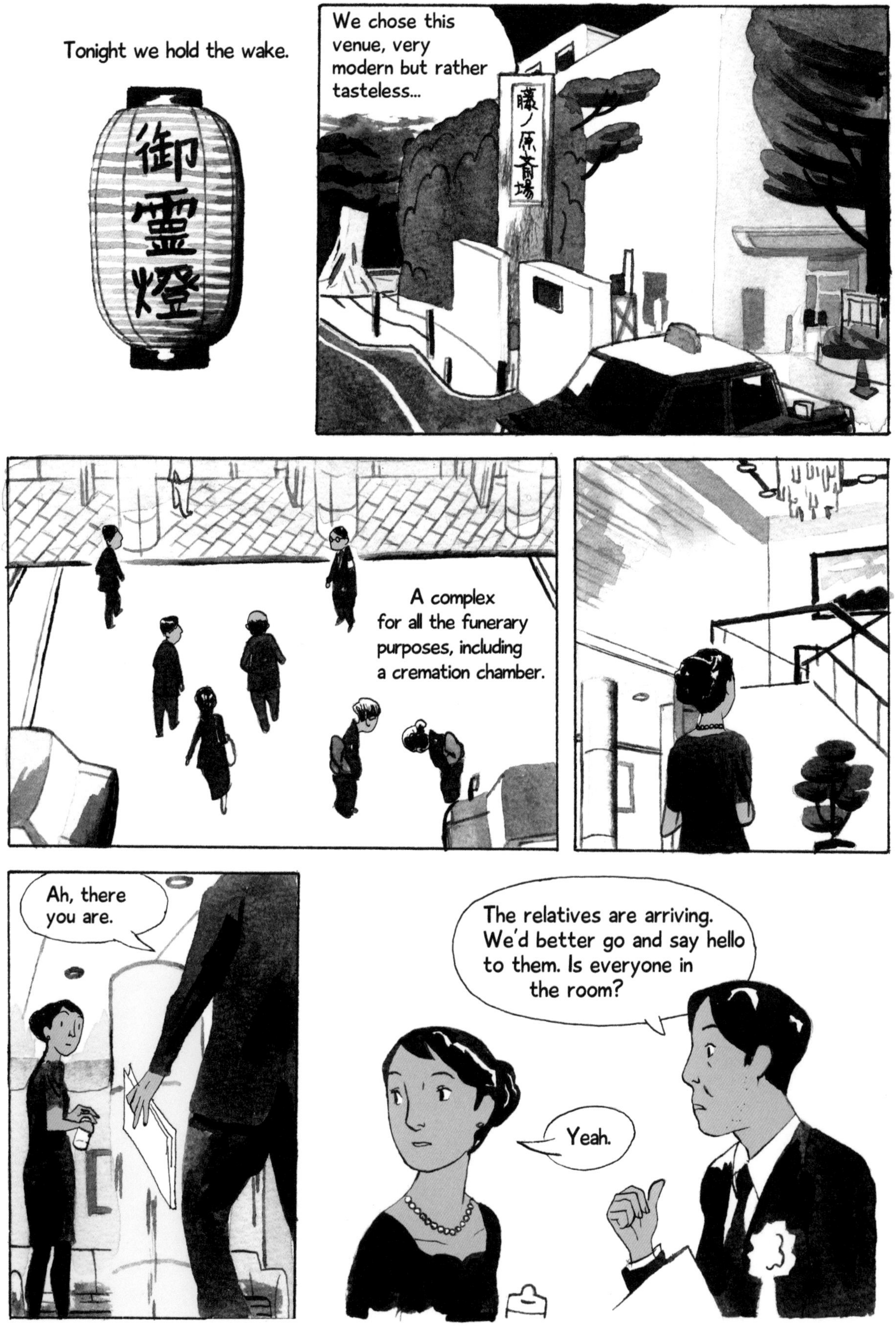
Tonight we hold the wake.
御霊燈
We chose this venue, very modern but rather tasteless...
A complex for all the funerary purposes, including a cremation chamber.
Ah, there you are.
The relatives are arriving. We'd better go and say hello to them. Is everyone in the room?
Yeah.

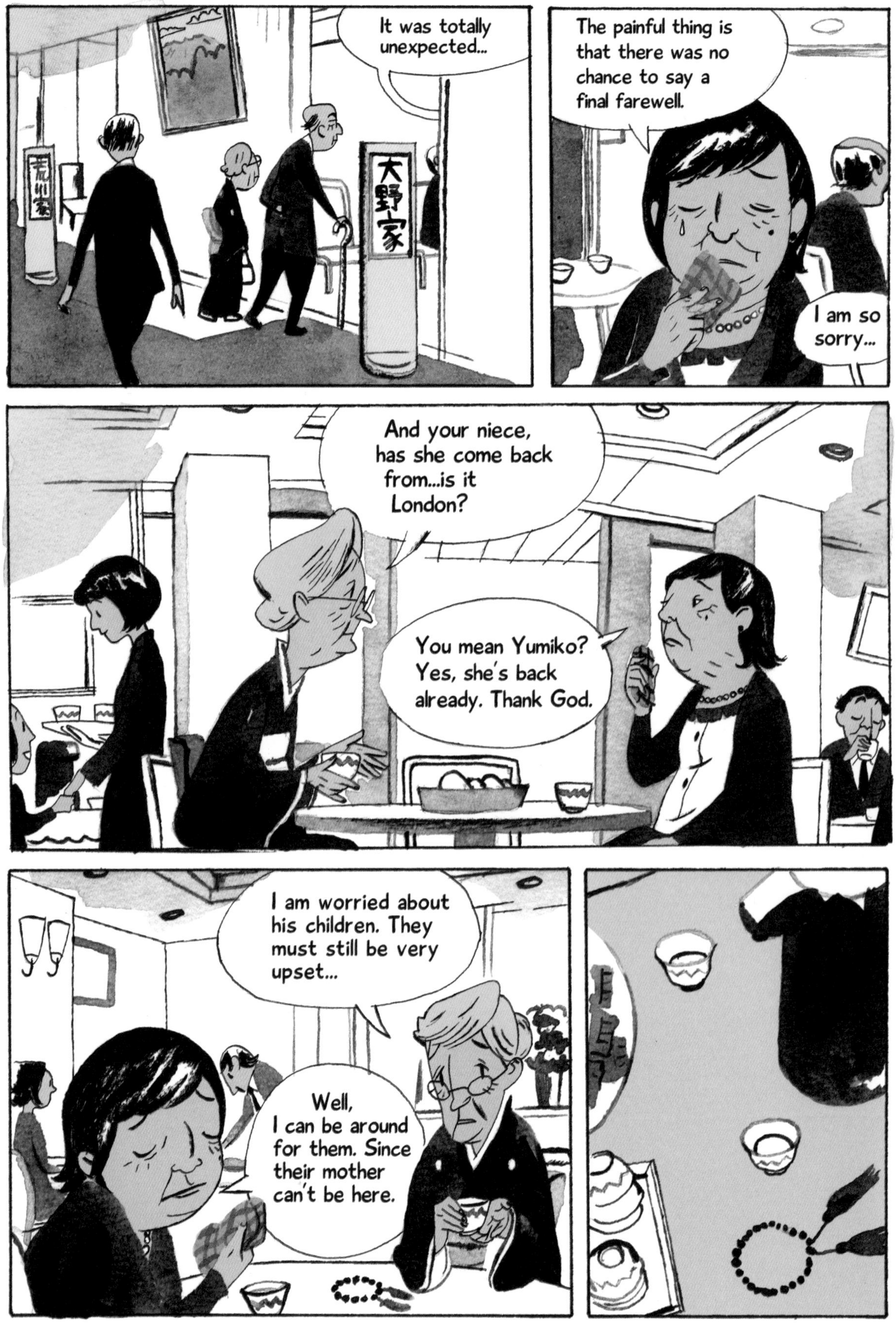
It was totally unexpected...
大野家
The painful thing is that there was no chance to say a final farewell.
I am so sorry...
And your niece, has she come back from...is it London?
You mean Yumiko? Yes, she's back already. Thank God.
I am worried about his children. They must still be very upset...
Well, I can be around for them. Since their mother can't be here.

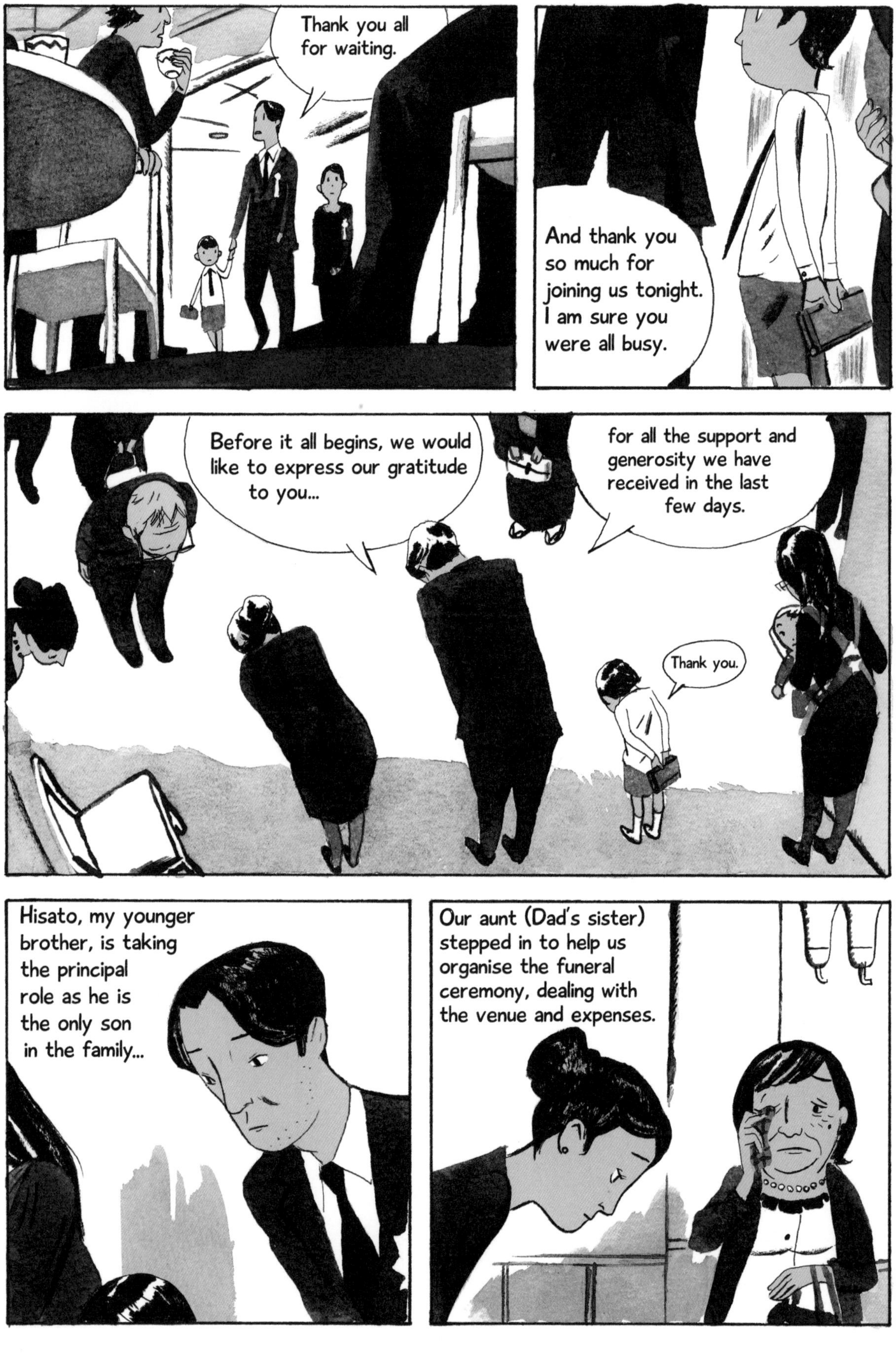
Thank you all for waiting.
And thank you so much for joining us tonight. I am sure you were all busy.
Before it all begins, we would like to express our gratitude to you...
for all the support and generosity we have received in the last few days.
Thank you.
Hisato, my younger brother, is taking the principal role as he is the only son in the family...
Our aunt (Dad's sister) stepped in to help us organise the funeral ceremony, dealing with the venue and expenses.

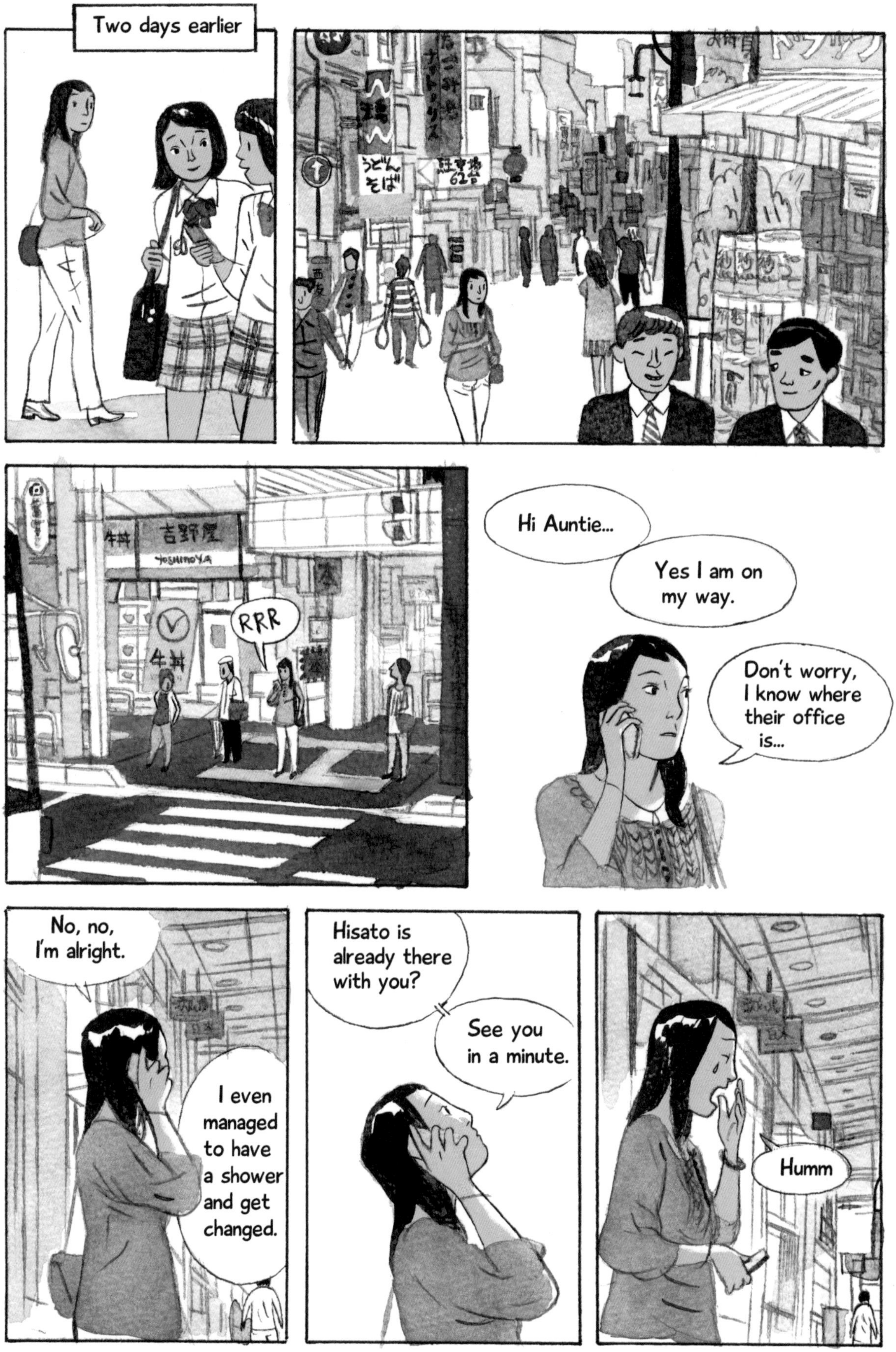
Two days earlier
うどん そば
牛丼
吉野屋
YOSHINOYA
RRR
Hi Auntie...
Yes I am on my way.
Don't worry, I know where their office is...
No, no, I'm alright.
I even managed to have a shower and get changed.
Hisato is already there with you?
See you in a minute.
Humm

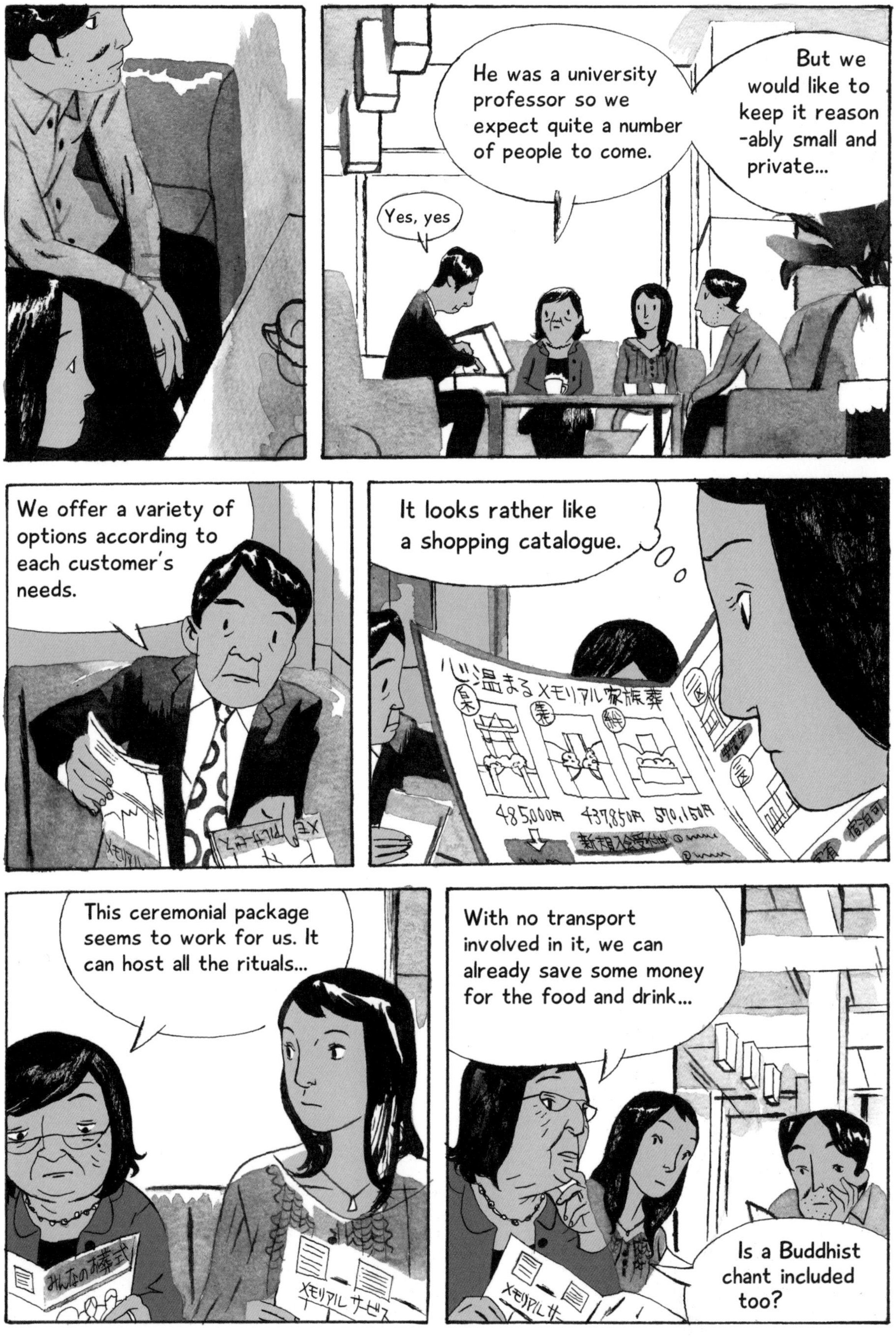
He was a university professor so we expect quite a number of people to come.
But we would like to keep it reason -ably small and private...
Yes, yes
We offer a variety of options according to each customer's needs.
It looks rather like a shopping catalogue.
心温まるメモリアル家族葬
485,000円
437,850円
570,150円
This ceremonial package seems to work for us. It can host all the rituals...
みんなのお葬式
メモリアルサービス
With no transport involved in it, we can already save some money for the food and drink...
Is a Buddhist chant included too?

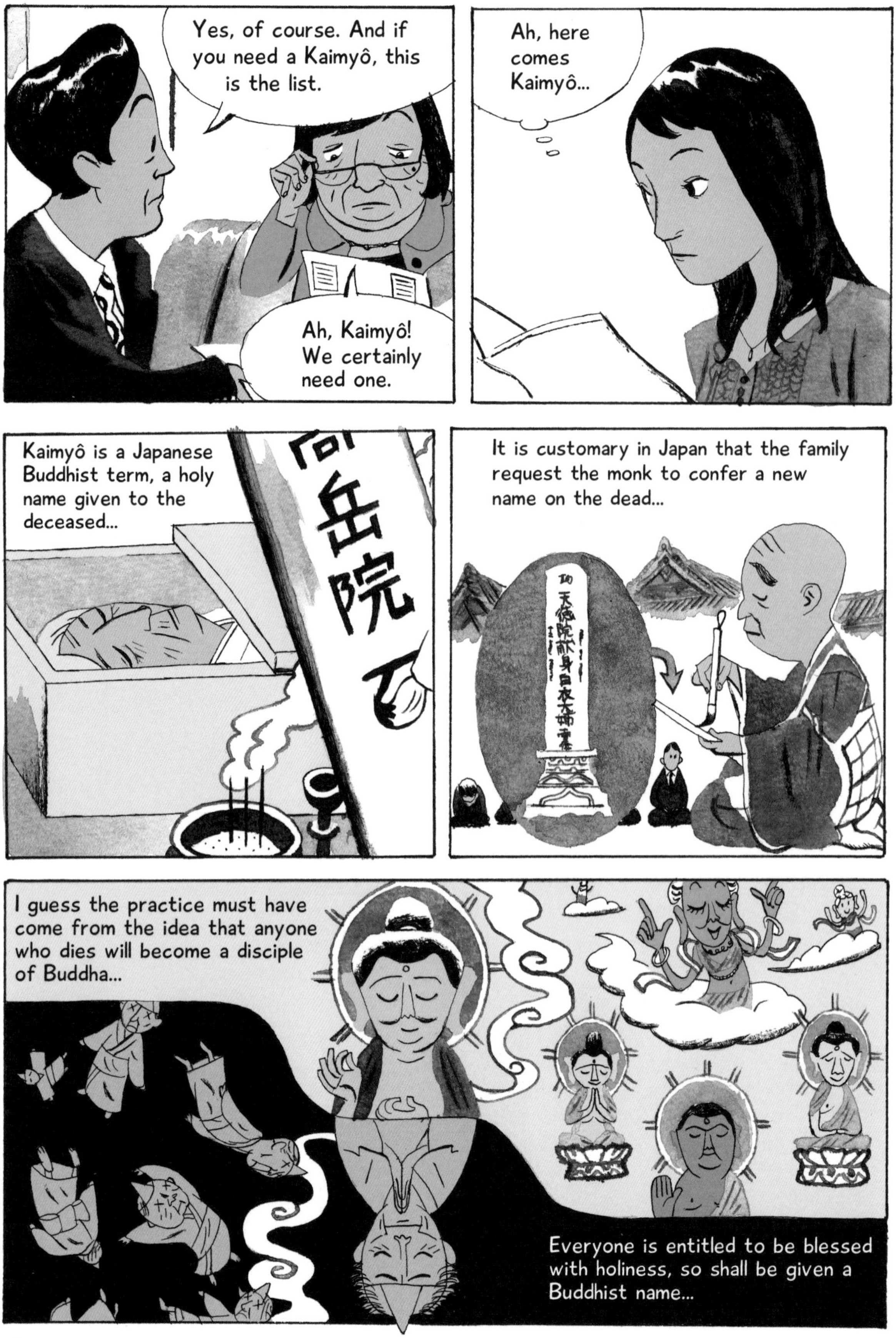

Yes, of course. And if you need a Kaimyô, this is the list.
Ah, Kaimyô! We certainly need one.
Ah, here comes Kaimyô...
Kaimyô is a Japanese Buddhist term, a holy name given to the deceased...
岳院
It is customary in Japan that the family request the monk to confer a new name on the dead...
I guess the practice must have come from the idea that anyone who dies will become a disciple of Buddha...
Everyone is entitled to be blessed with holiness, so shall be given a Buddhist name...

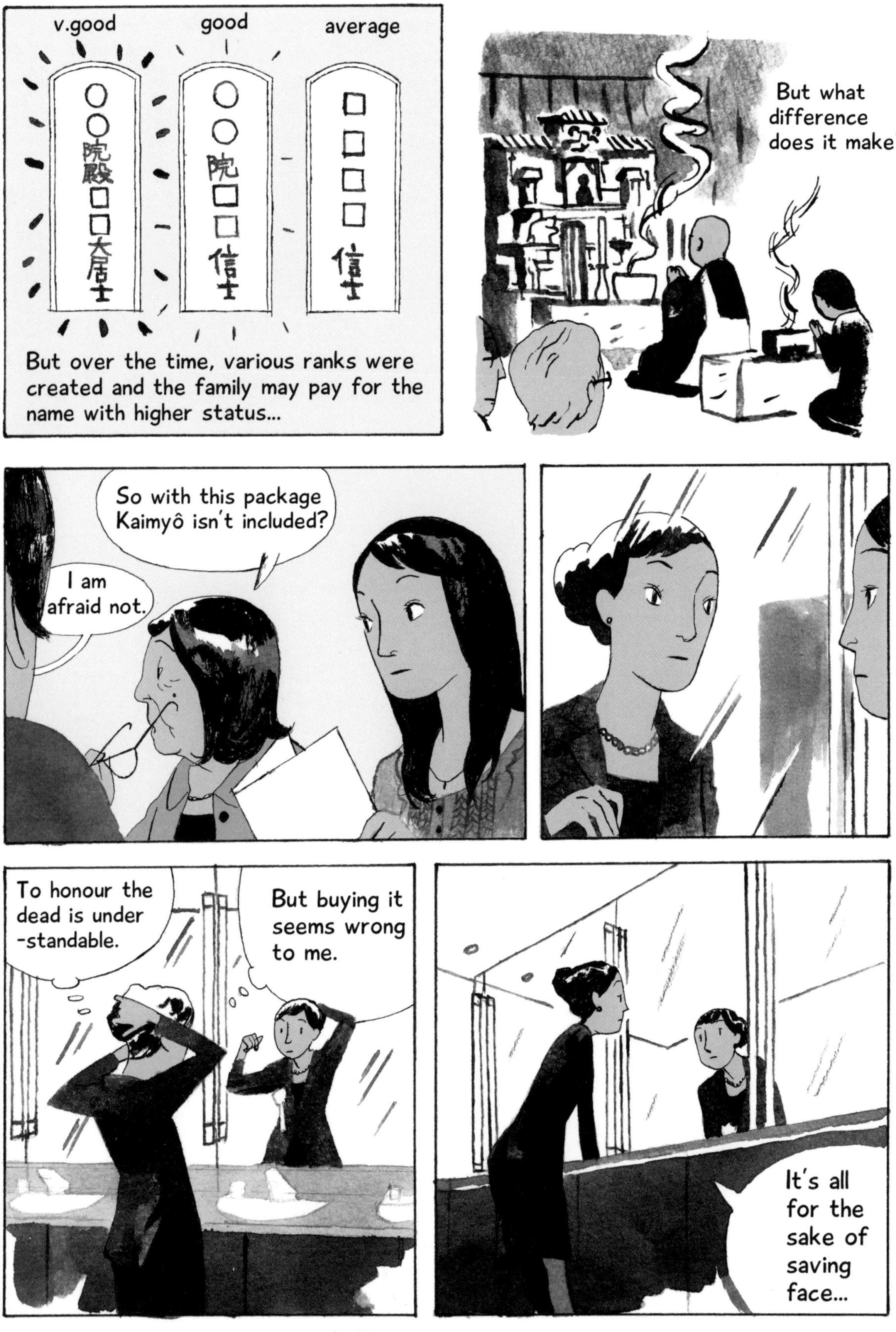
v.good
good
average
○○院殿□□大居士
○○院□□信士
□□□□信士
But over the time, various ranks were created and the family may pay for the name with higher status...
But what difference does it make?
So with this package Kaimyô isn't included?
I am afraid not.
To honour the dead is under -standable.
But buying it seems wrong to me.
It's all for the sake of saving face...

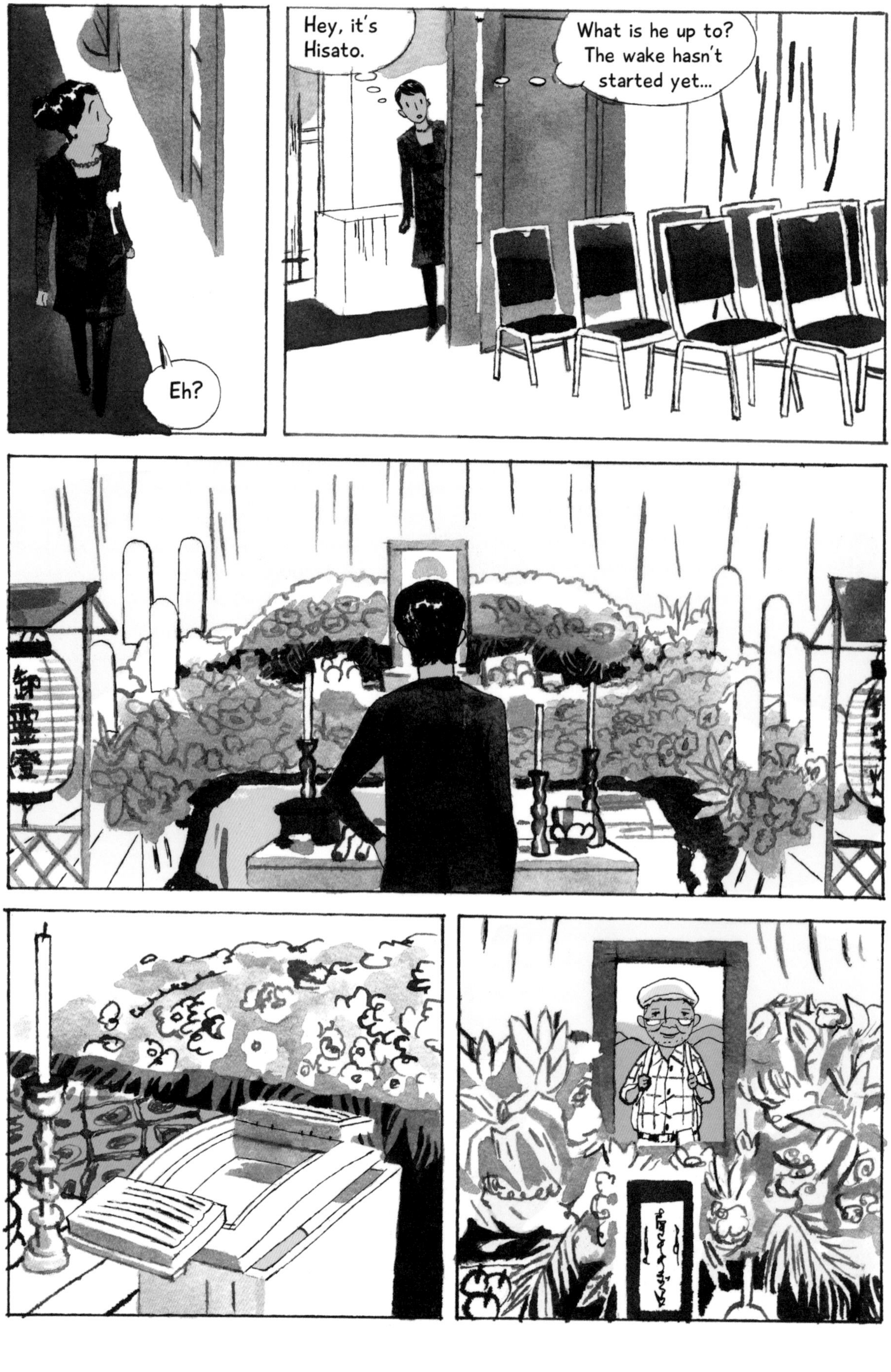
Eh?
Hey, it's Hisato.
What is he up to? The wake hasn't started yet...

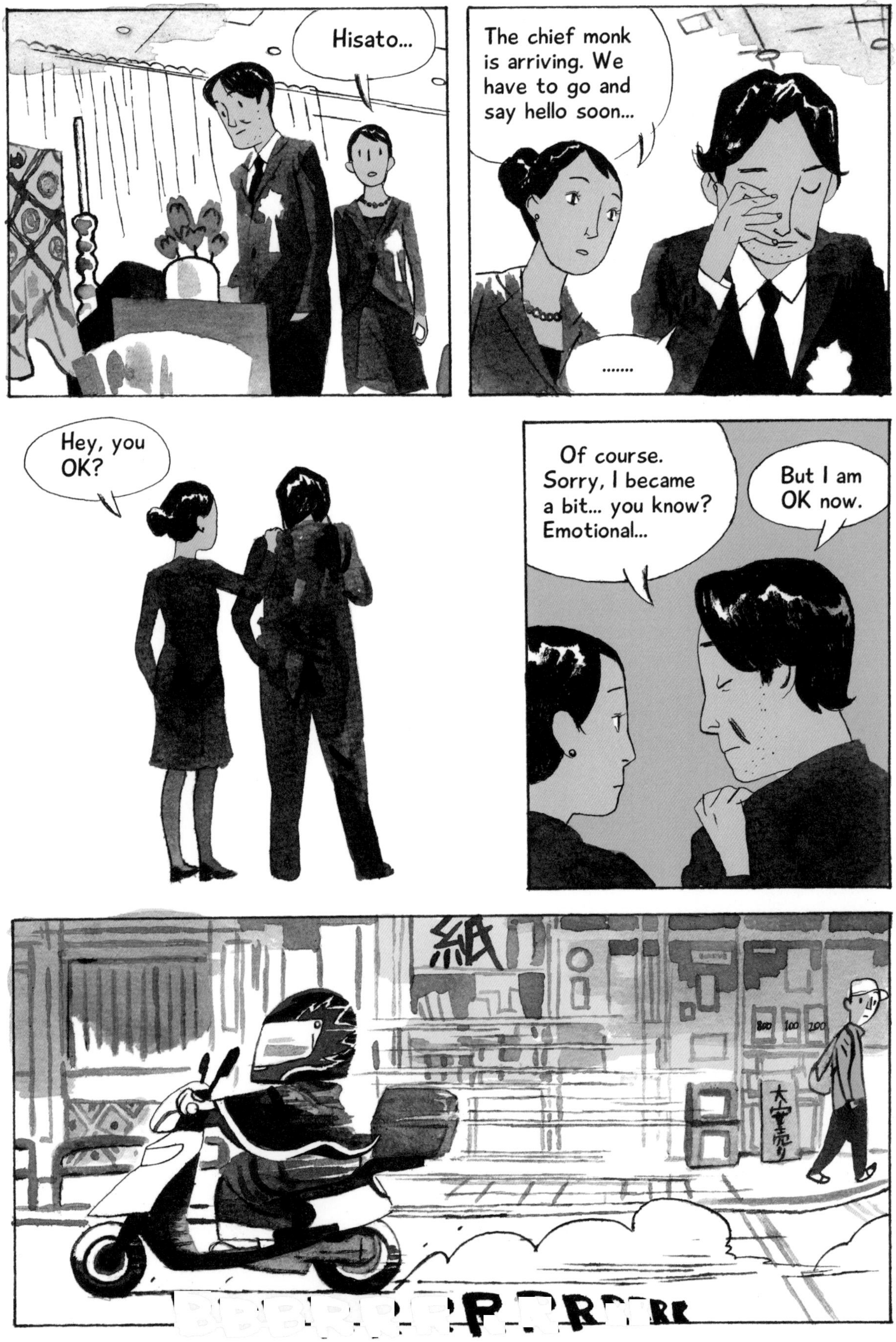
Hisato...
The chief monk is arriving. We have to go and say hello soon...
....
Hey, you OK?
Of course. Sorry, I became a bit... you know? Emotional...
But I am OK now.
紙

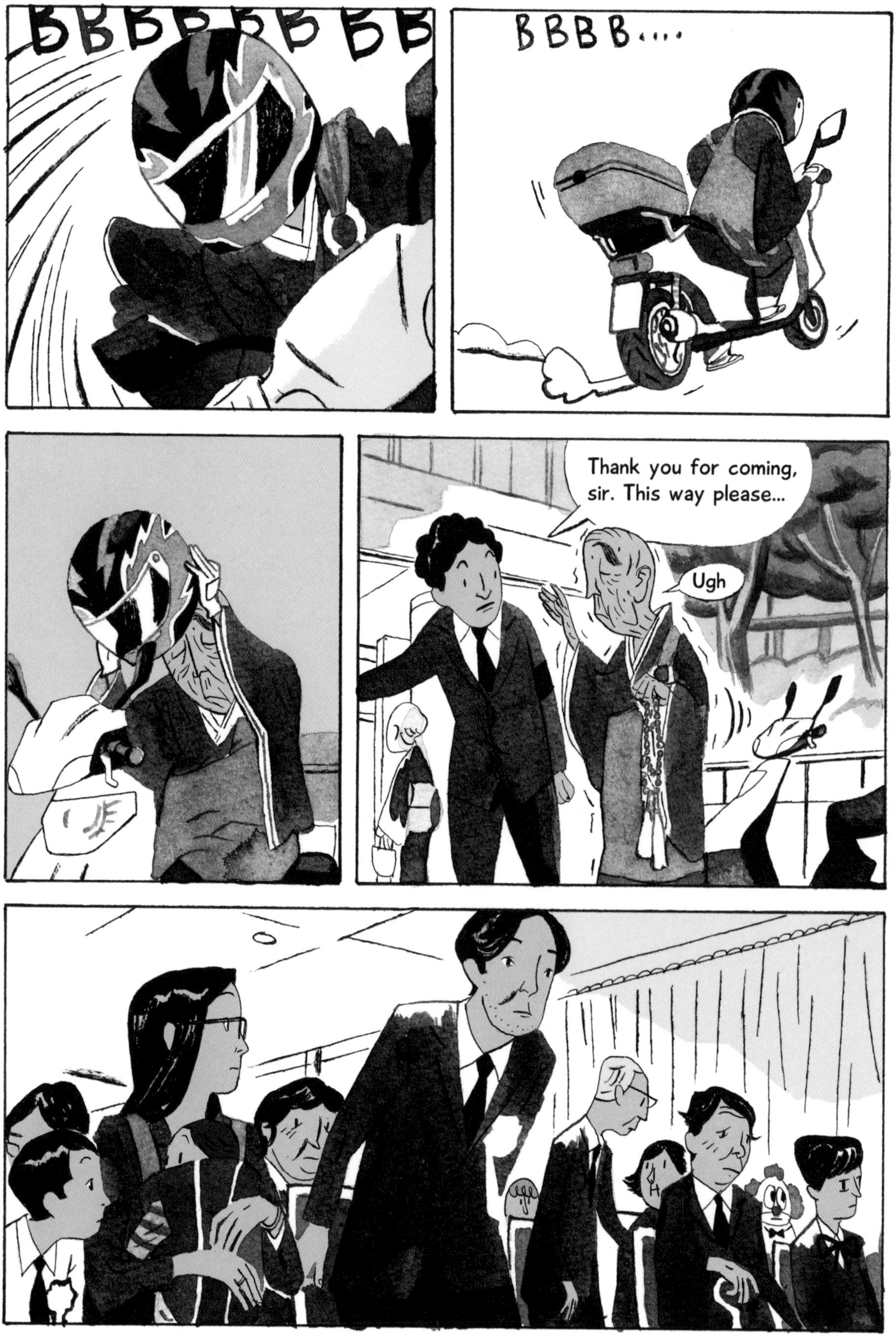
BBBBBBBBB
BBBB....
Thank you for coming, sir. This way please...
Ugh

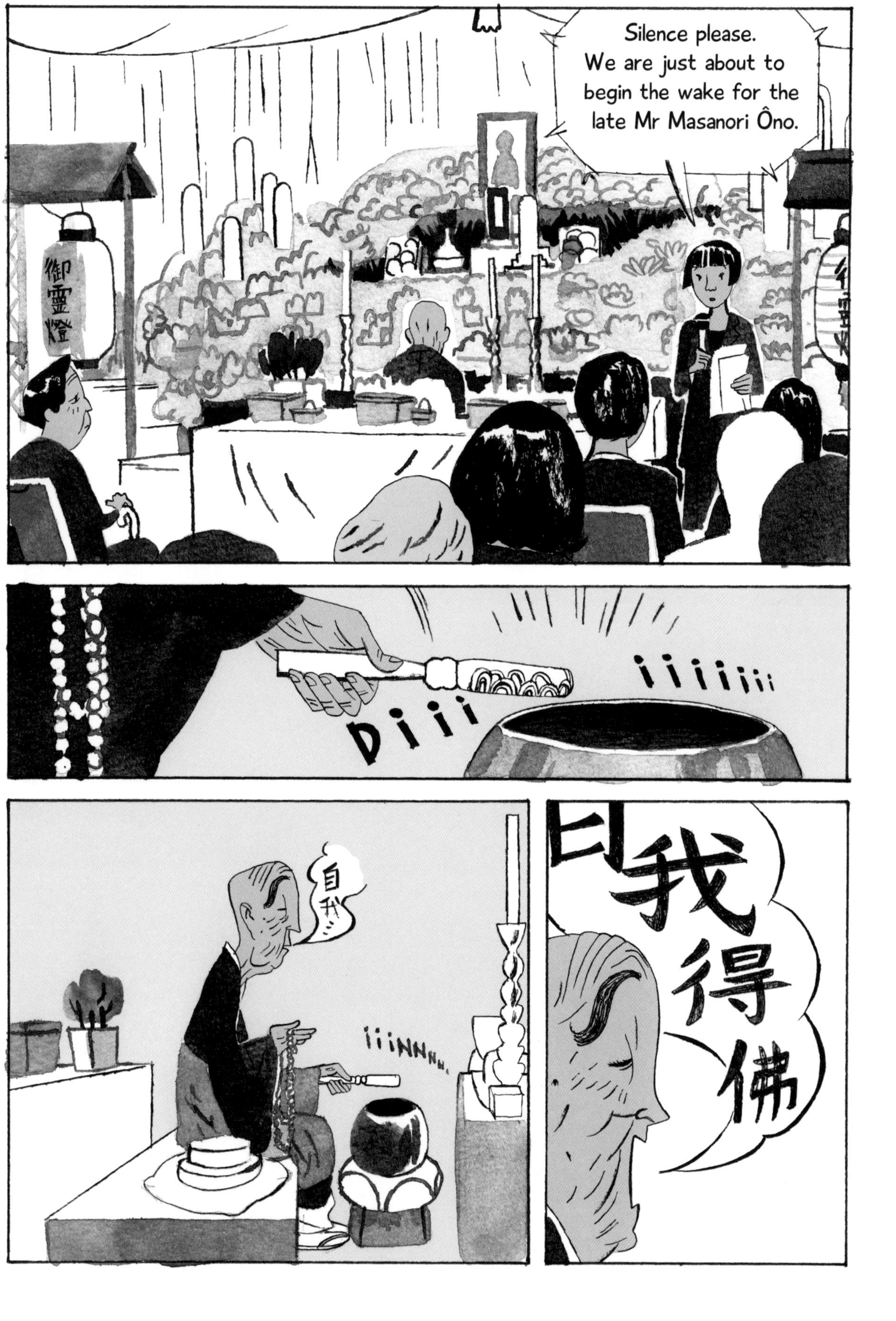
Silence please. We are just about to begin the wake for the late Mr Masanori Ôno.
御霊燈
Diii
iiiiiii
自我…
iiiNNnn..
我得佛

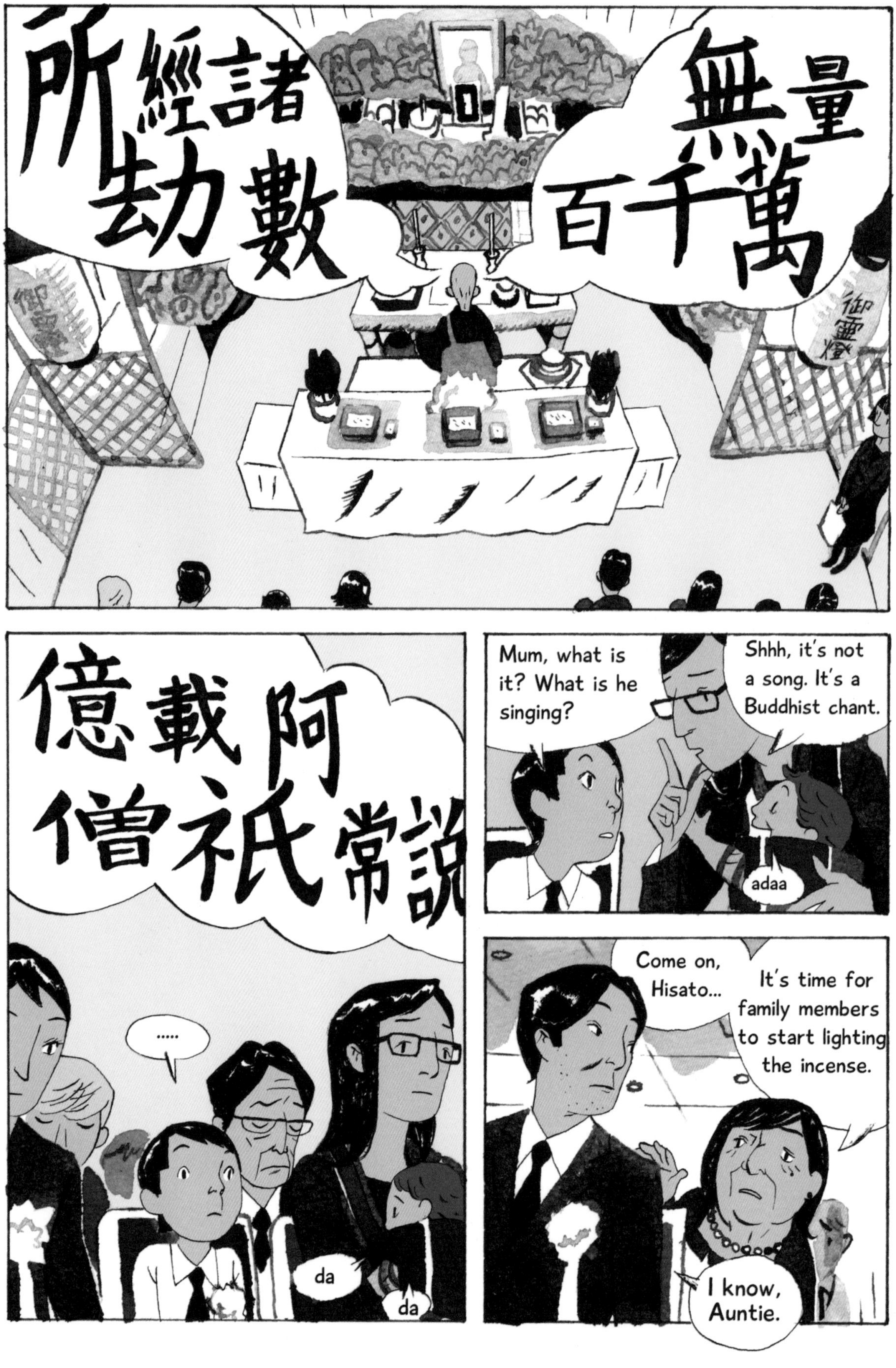

所經諸劫數
無量百千萬
億載阿僧祇常說
.....
da
da
Mum, what is it? What is he singing?
Shhh, it's not a song. It's a Buddhist chant.
adaa
Come on, Hisato...
It's time for family members to start lighting the incense.
I know, Auntie.

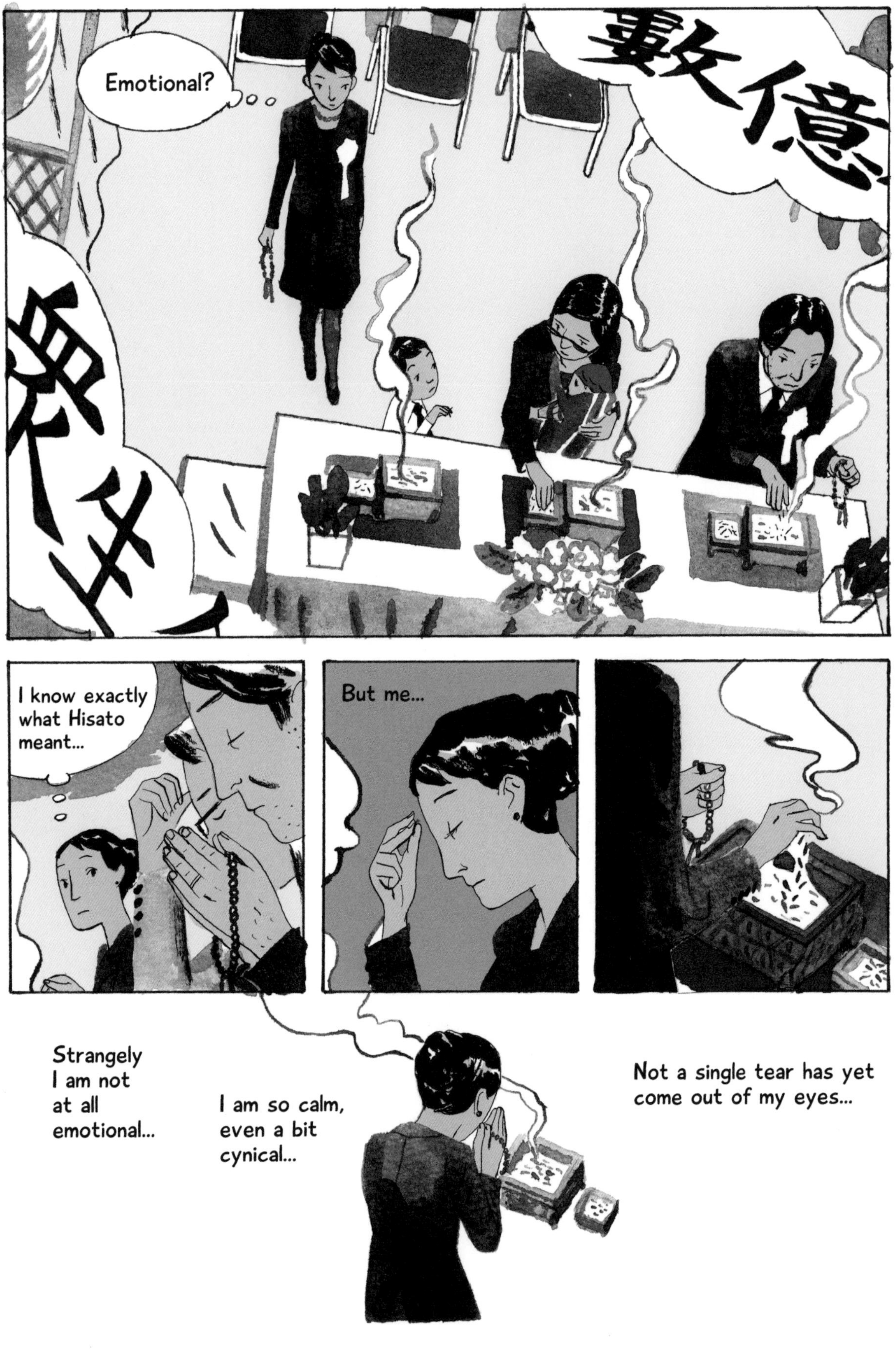

Emotional?
數億
I know exactly what Hisato meant...
But me...
Strangely I am not at all emotional...
I am so calm, even a bit cynical...
Not a single tear has yet come out of my eyes...

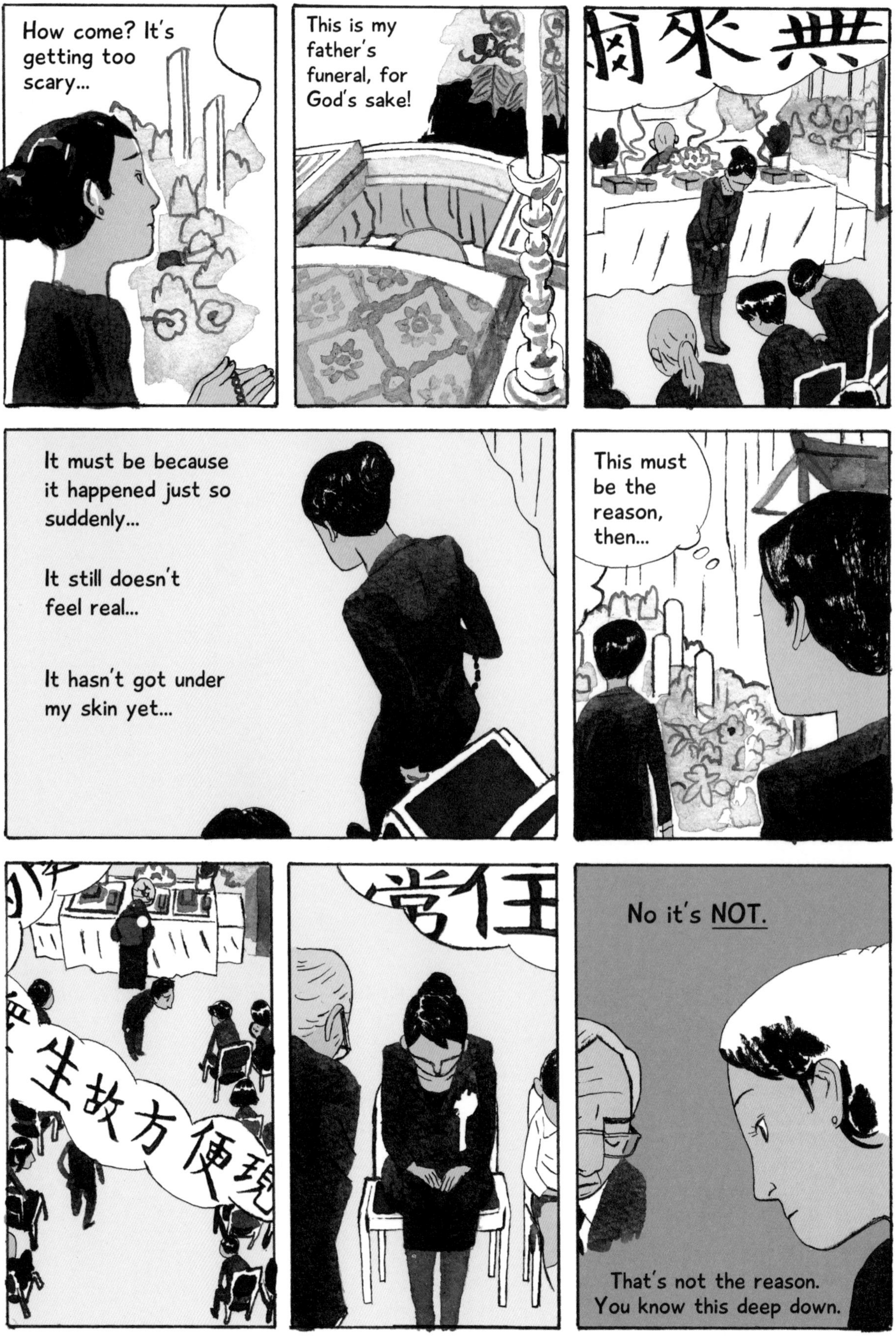
How come? It's getting too scary...
This is my father's funeral, for God's sake!
It must be because it happened just so suddenly...
It still doesn't feel real...
It hasn't got under my skin yet...
This must be the reason, then...
生故方便現
No it's NOT.
That's not the reason. You know this deep down.

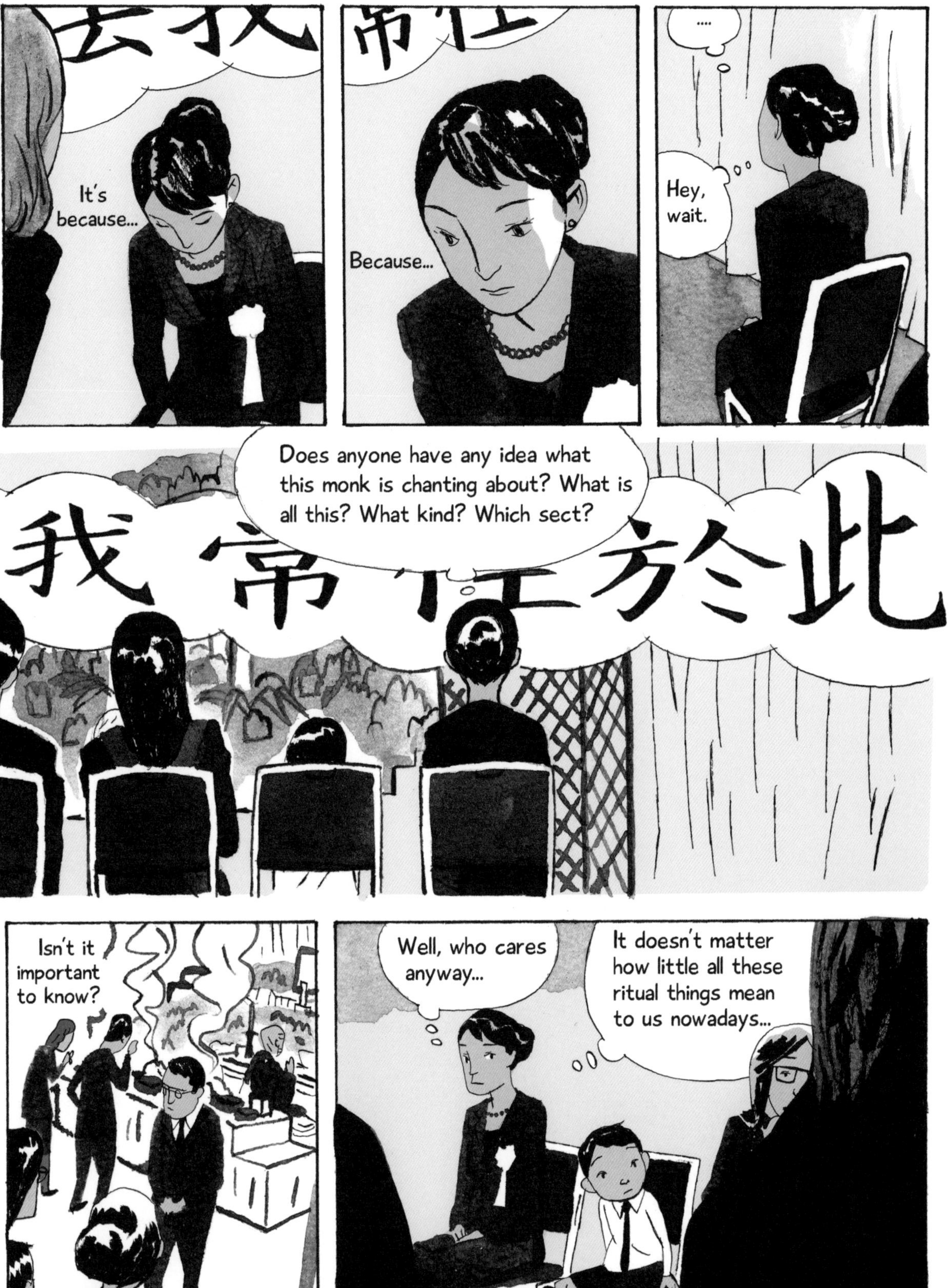
It's because...
Because...
....
Hey, wait.
Does anyone have any idea what this monk is chanting about? What is all this? What kind? Which sect?
Isn't it important to know?
Well, who cares anyway...
It doesn't matter how little all these ritual things mean to us nowadays...

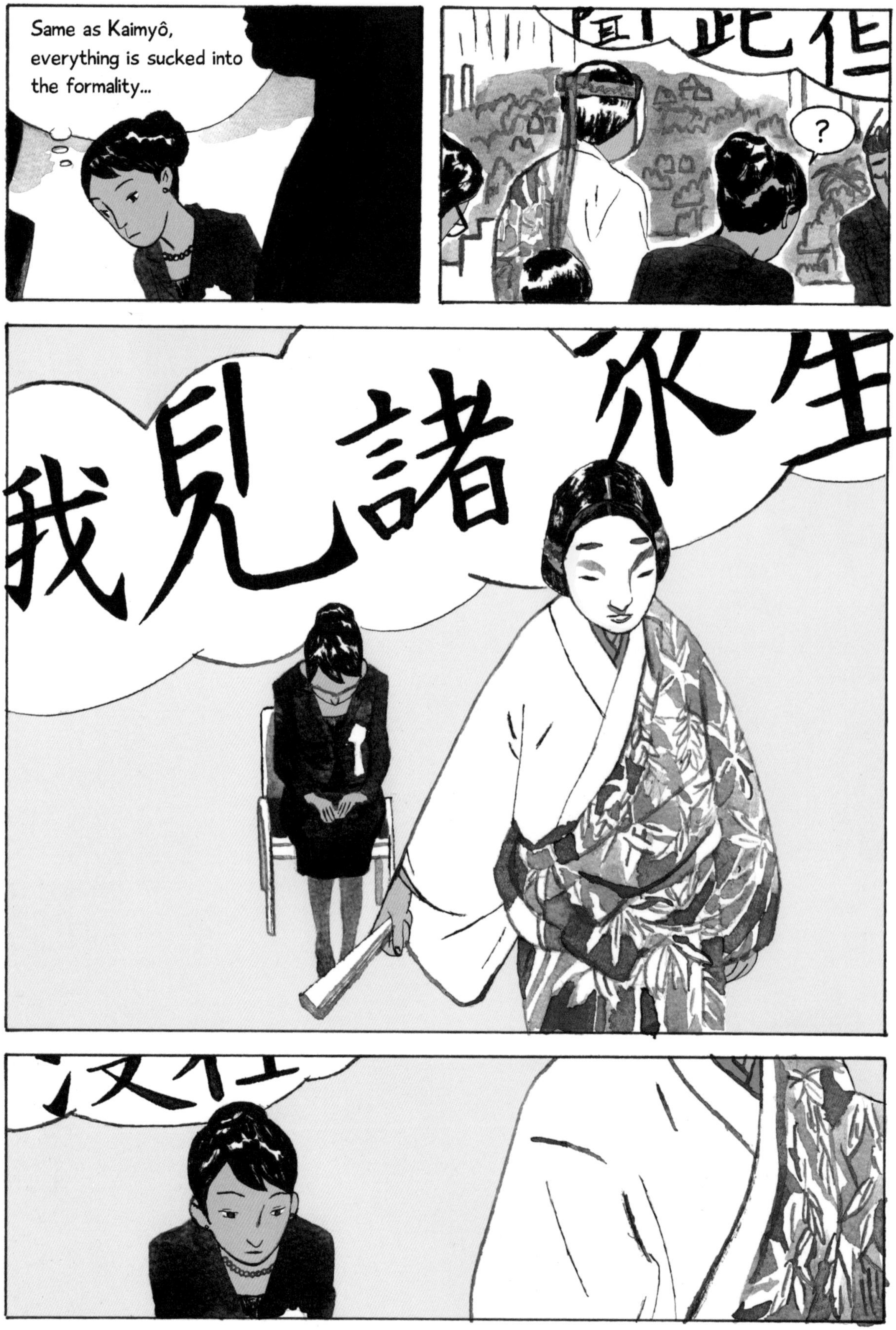
Same as Kaimyô, everything is sucked into the formality...
?
我見諸

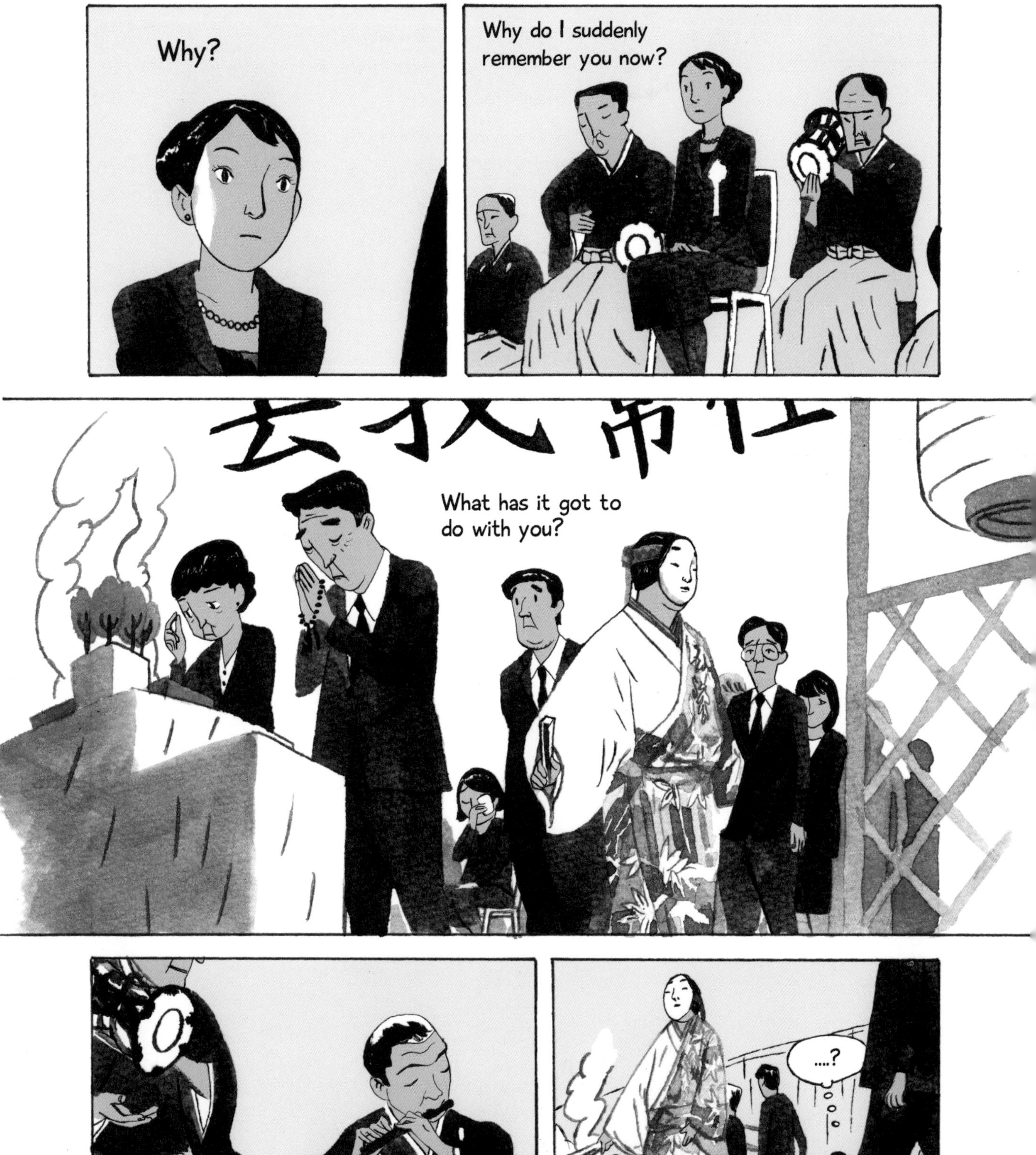
Why?
Why do I suddenly remember you now?
What has it got to do with you?
....?

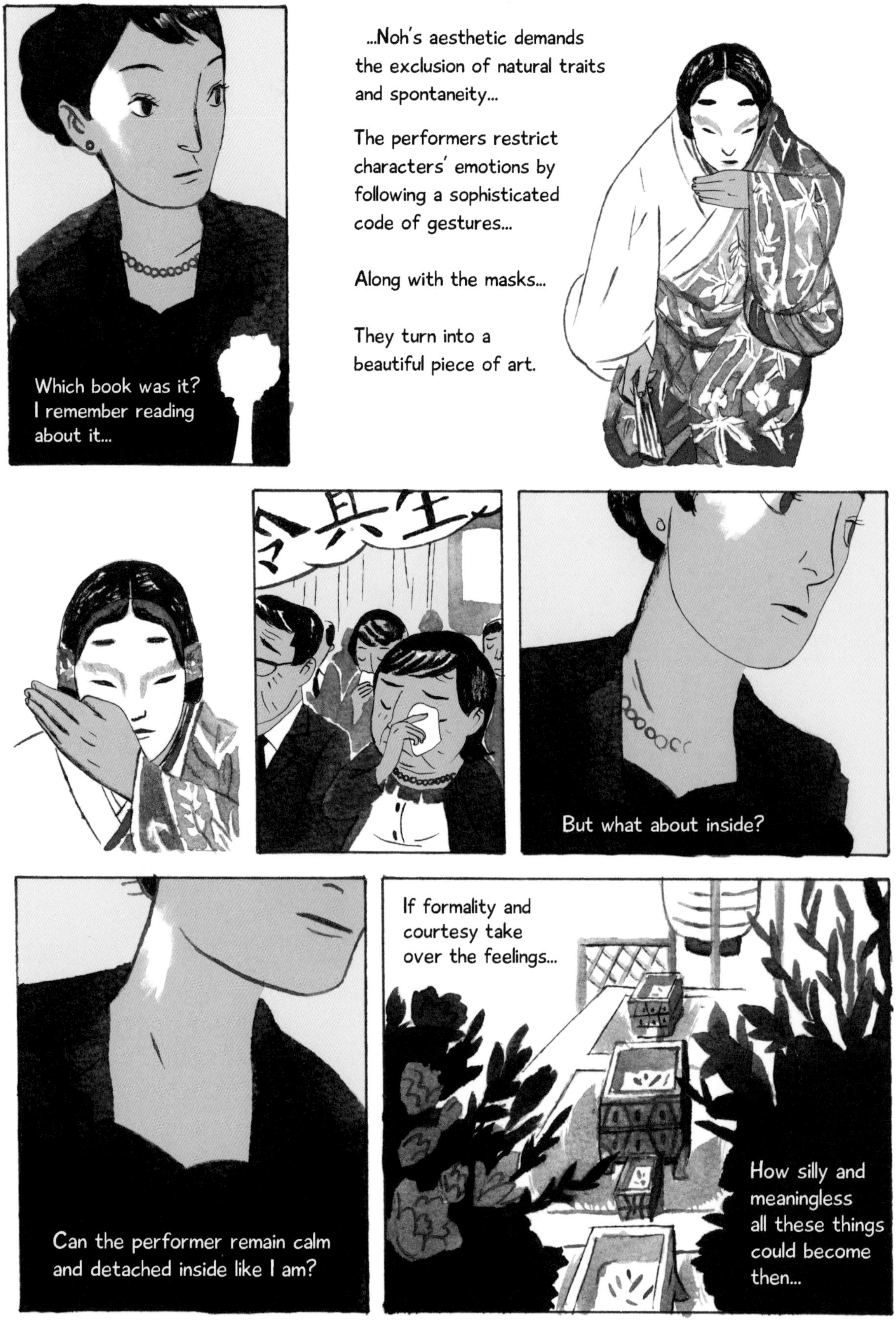

Which book was it?
I remember reading about it...
...Noh's aesthetic demands the exclusion of natural traits and spontaneity...
The performers restrict characters' emotions by following a sophisticated code of gestures...
Along with the masks...
They turn into a beautiful piece of art.
But what about inside?
Can the performer remain calm and detached inside like I am?
If formality and courtesy take over the feelings...
How silly and meaningless all these things could become then...

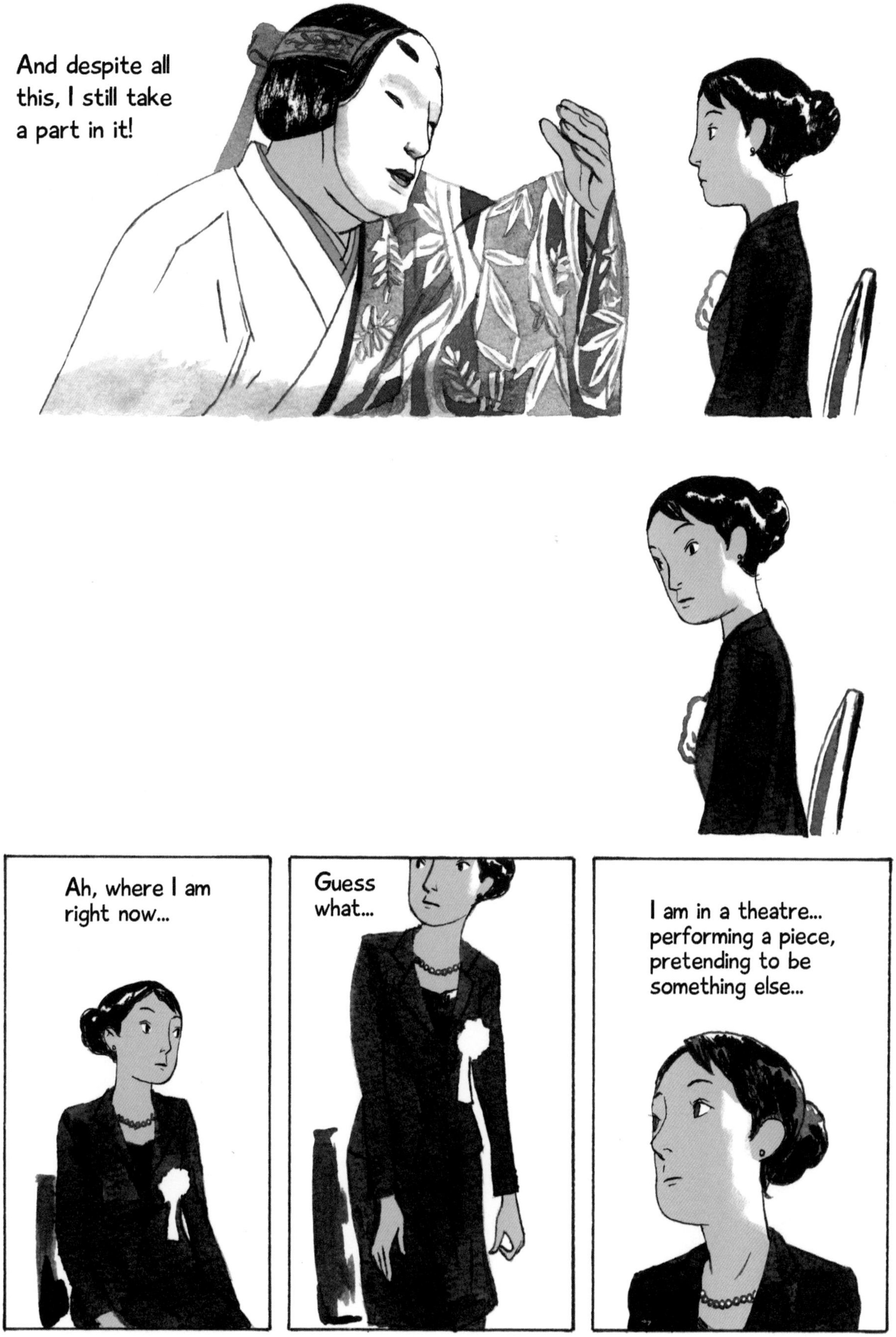

And despite all this, I still take a part in it!
Ah, where I am right now...
Guess what...
I am in a theatre... performing a piece, pretending to be something else...

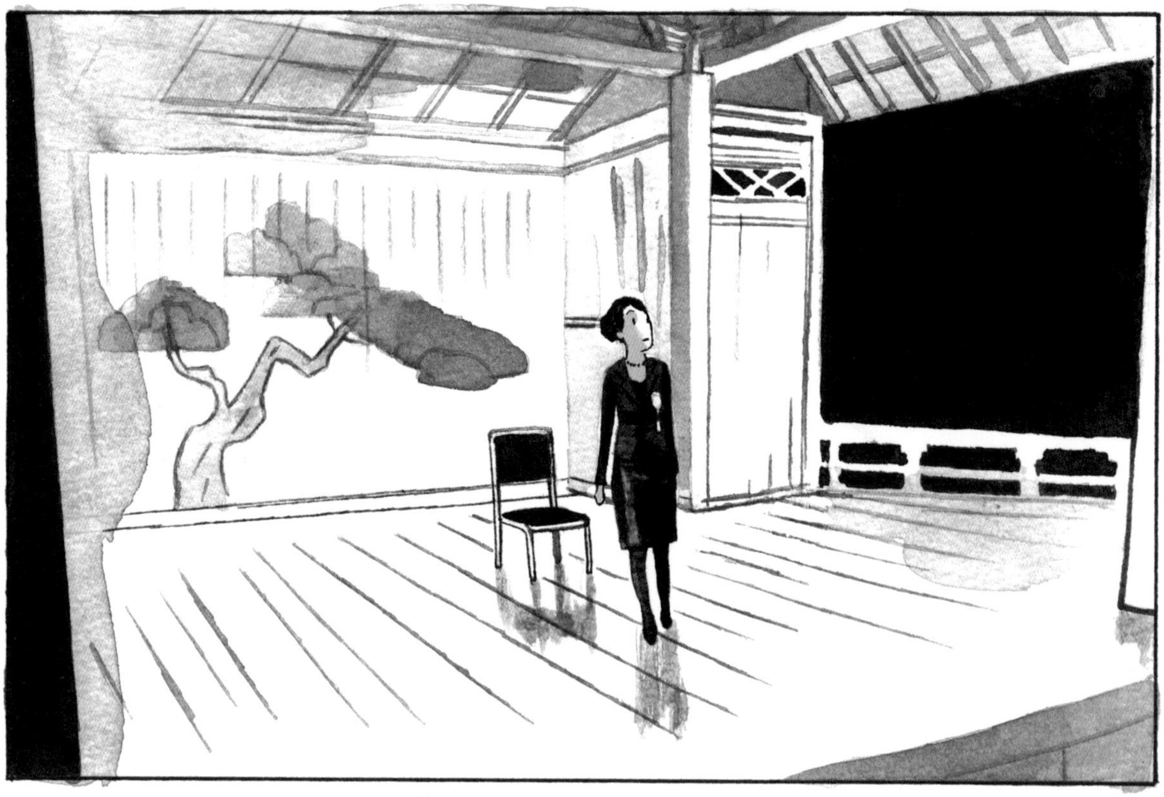

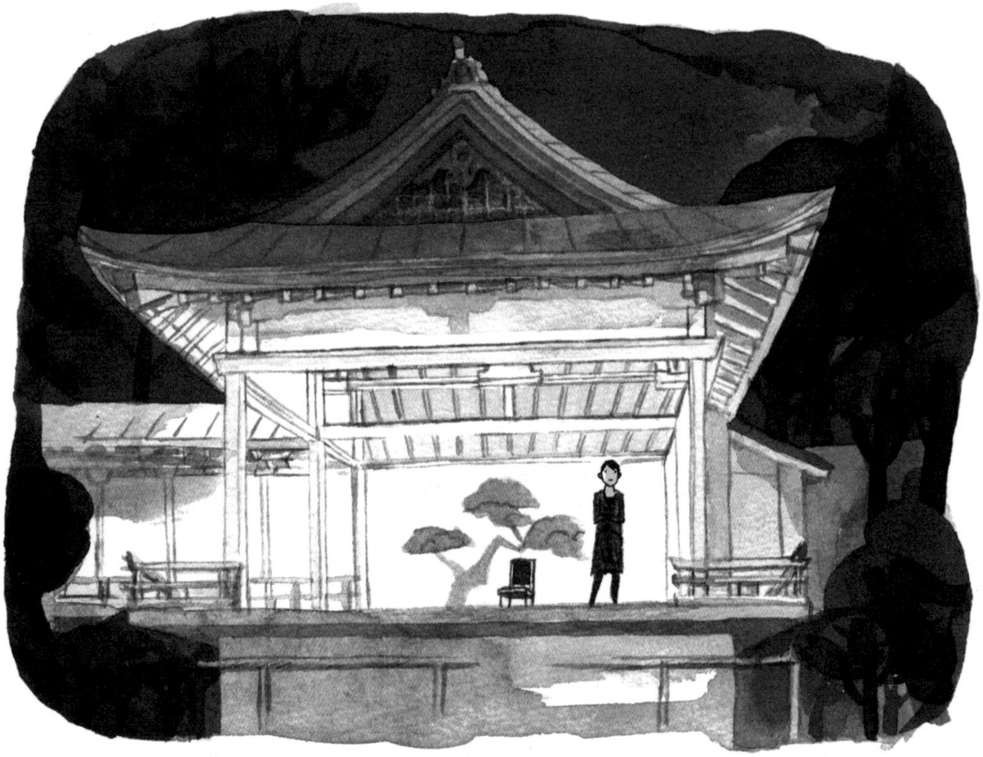

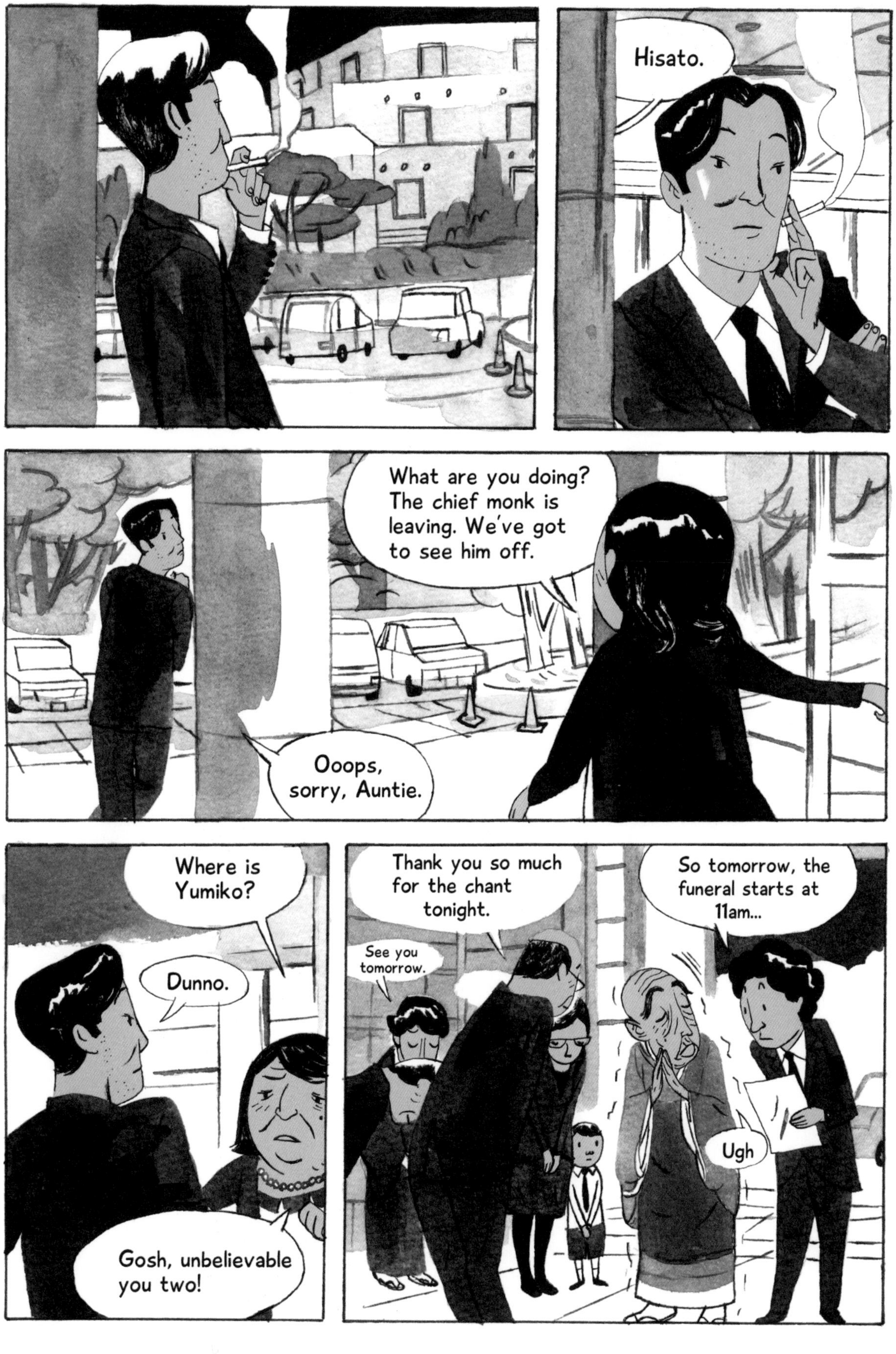

Hisato.
What are you doing? The chief monk is leaving. We've got to see him off.
Ooops, sorry, Auntie.
Where is Yumiko?
Dunno.
Gosh, unbelievable you two!
Thank you so much for the chant tonight.
See you tomorrow.
So tomorrow, the funeral starts at 11am...
Ugh

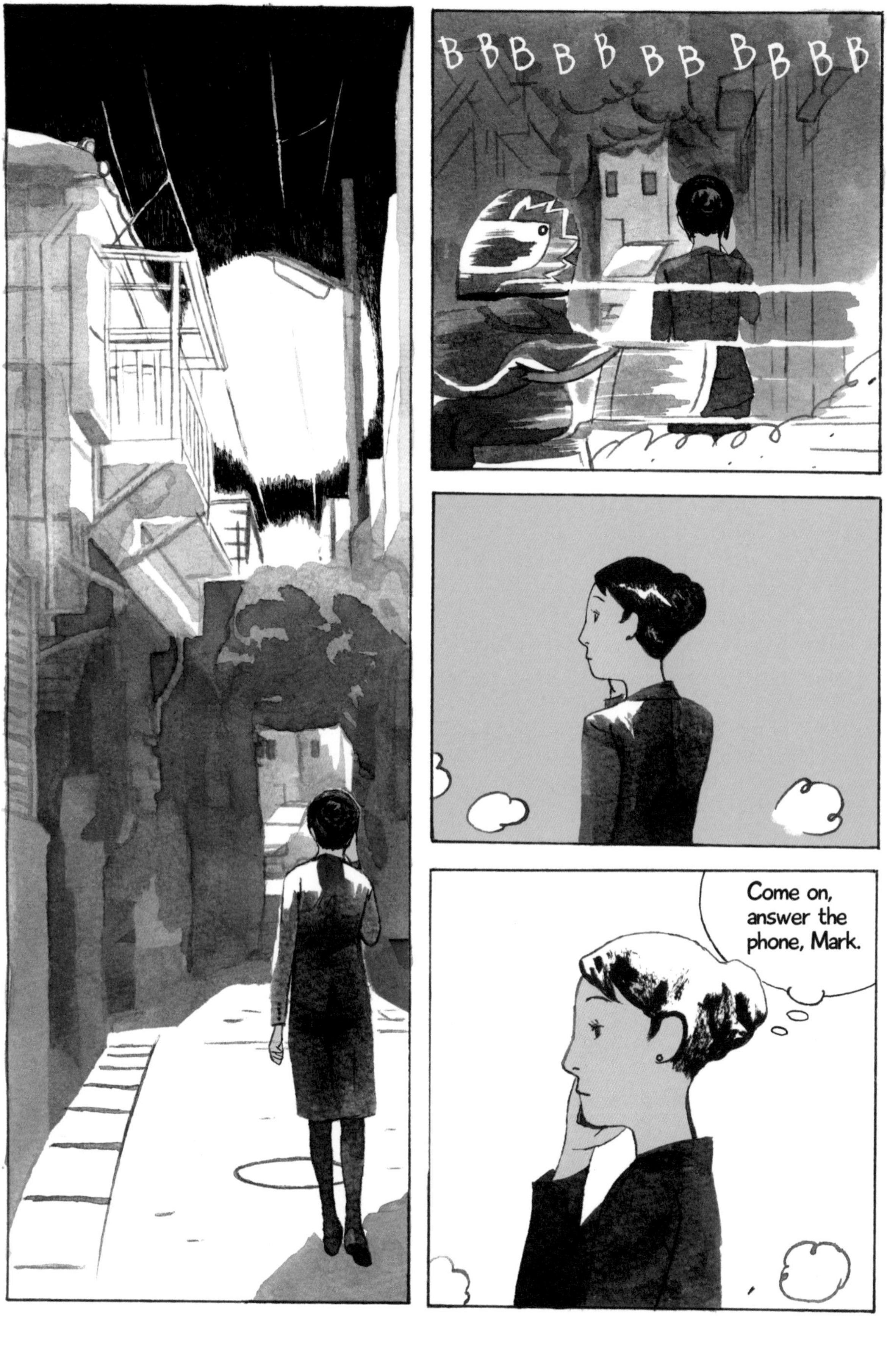
BBBBBBBBBBB
Come on, answer the phone, Mark.

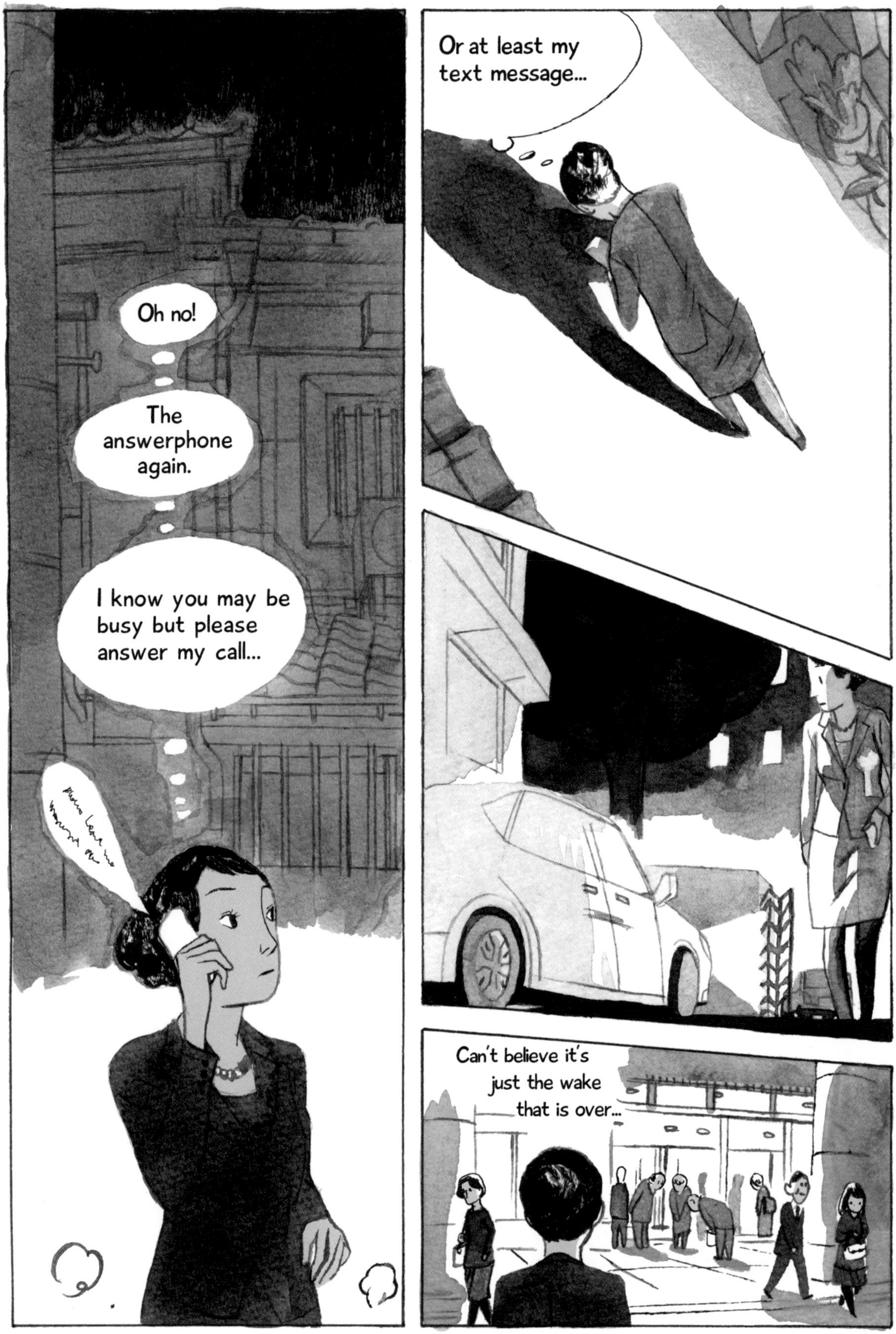
Oh no!
The answerphone again.
I know you may be busy but please answer my call...
Or at least my text message...
Can't believe it's just the wake that is over...

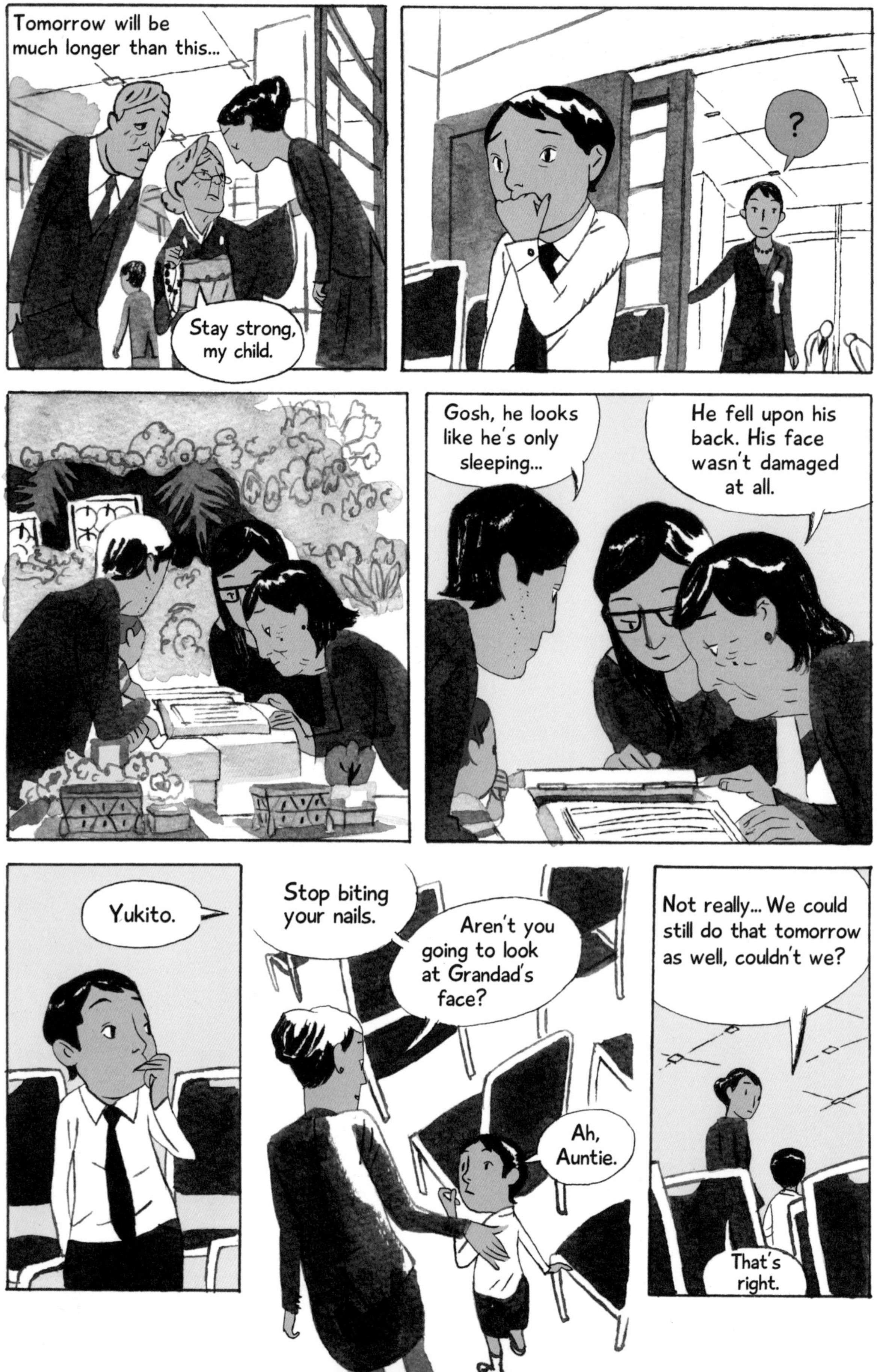

Tomorrow will be much longer than this...
Stay strong, my child.
?
Gosh, he looks like he's only sleeping...
He fell upon his back. His face wasn't damaged at all.
Yukito.
Stop biting your nails.
Aren't you going to look at Grandad's face?
Ah, Auntie.
Not really... We could still do that tomorrow as well, couldn't we?
That's right.

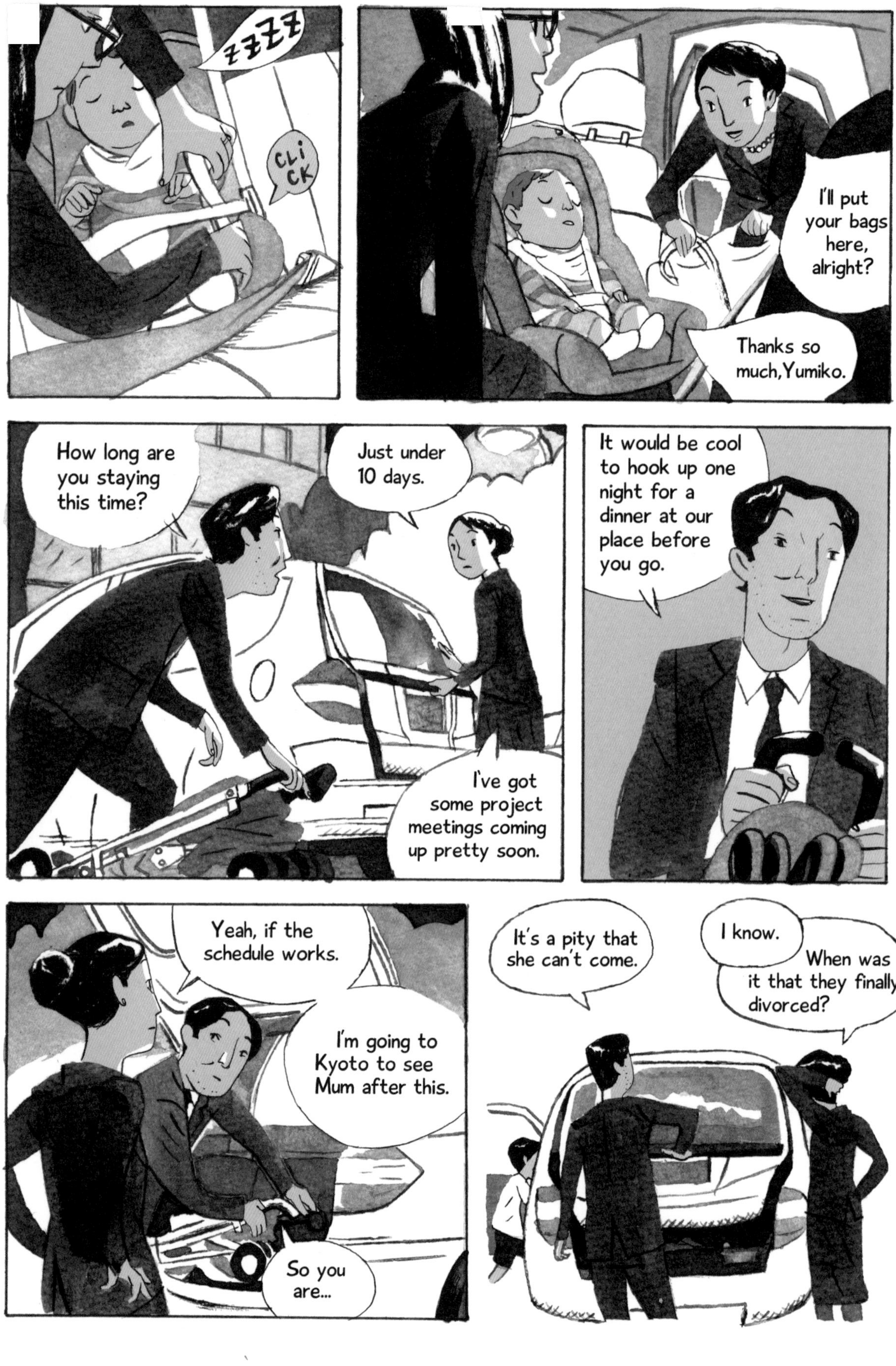
ZZZZ
CLICK
I'll put your bags here, alright?
Thanks so much, Yumiko.
How long are you staying this time?
Just under 10 days.
I've got some project meetings coming up pretty soon.
It would be cool to hook up one night for a dinner at our place before you go.
Yeah, if the schedule works.
I'm going to Kyoto to see Mum after this.
So you are...
It's a pity that she can't come.
I know.
When was it that they finally divorced?

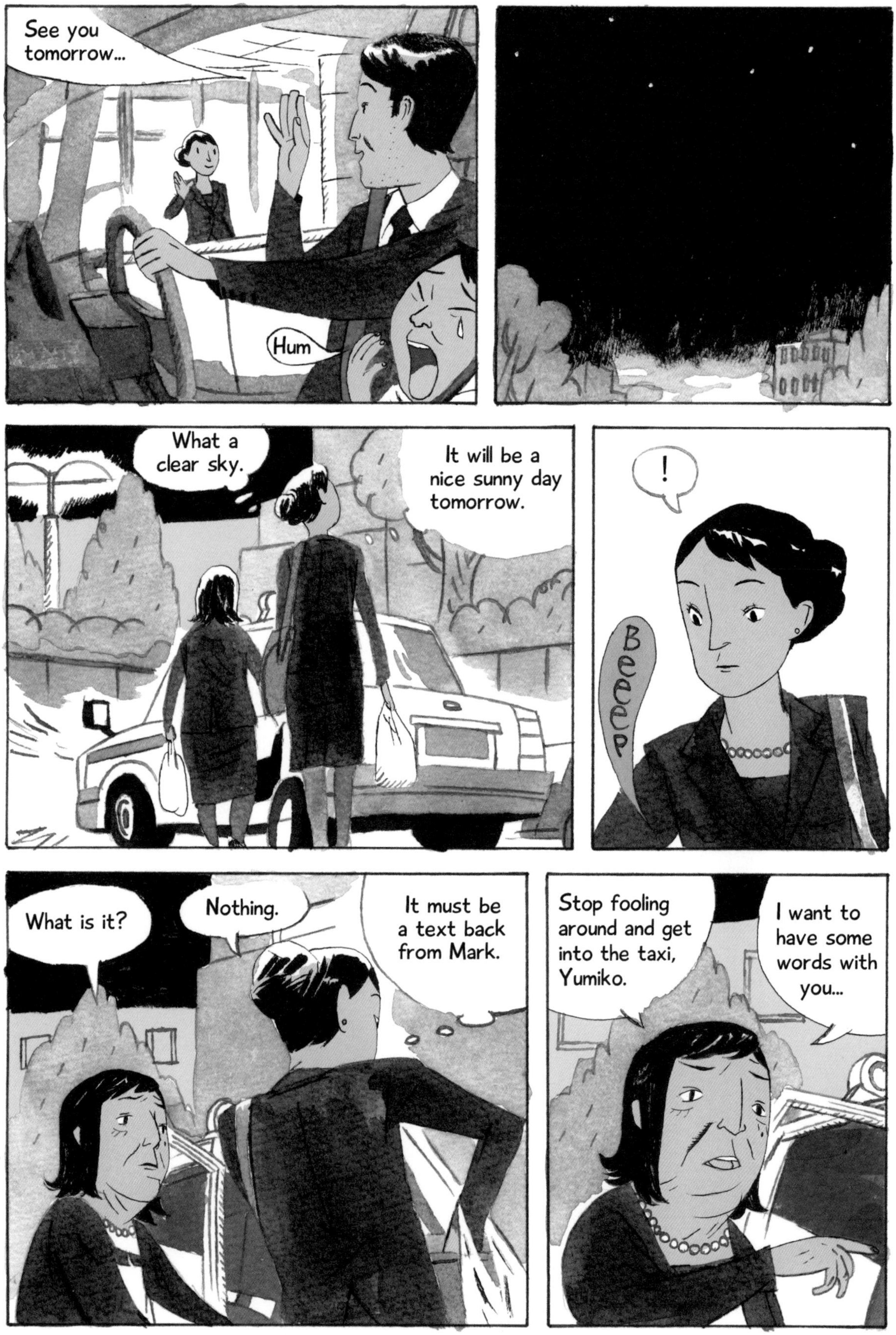
See you tomorrow...
Hum
What a clear sky.
It will be a nice sunny day tomorrow.
!
Beeep
What is it?
Nothing.
It must be a text back from Mark.
Stop fooling around and get into the taxi, Yumiko.
I want to have some words with you...

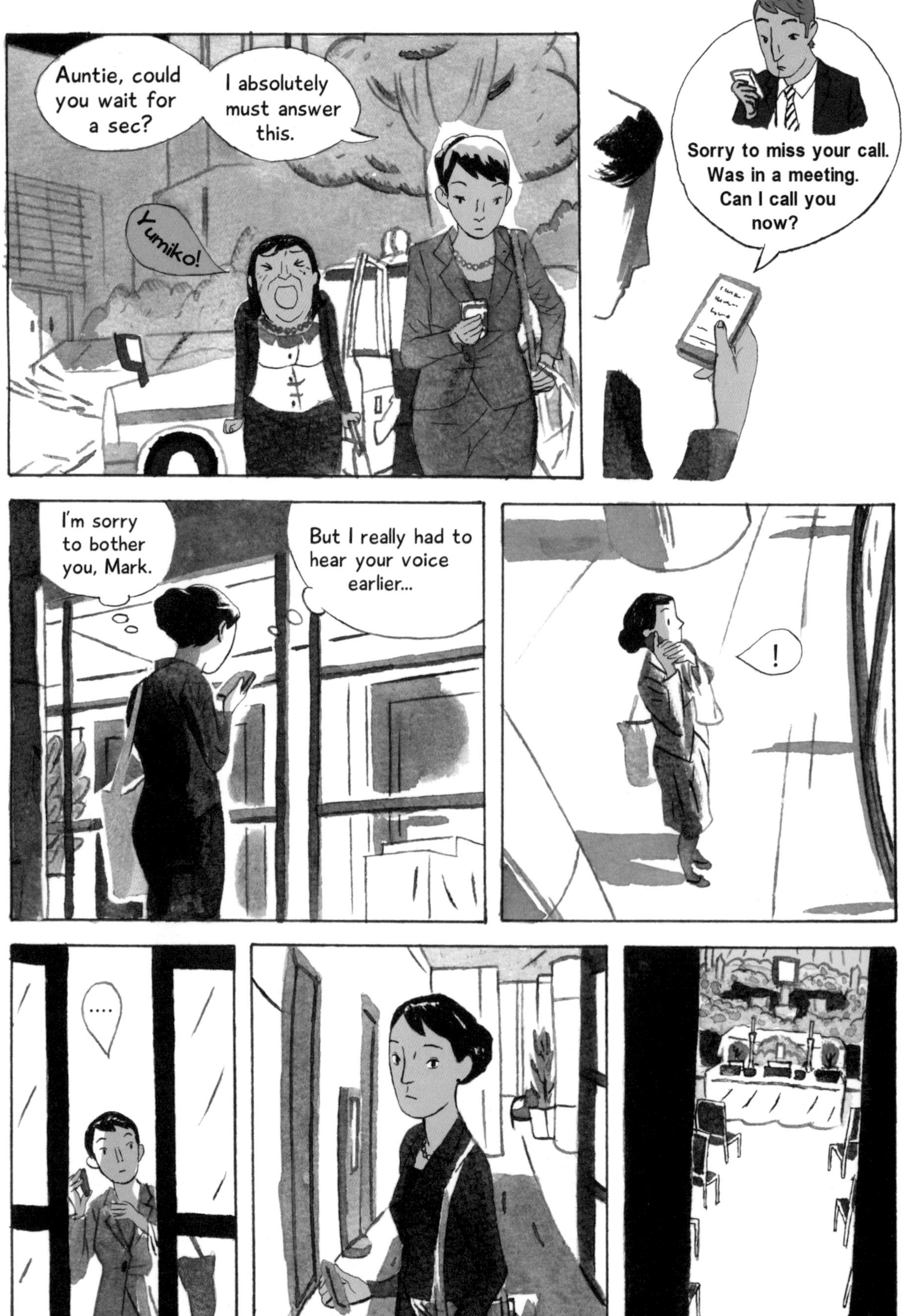
Auntie, could you wait for a sec?
I absolutely must answer this.
Yumiko!
Sorry to miss your call. Was in a meeting. Can I call you now?
I'm sorry to bother you, Mark.
But I really had to hear your voice earlier...
!
....

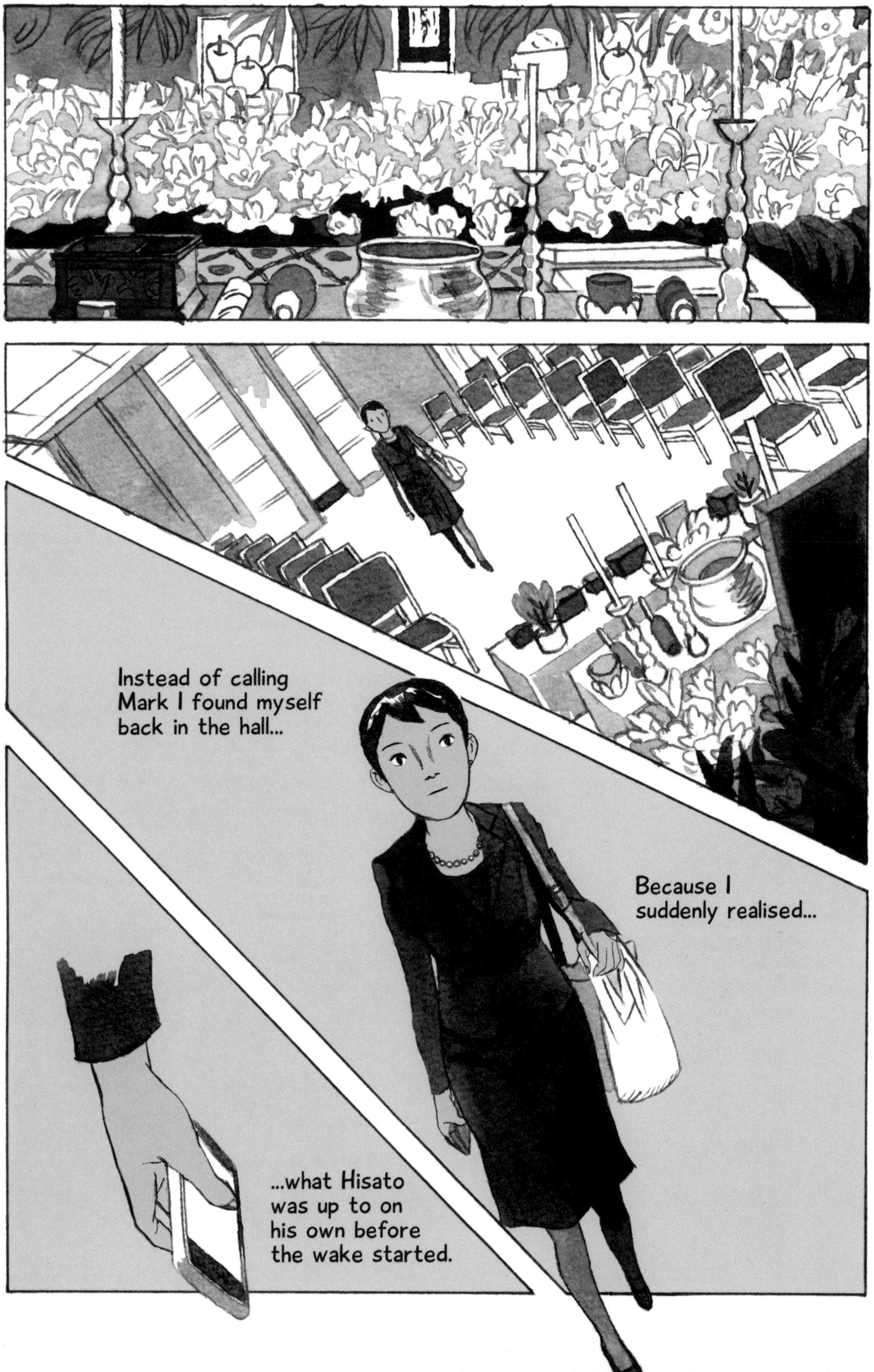
Instead of calling Mark I found myself back in the hall...
Because I suddenly realised...
...what Hisato was up to on his own before the wake started.

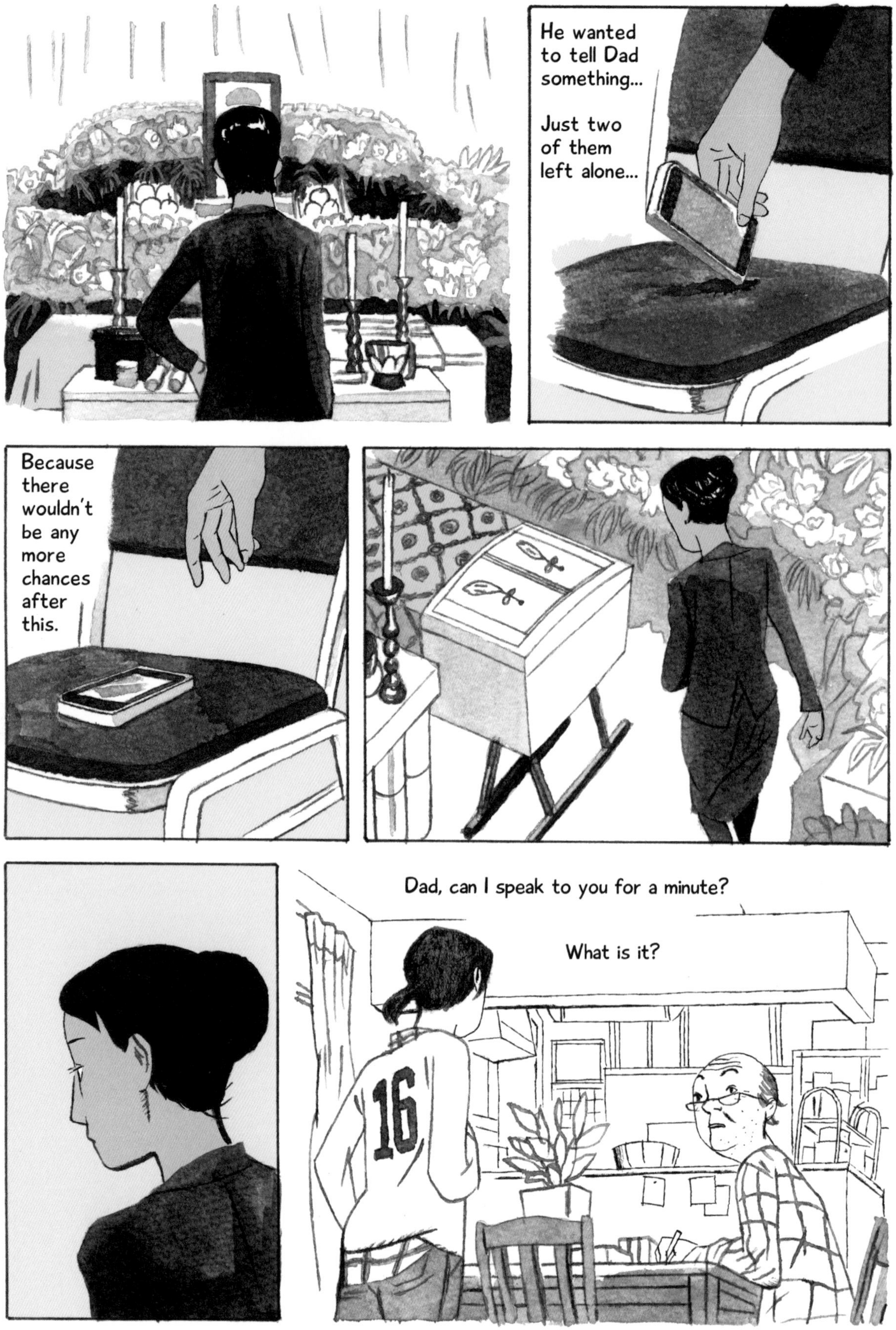
He wanted to tell Dad something...
Just two of them left alone...
Because there wouldn't be any more chances after this.
Dad, can I speak to you for a minute?
What is it?
16

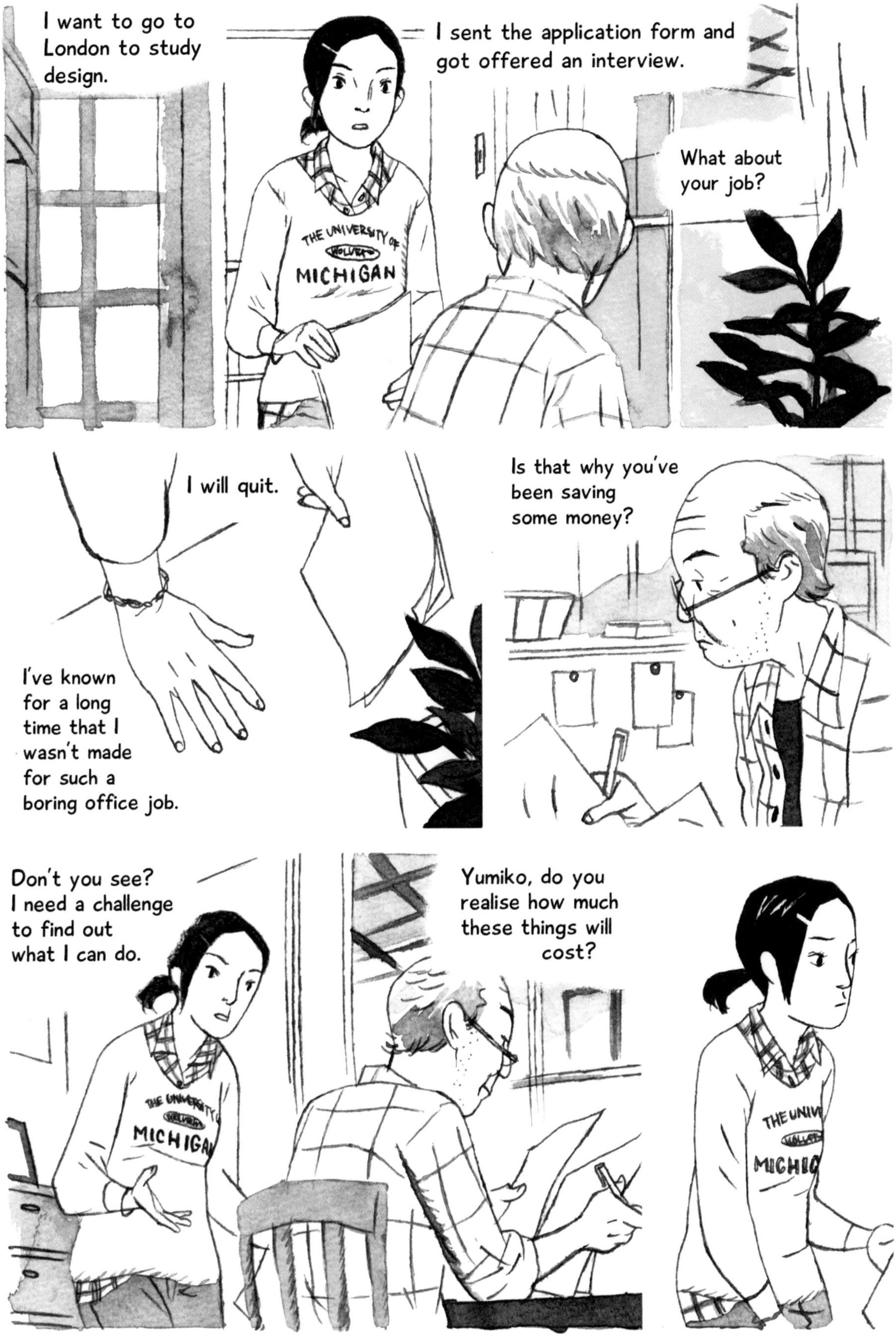
I want to go to London to study design.
I sent the application form and got offered an interview.
What about your job?
I will quit.
I've known for a long time that I wasn't made for such a boring office job.
Is that why you've been saving some money?
Don't you see? I need a challenge to find out what I can do.
Yumiko, do you realise how much these things will cost?
THE UNIVERSITY OF
MICHIGAN

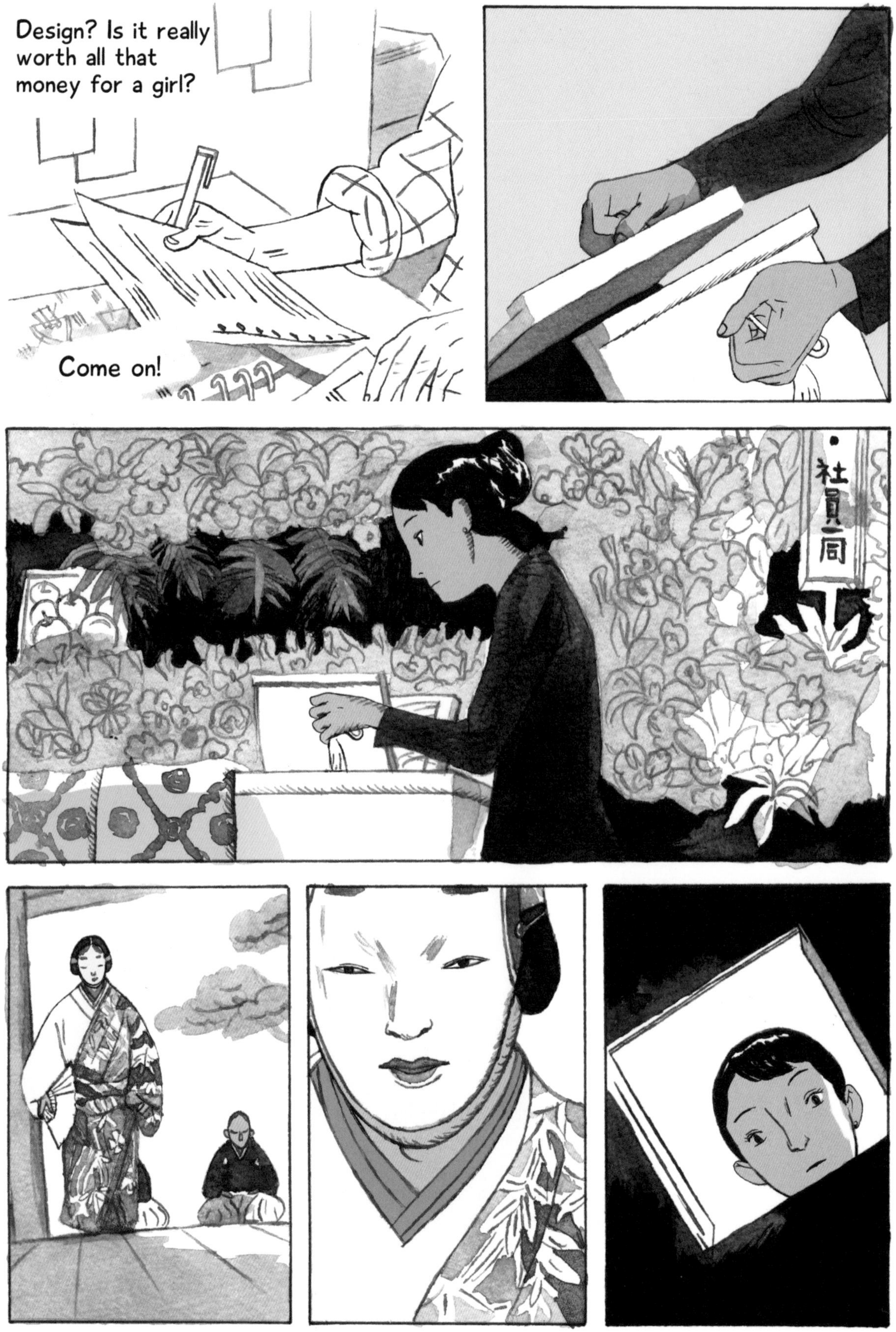
Design? Is it really worth all that money for a girl?
Come on!

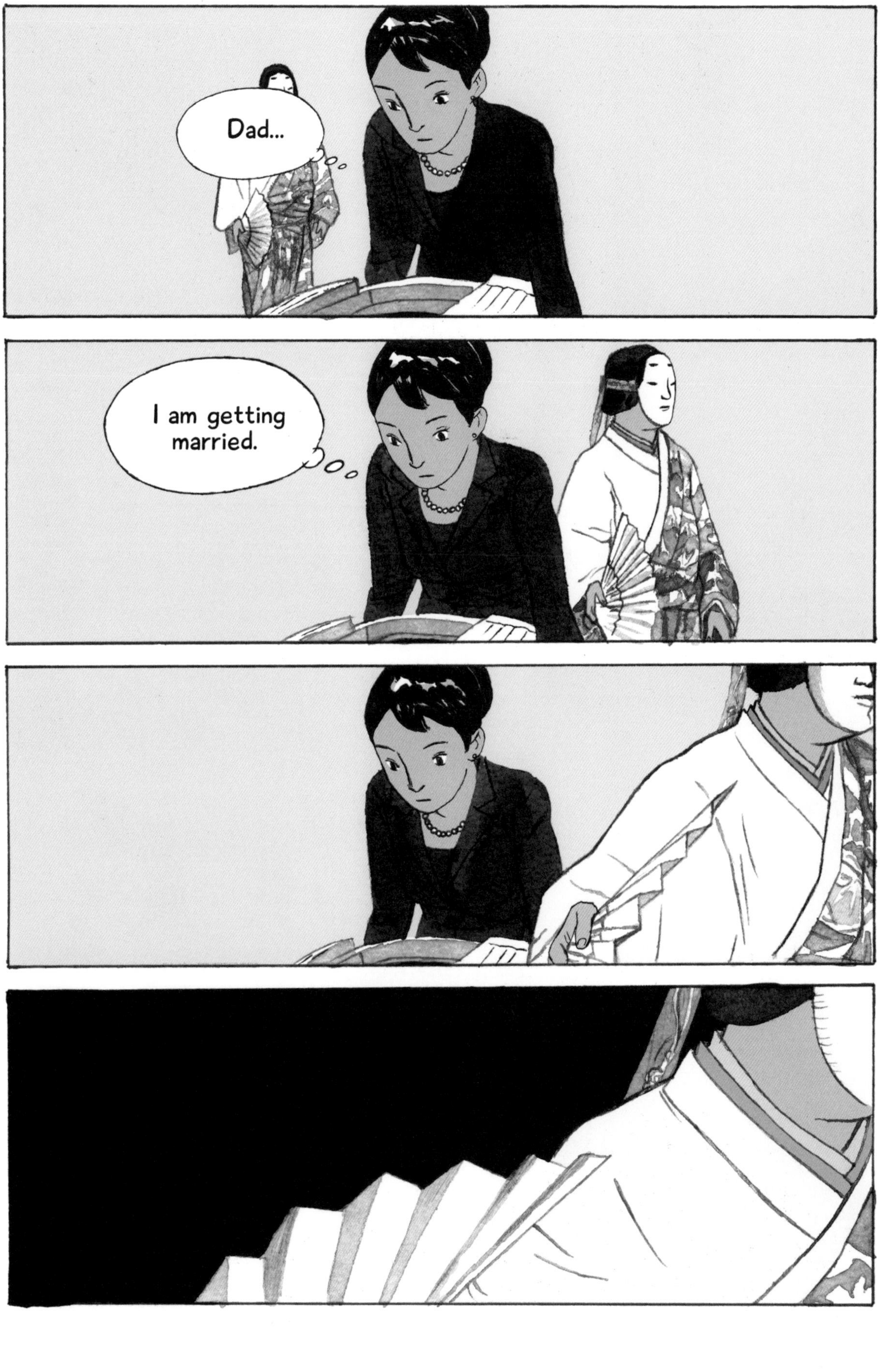
Dad...
I am getting married.

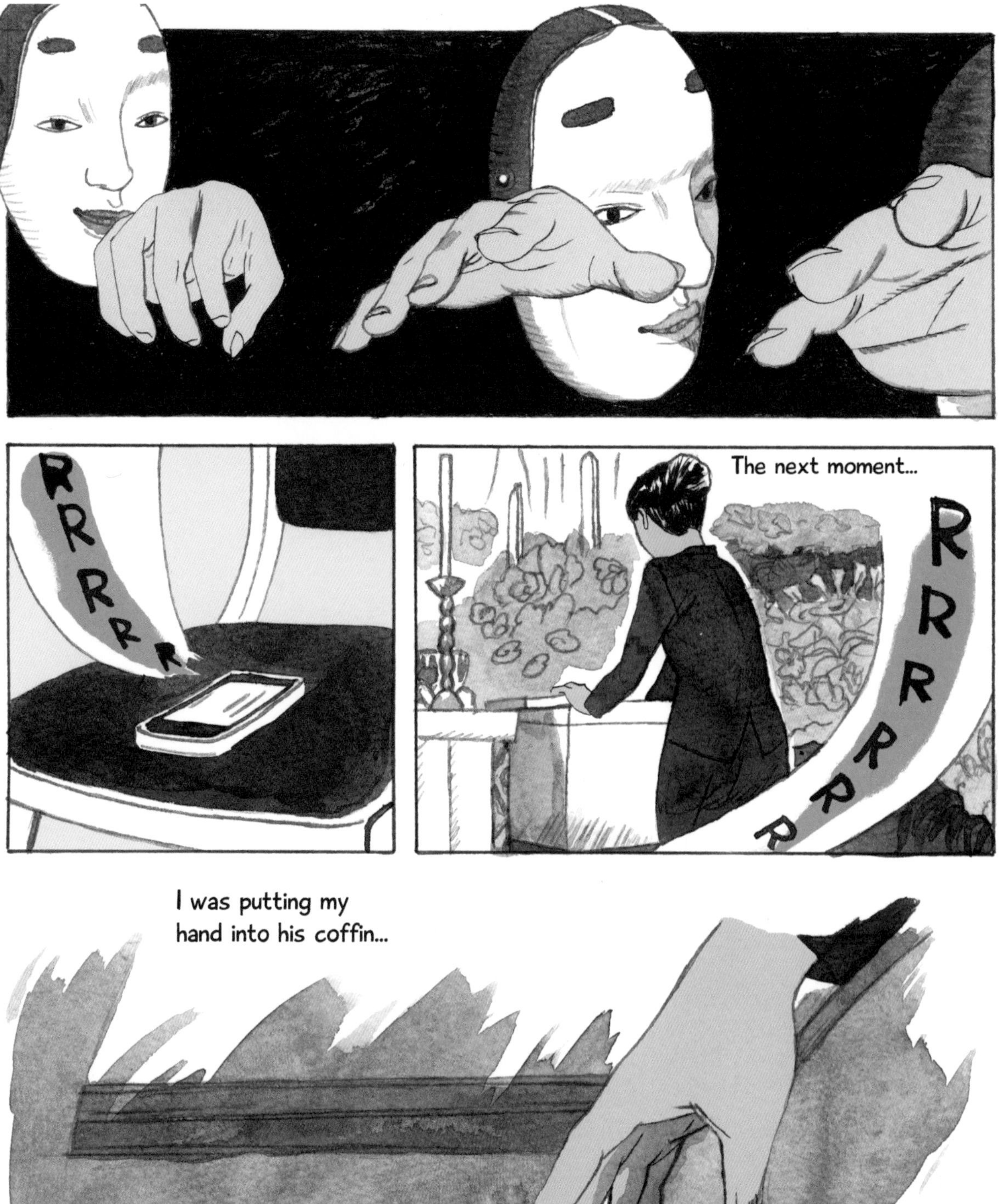
RRRRR
The next moment...
RRRRRR
I was putting my hand into his coffin...
Touching his dead flesh...
Stroking...

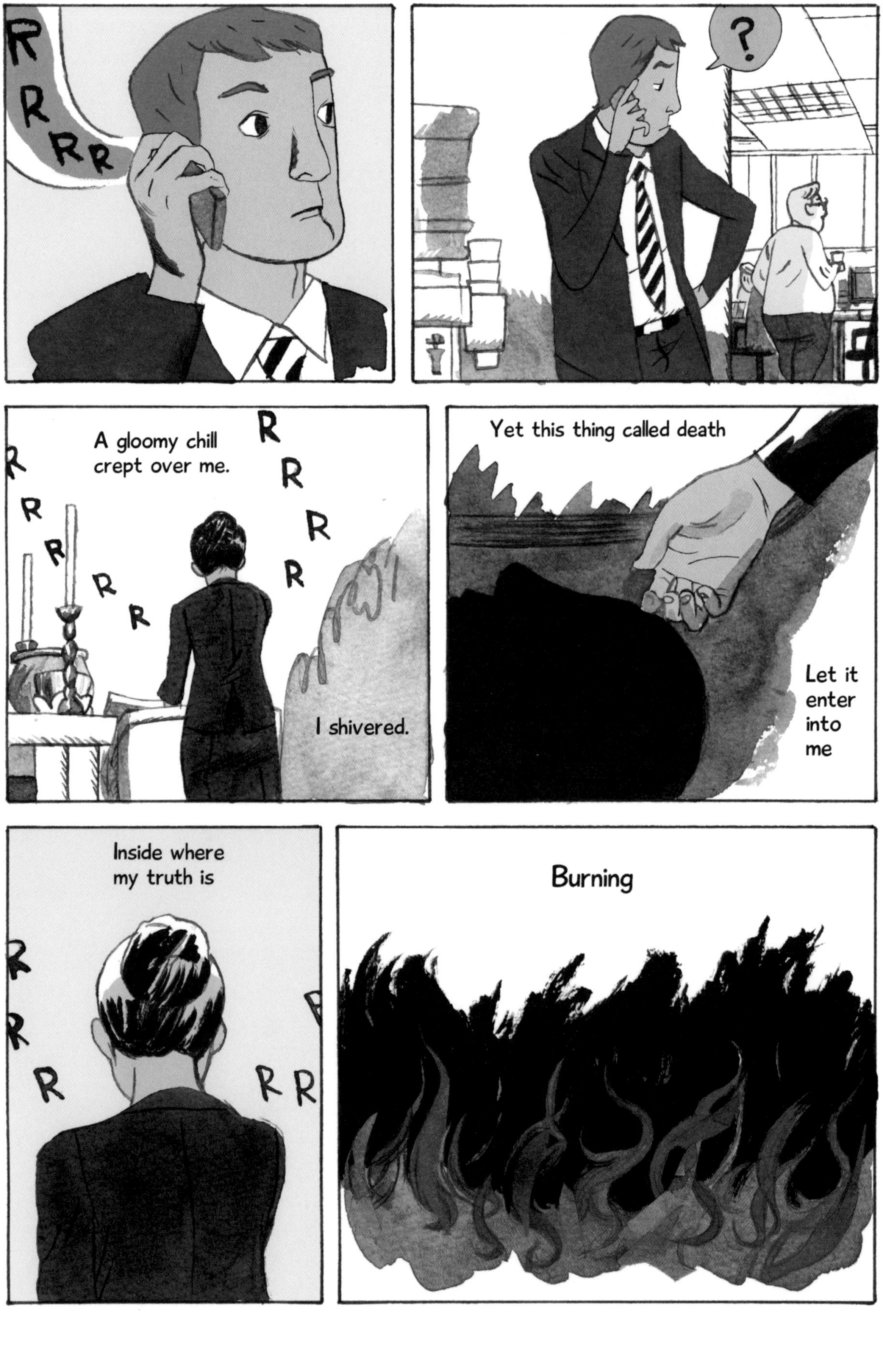
RRRR
?
A gloomy chill crept over me.
RRRRRR
RRRRR
I shivered.
Yet this thing called death
Let it enter into me
Inside where my truth is
RRR
RR
Burning

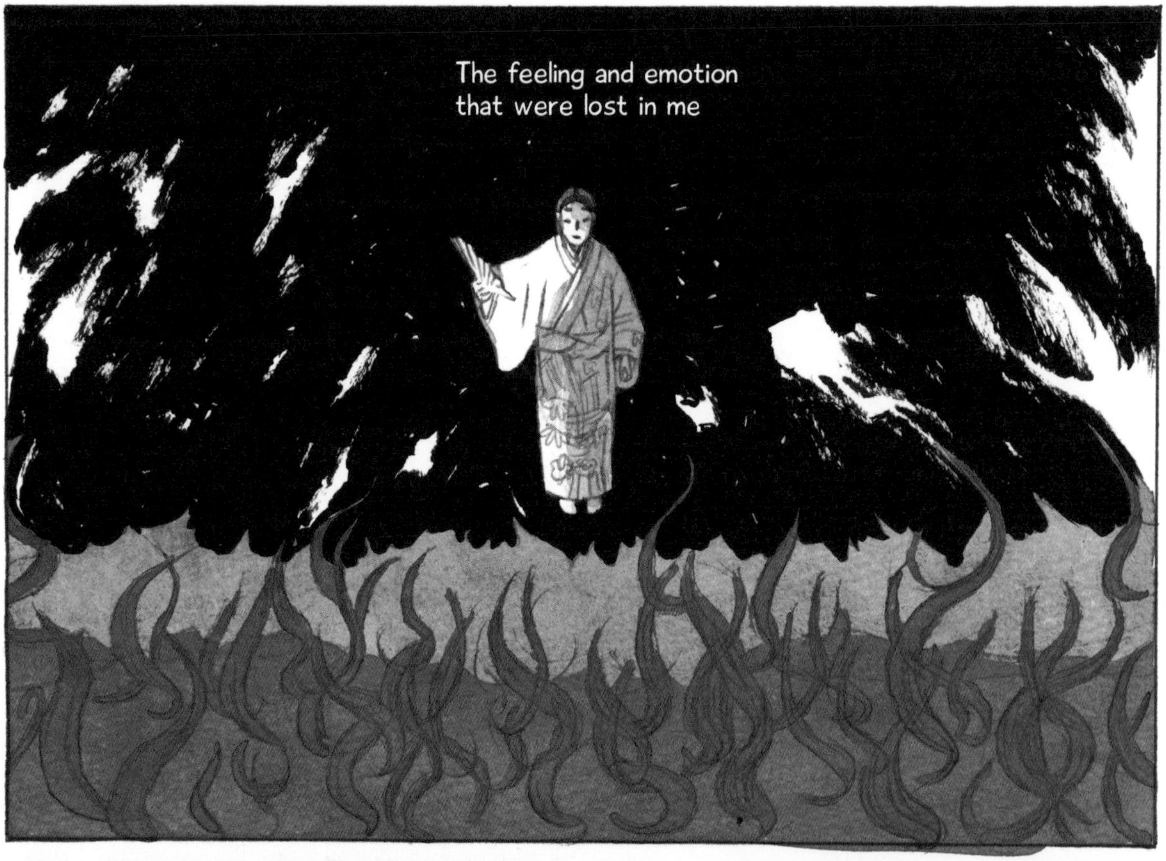
The feeling and emotion
that were lost in me

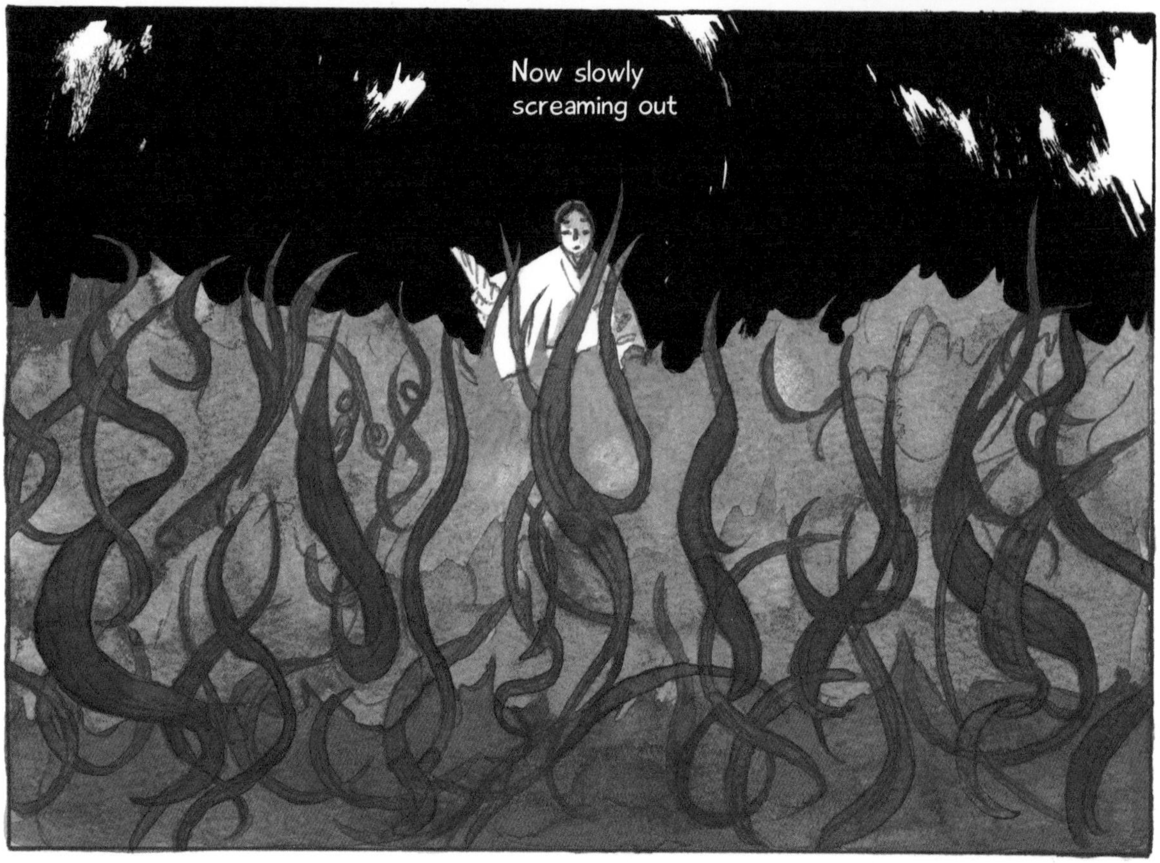
Now slowly
screaming out

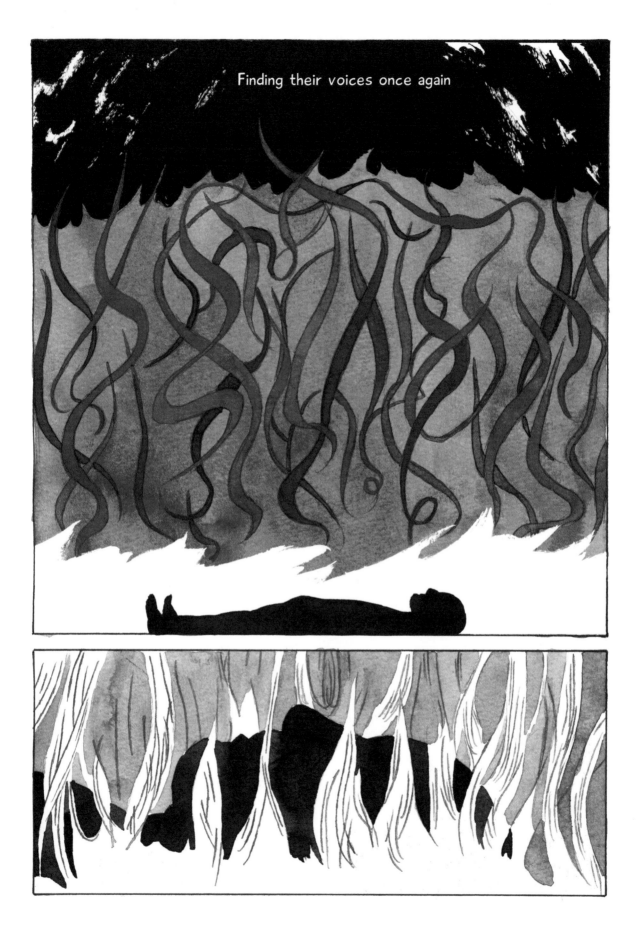

Finding their voices once again

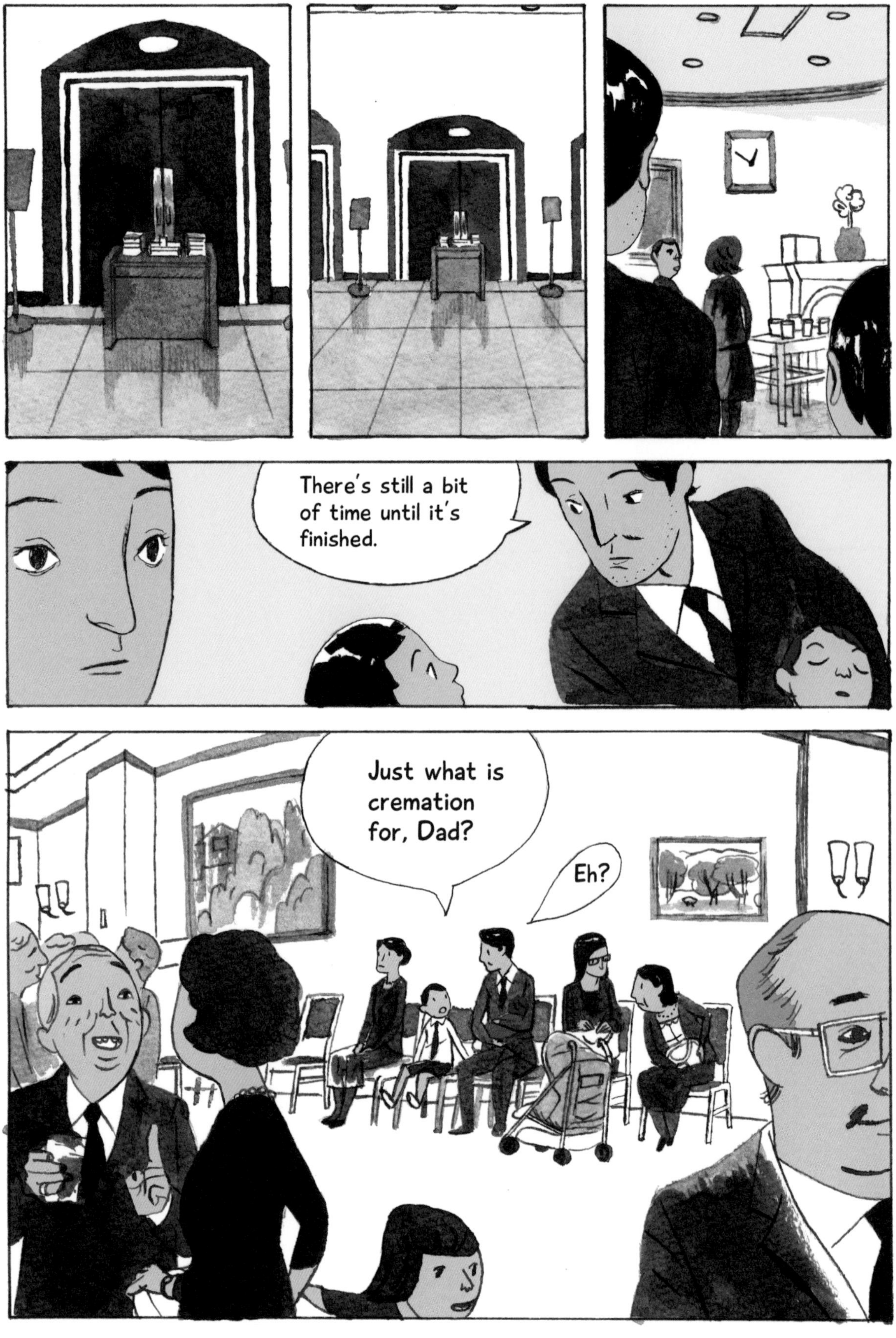
There's still a bit of time until it's finished.
Just what is cremation for, Dad?
Eh?

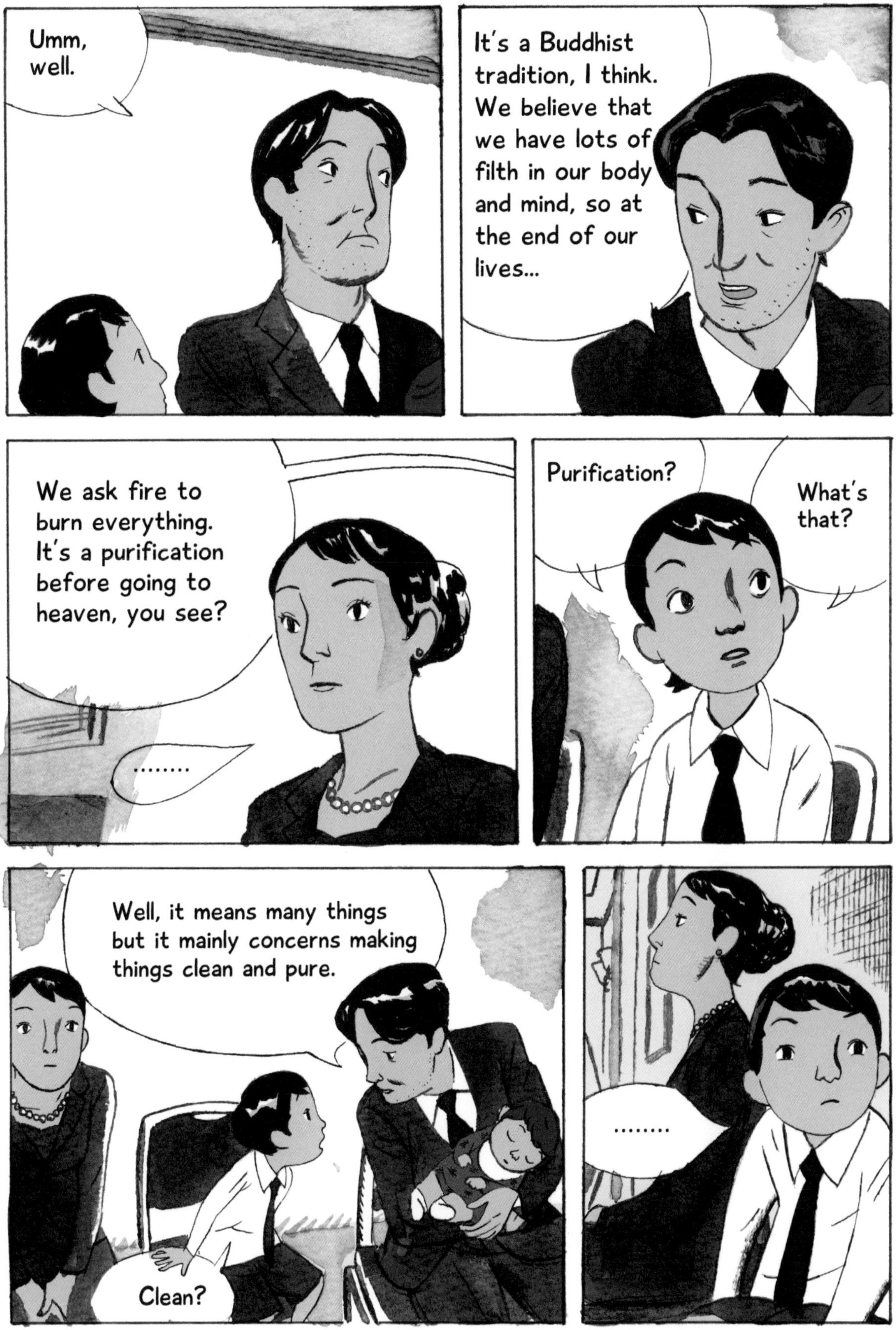

Umm, well.
It's a Buddhist tradition, I think. We believe that we have lots of filth in our body and mind, so at the end of our lives...
We ask fire to burn everything. It's a purification before going to heaven, you see?
....
Purification?
What's that?
Well, it means many things but it mainly concerns making things clean and pure.
Clean?
....

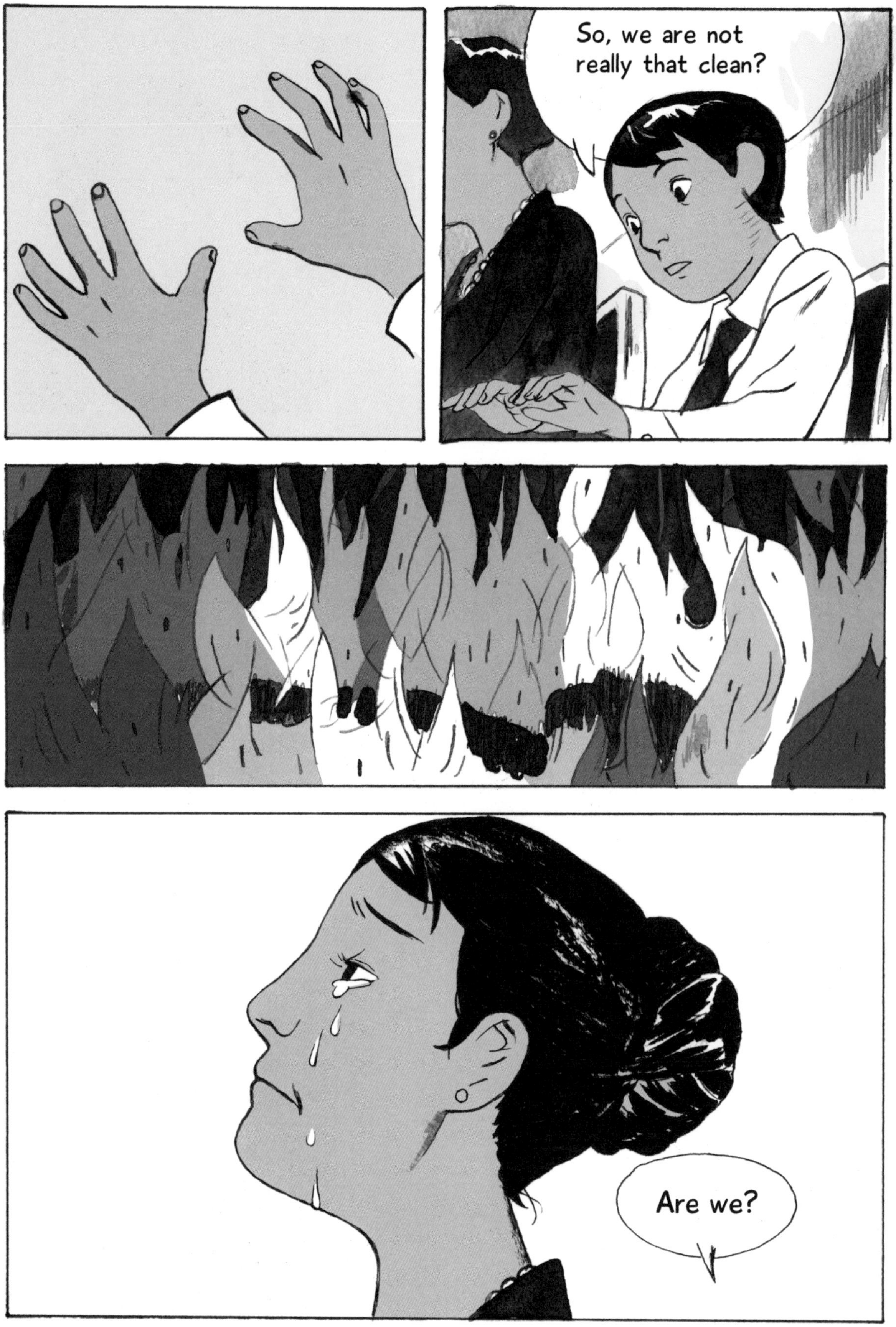
So, we are not really that clean?
Are we?

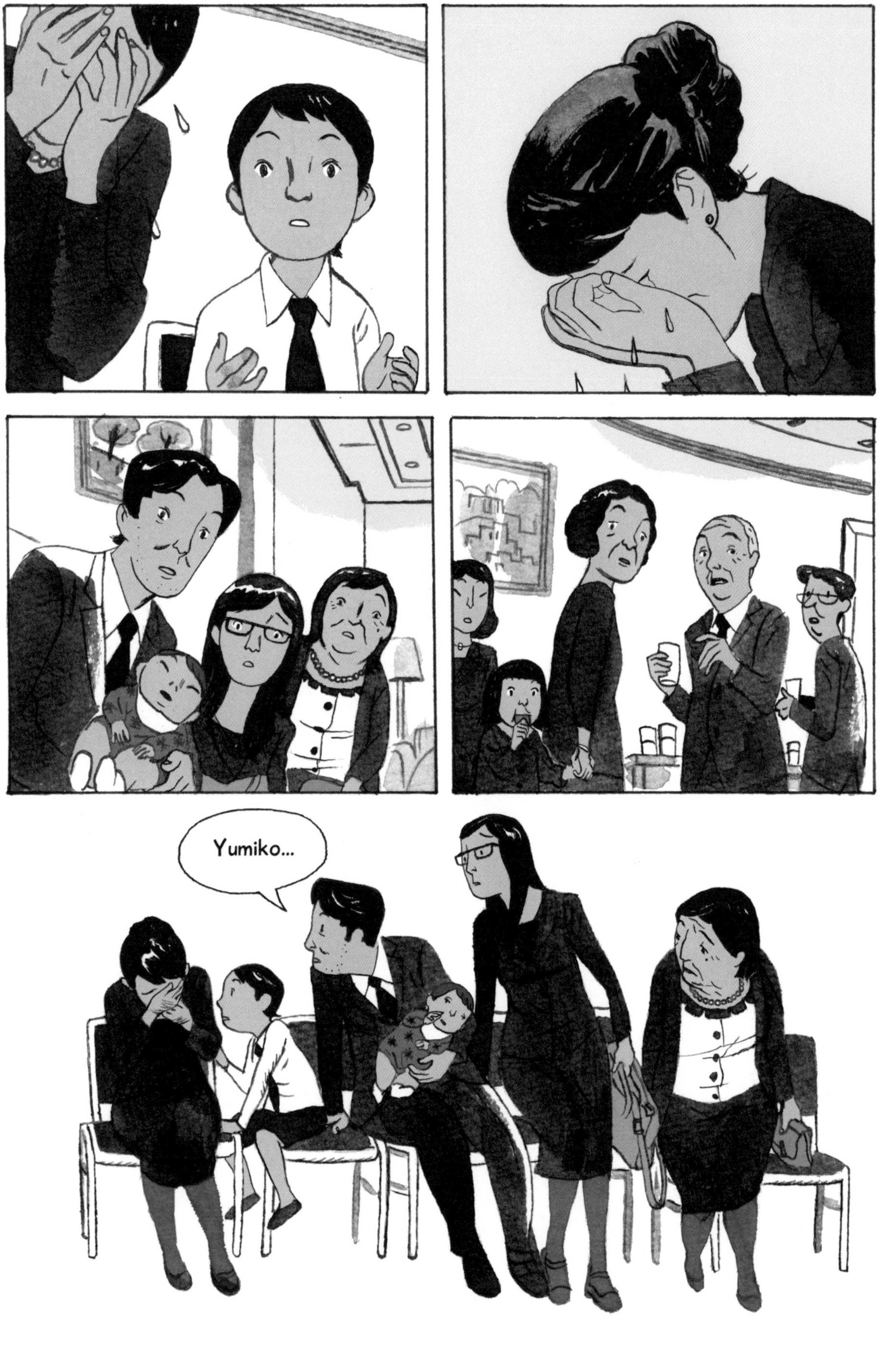
Yumiko...

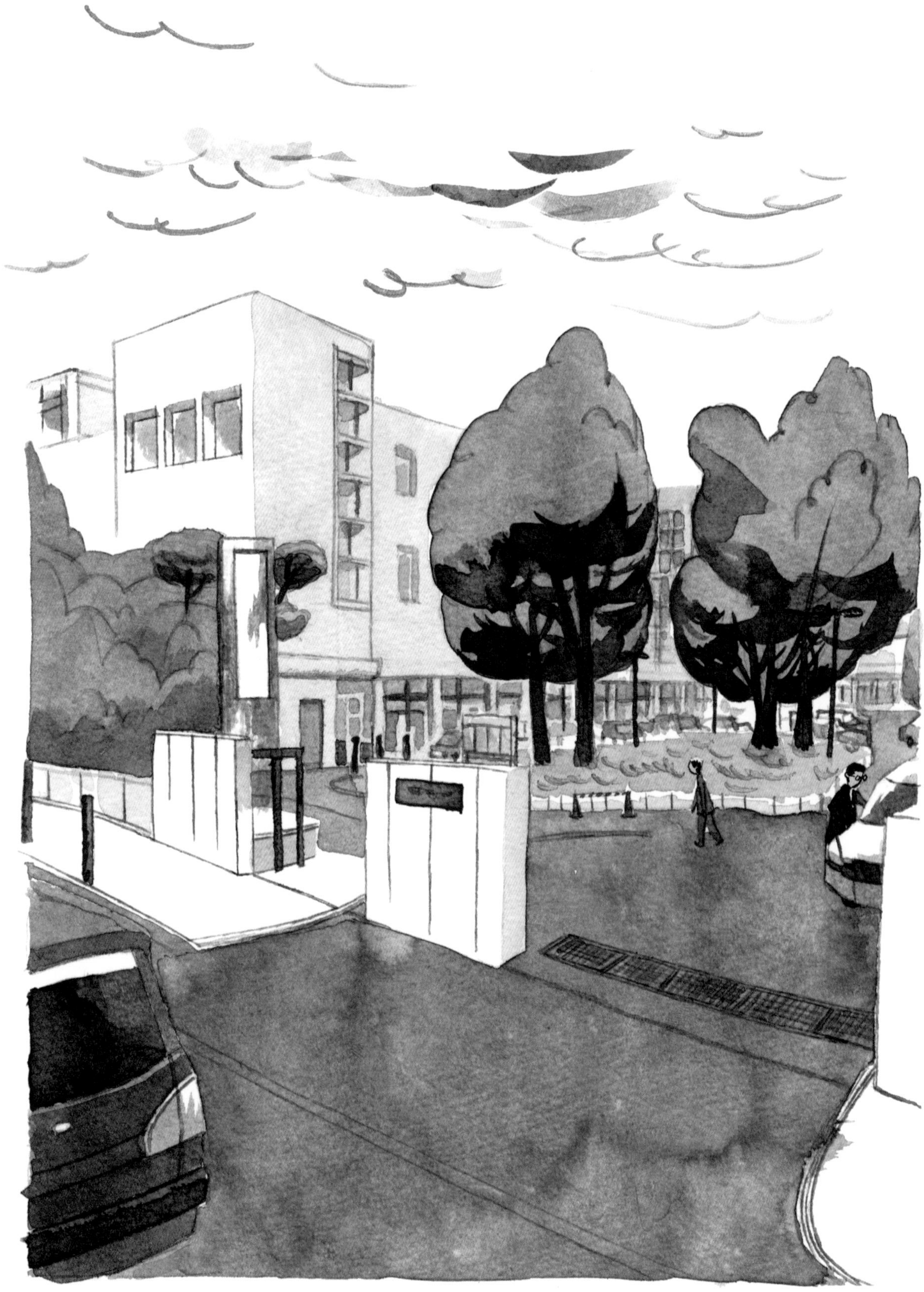

III

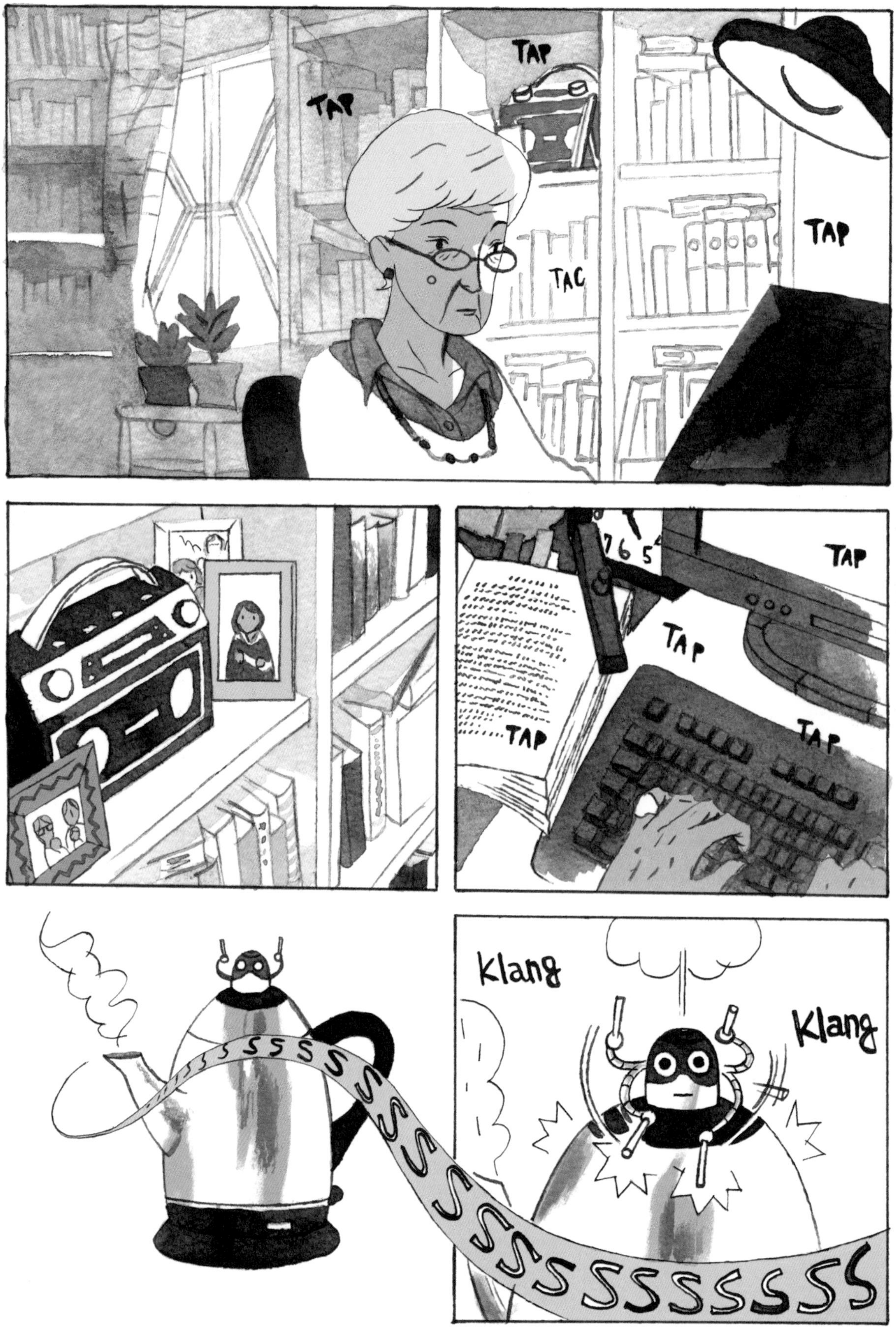
TAP
TAP
TAC
TAP
TAP
TAP
TAP
TAP
SSSSSSSSSSSSSSSSSSSSSSSS
Klang
Klang

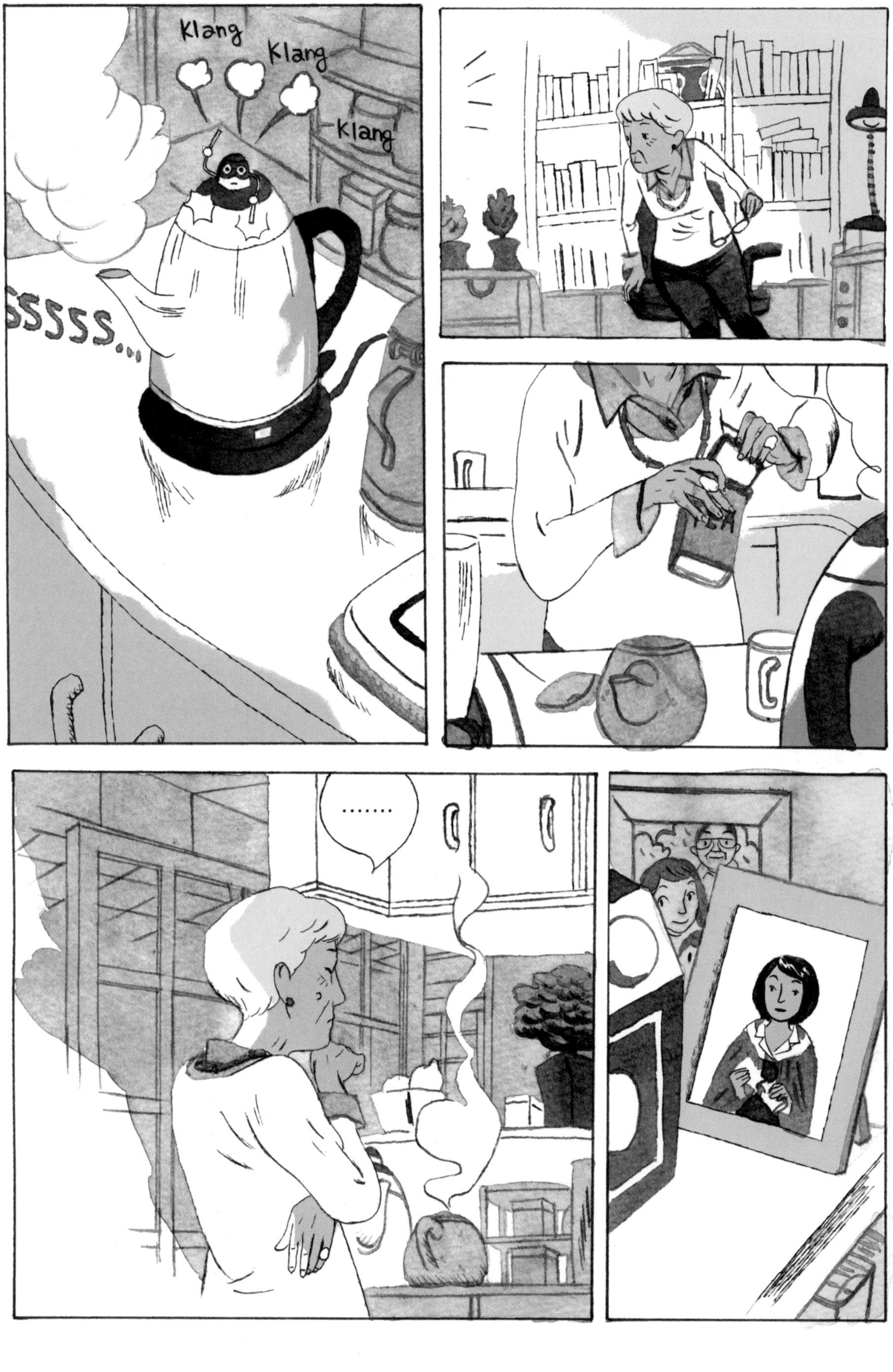
Klang
Klang
Klang
SSSSS...
....

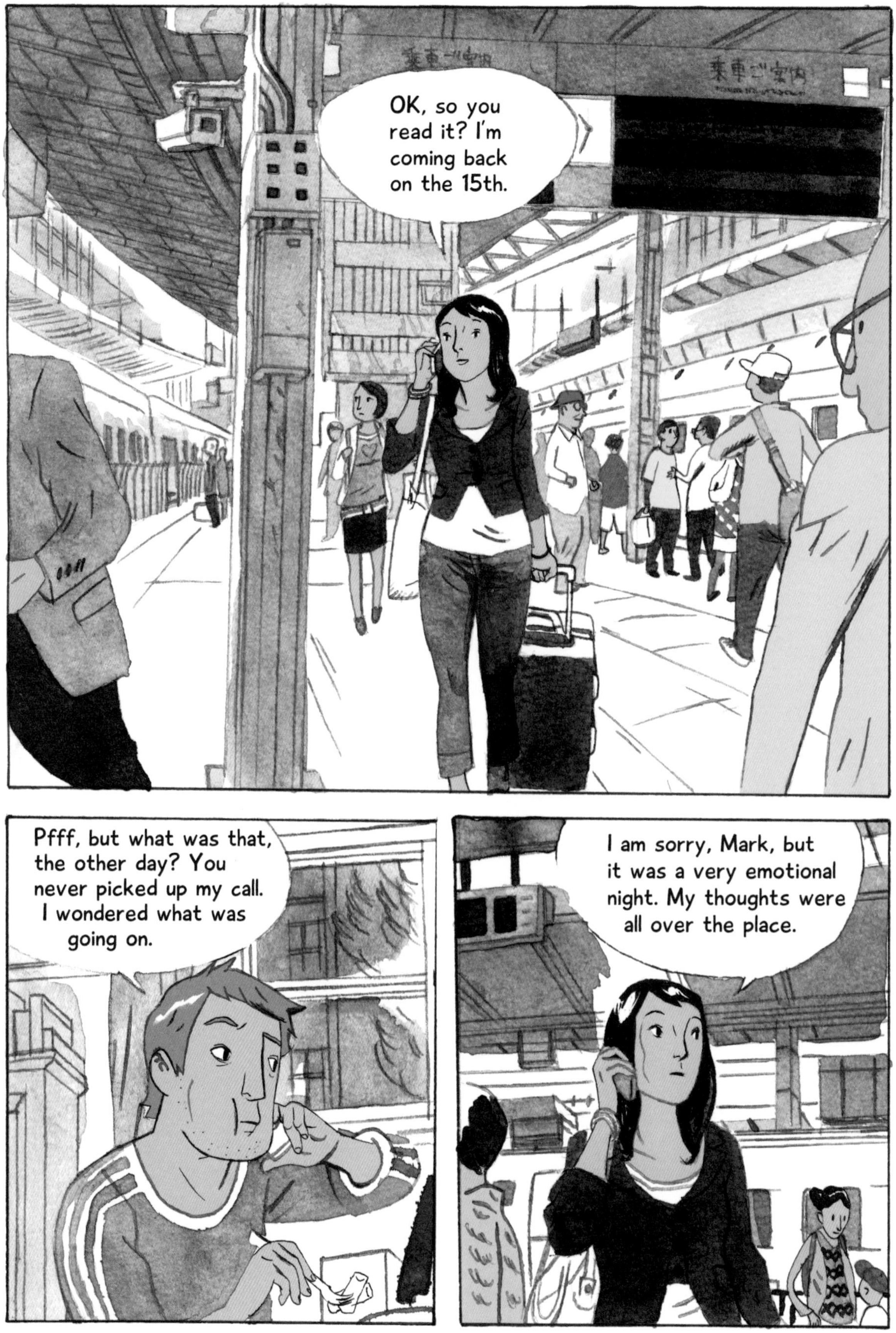
OK, so you read it? I'm coming back on the 15th.
Pfff, but what was that, the other day? You never picked up my call. I wondered what was going on.
I am sorry, Mark, but it was a very emotional night. My thoughts were all over the place.

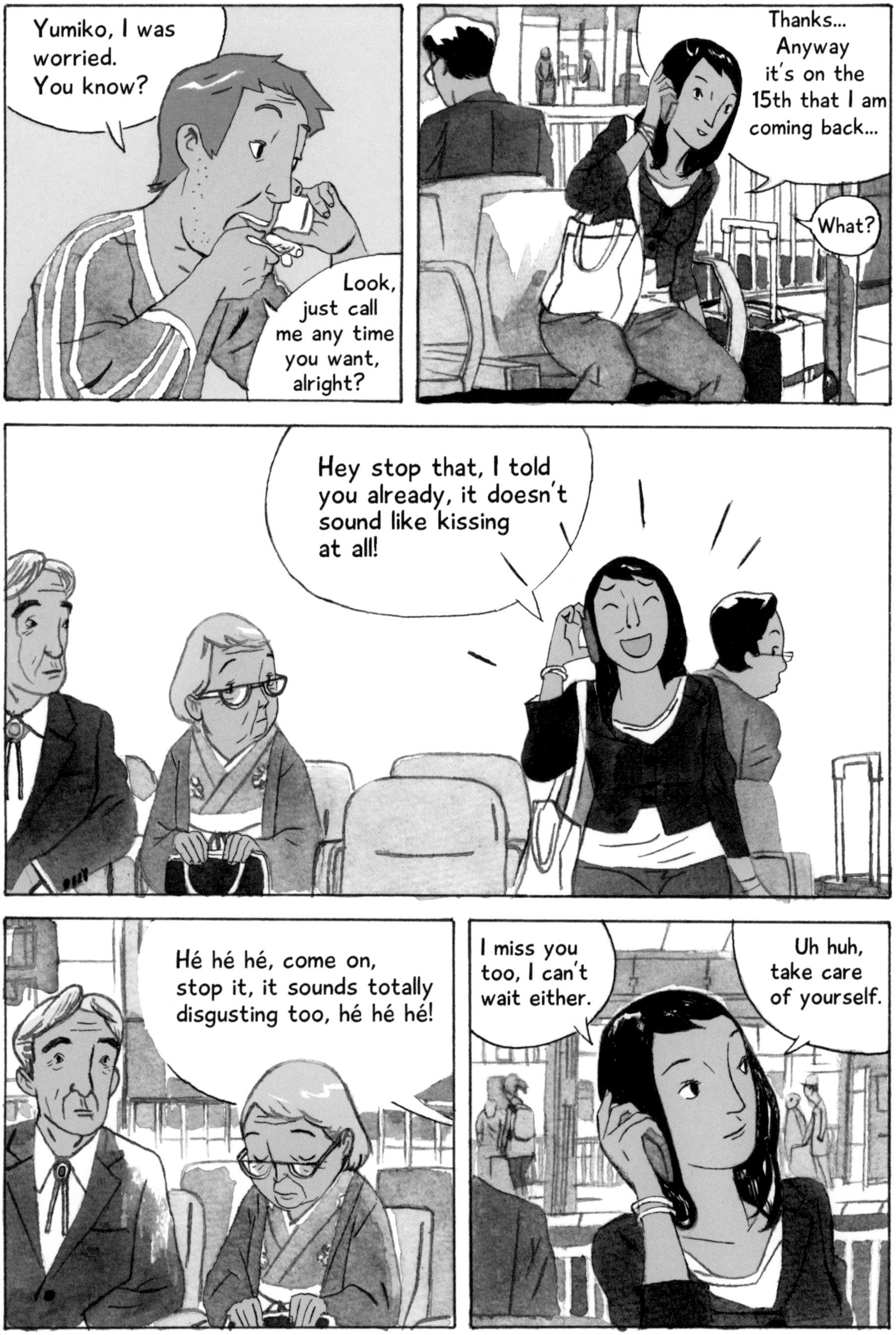
Yumiko, I was worried. You know?
Look, just call me any time you want, alright?
Thanks... Anyway it's on the 15th that I am coming back...
What?
Hey stop that, I told you already, it doesn't sound like kissing at all!
Hé hé hé, come on, stop it, it sounds totally disgusting too, hé hé hé!
I miss you too, I can't wait either.
Uh huh, take care of yourself.

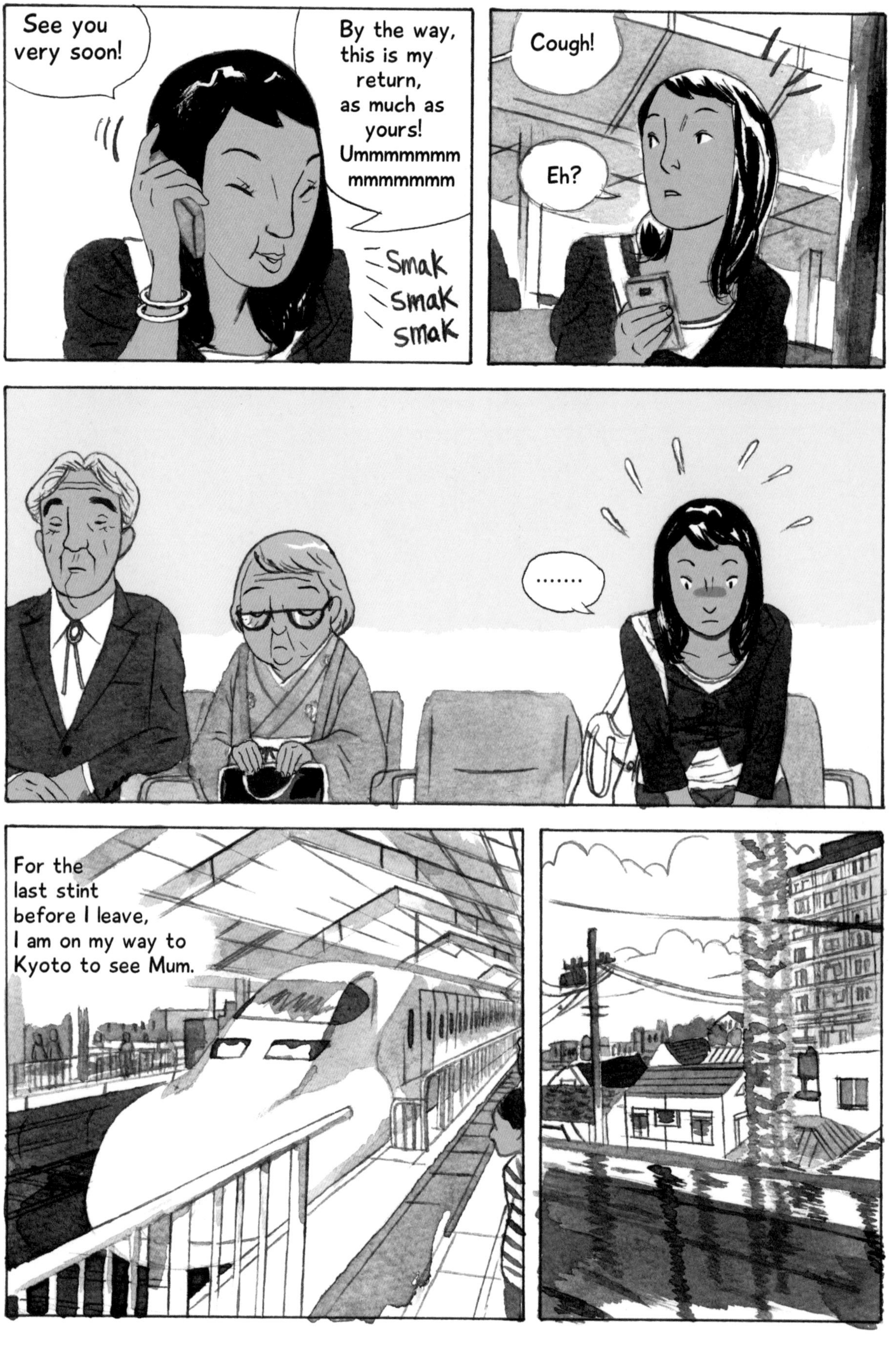
See you very soon!
By the way, this is my return, as much as yours! Ummmmmmm mmmmmmm
Smak smak smak
Cough!
Eh?
....
For the last stint before I leave, I am on my way to Kyoto to see Mum.

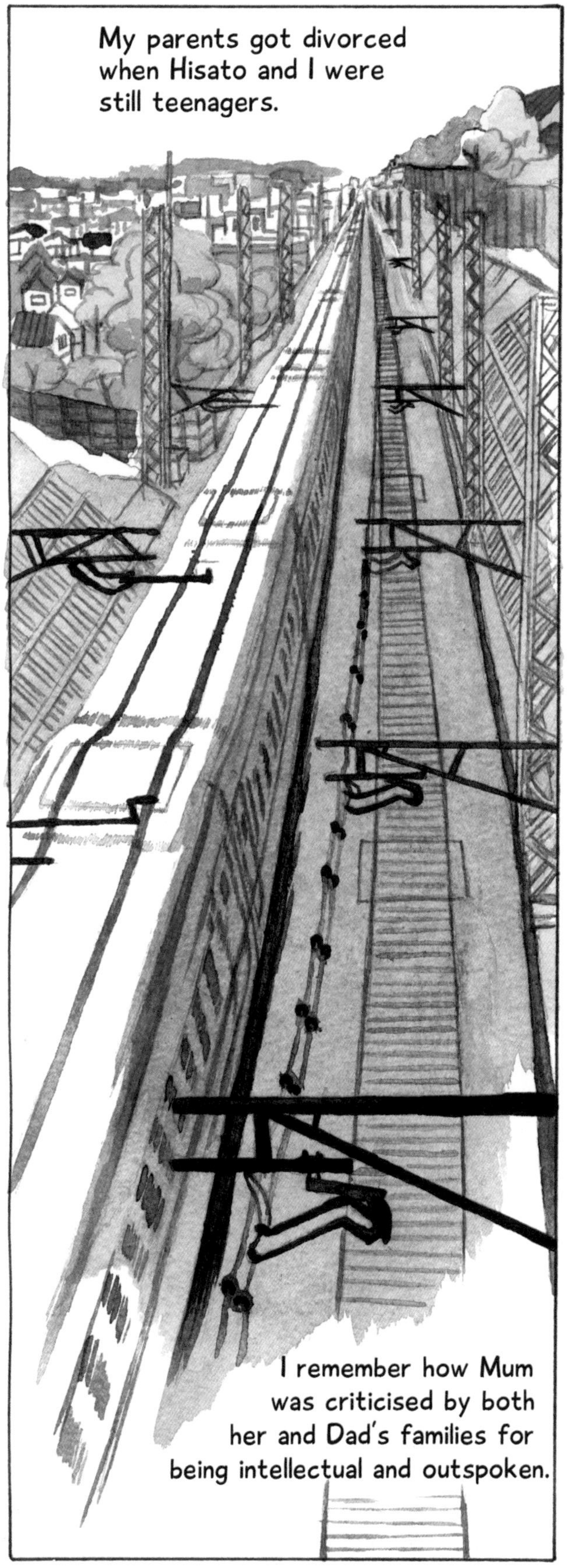
My parents got divorced when Hisato and I were still teenagers.
I remember how Mum was criticised by both her and Dad's families for being intellectual and outspoken.

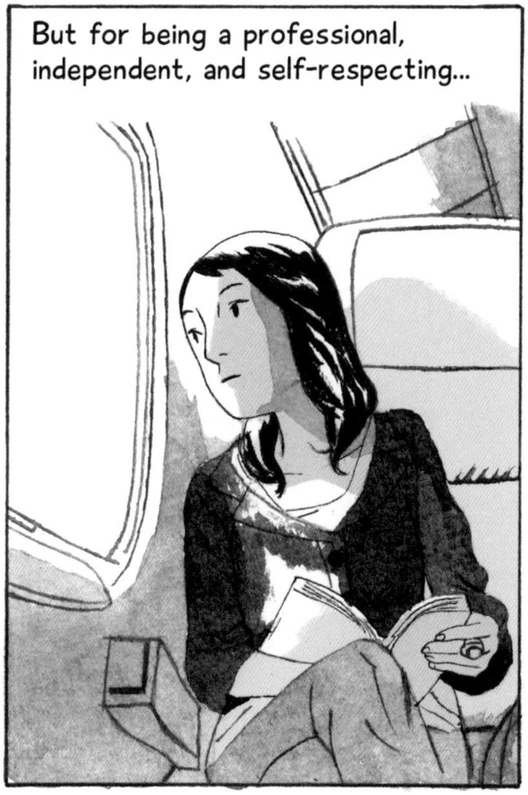
But for being a professional, independent, and self-respecting...

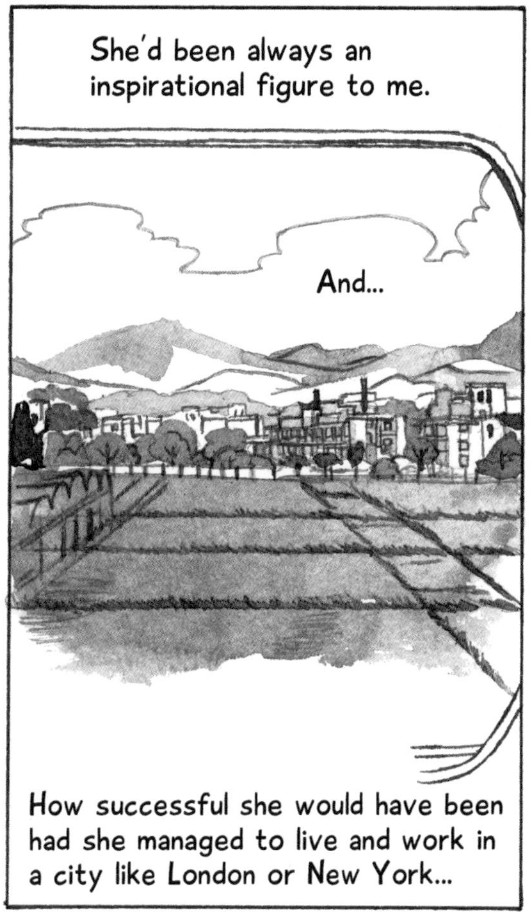
She'd been always an inspirational figure to me.
And...
How successful she would have been had she managed to live and work in a city like London or New York...

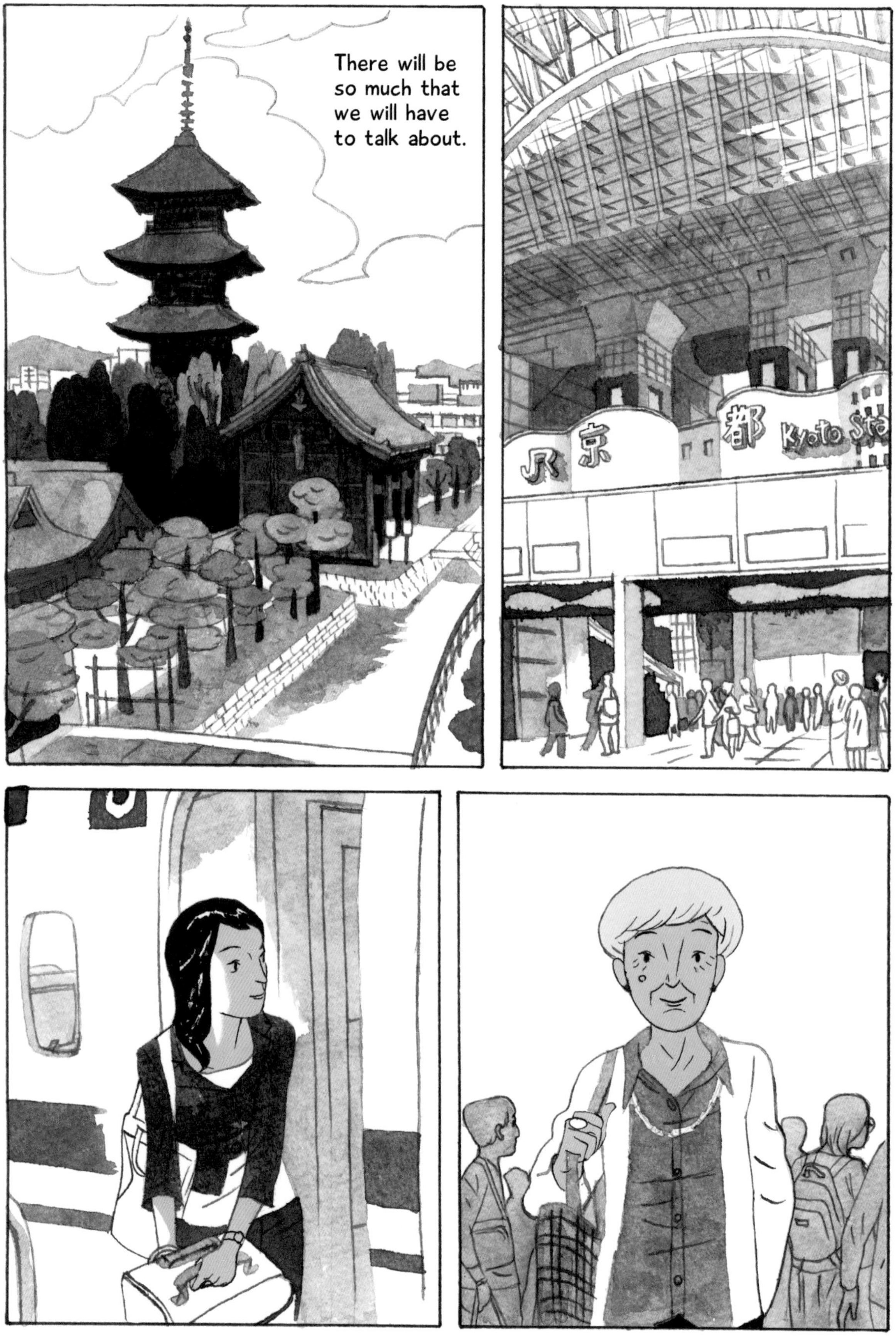
There will be so much that we will have to talk about.
京 都

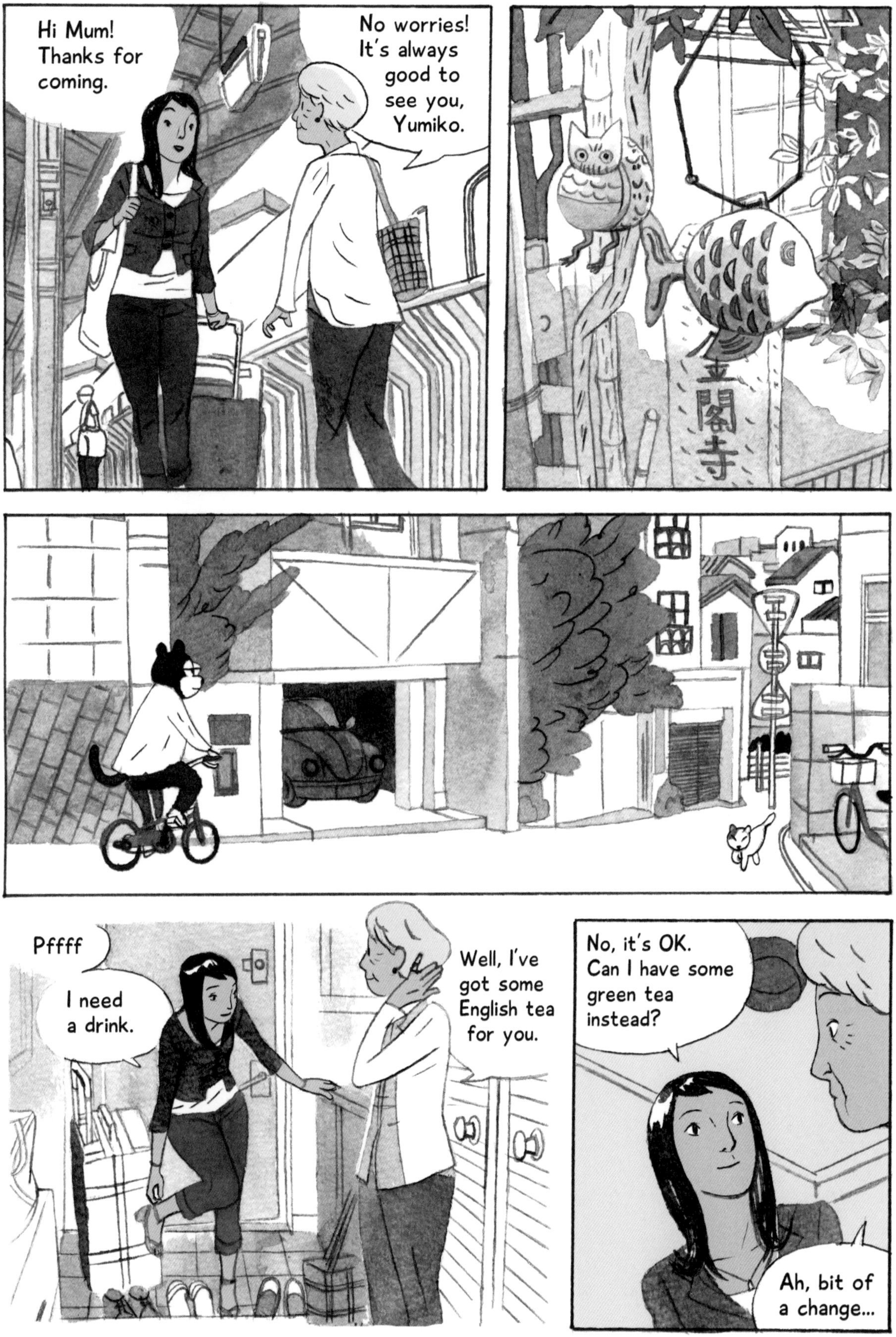
Hi Mum! Thanks for coming.
No worries! It's always good to see you, Yumiko.
Pffff
I need a drink.
Well, I've got some English tea for you.
No, it's OK. Can I have some green tea instead?
Ah, bit of a change...

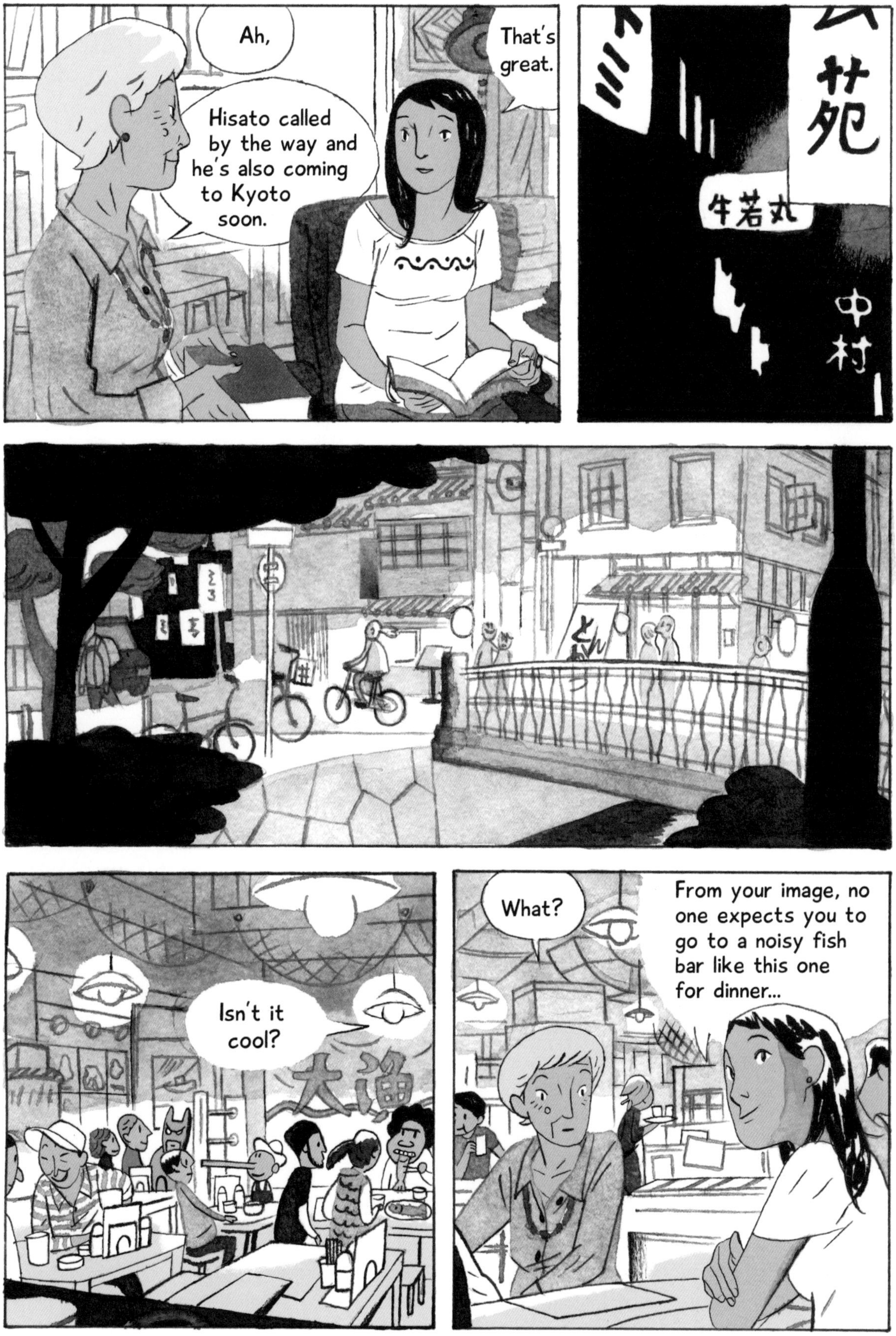
Ah,
Hisato called by the way and he's also coming to Kyoto soon.
That's great.
苑
牛若丸
中村
Isn't it cool?
大漁
What?
From your image, no one expects you to go to a noisy fish bar like this one for dinner...

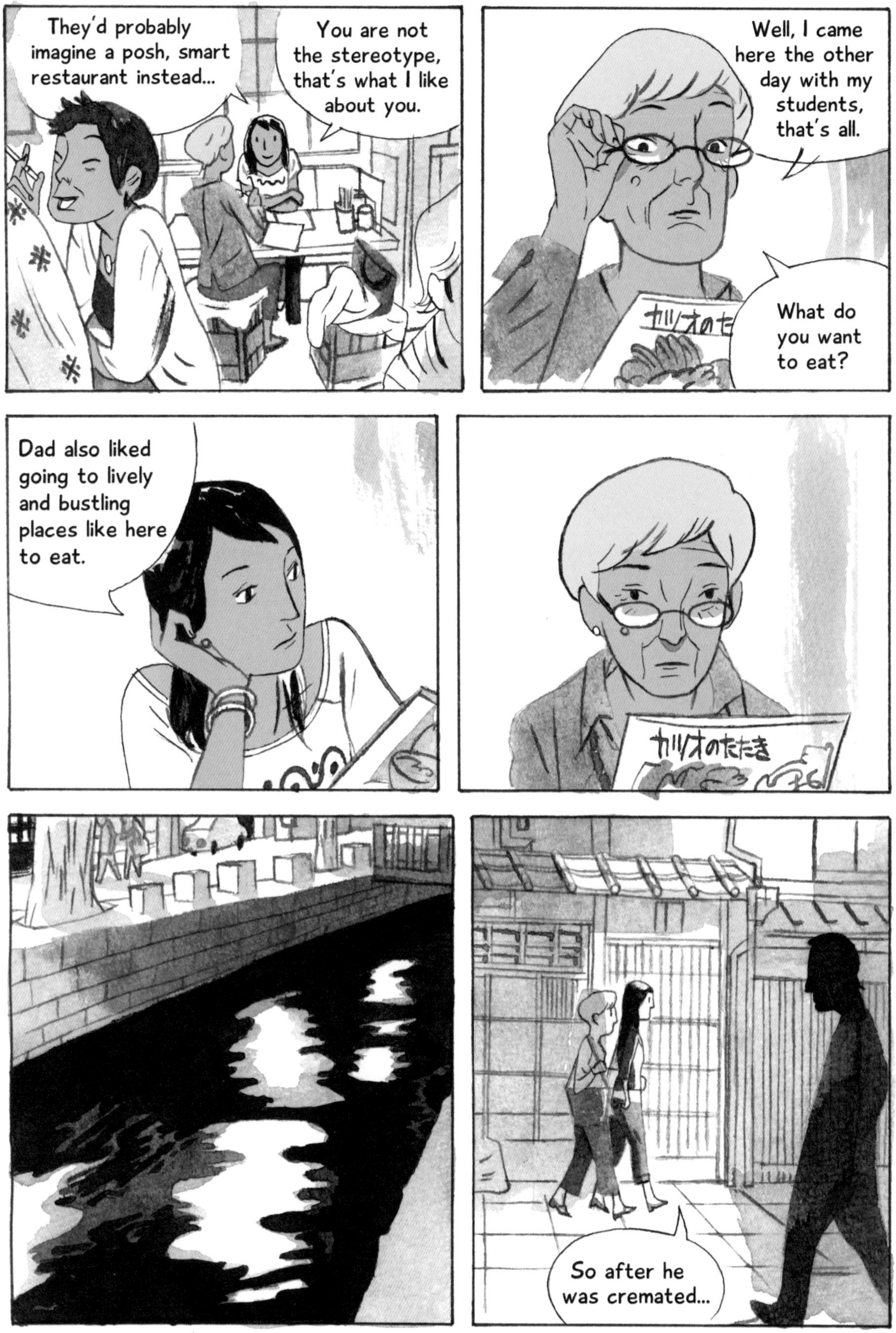
They'd probably imagine a posh, smart restaurant instead...
You are not the stereotype, that's what I like about you.
Well, I came here the other day with my students, that's all.
What do you want to eat?
Dad also liked going to lively and bustling places like here to eat.
カツオのたたき
So after he was cremated...

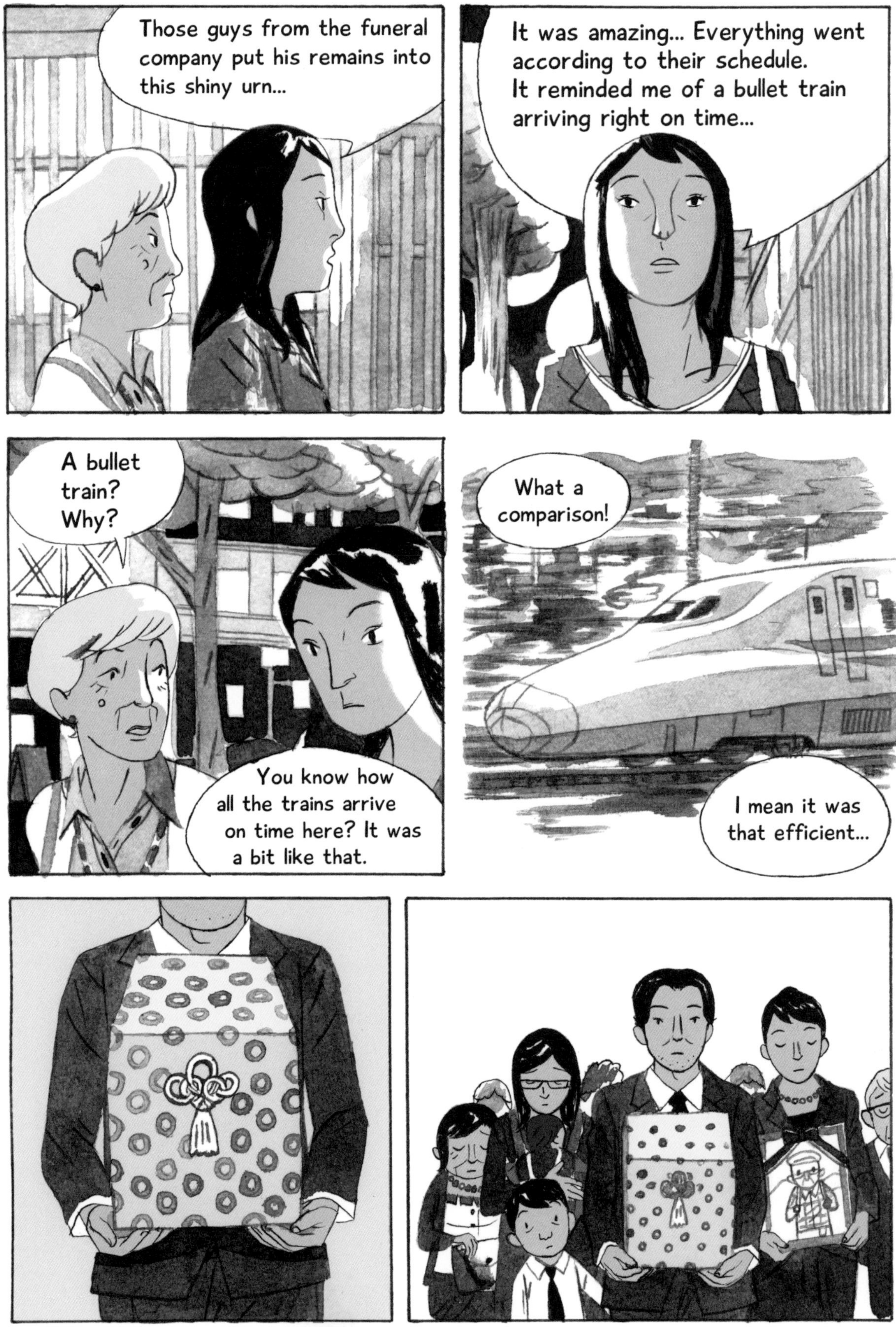
Those guys from the funeral company put his remains into this shiny urn...
It was amazing... Everything went according to their schedule.
It reminded me of a bullet train arriving right on time...
A bullet train? Why?
You know how all the trains arrive on time here? It was a bit like that.
What a comparison!
I mean it was that efficient...

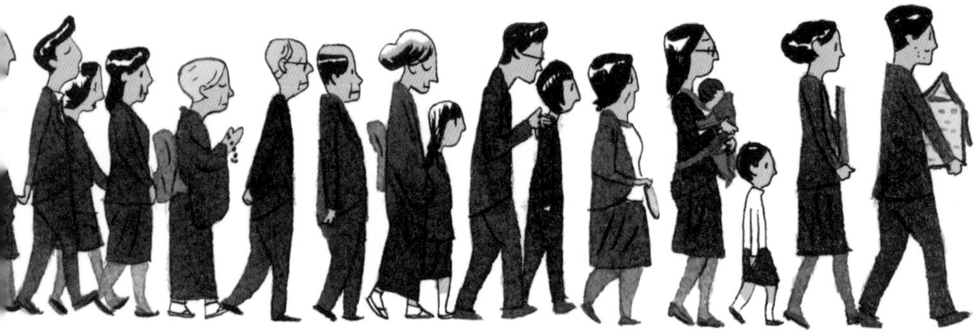

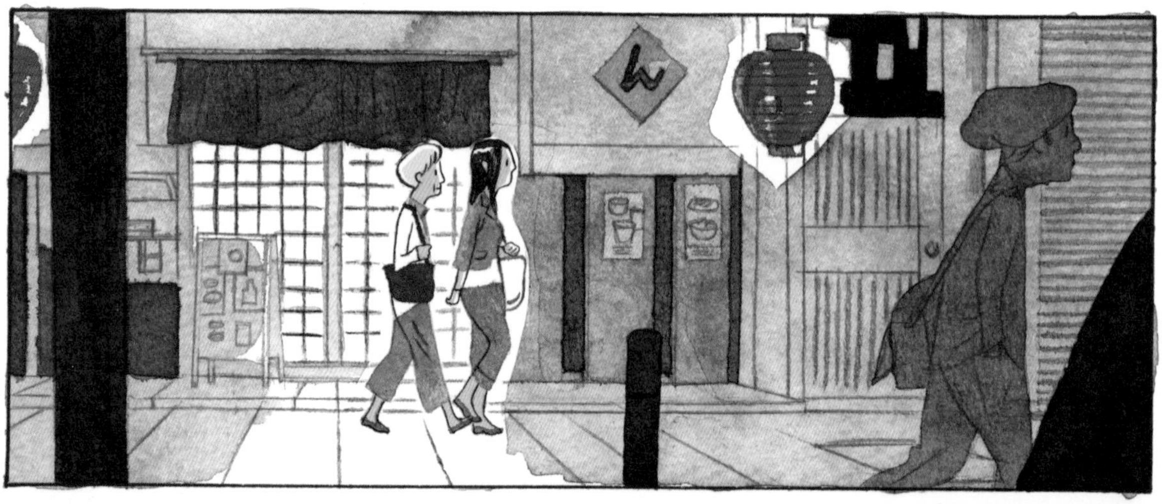

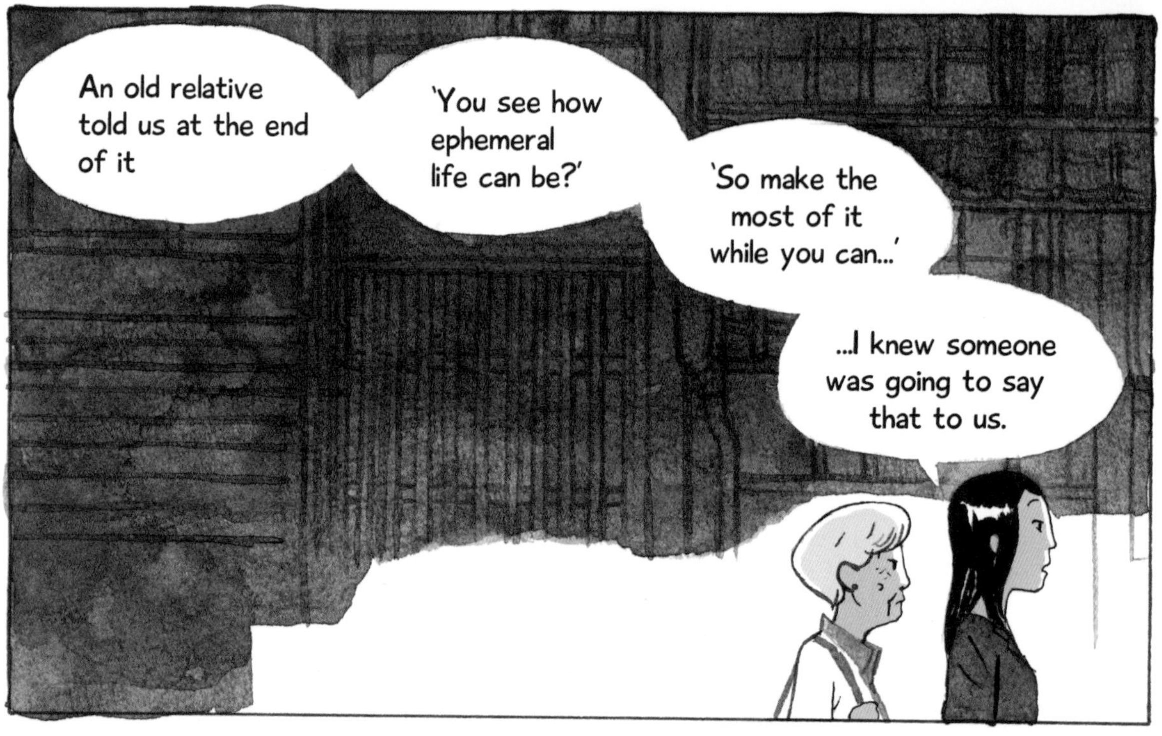
An old relative told us at the end of it
'You see how ephemeral life can be?'
'So make the most of it while you can...'
...I knew someone was going to say that to us.

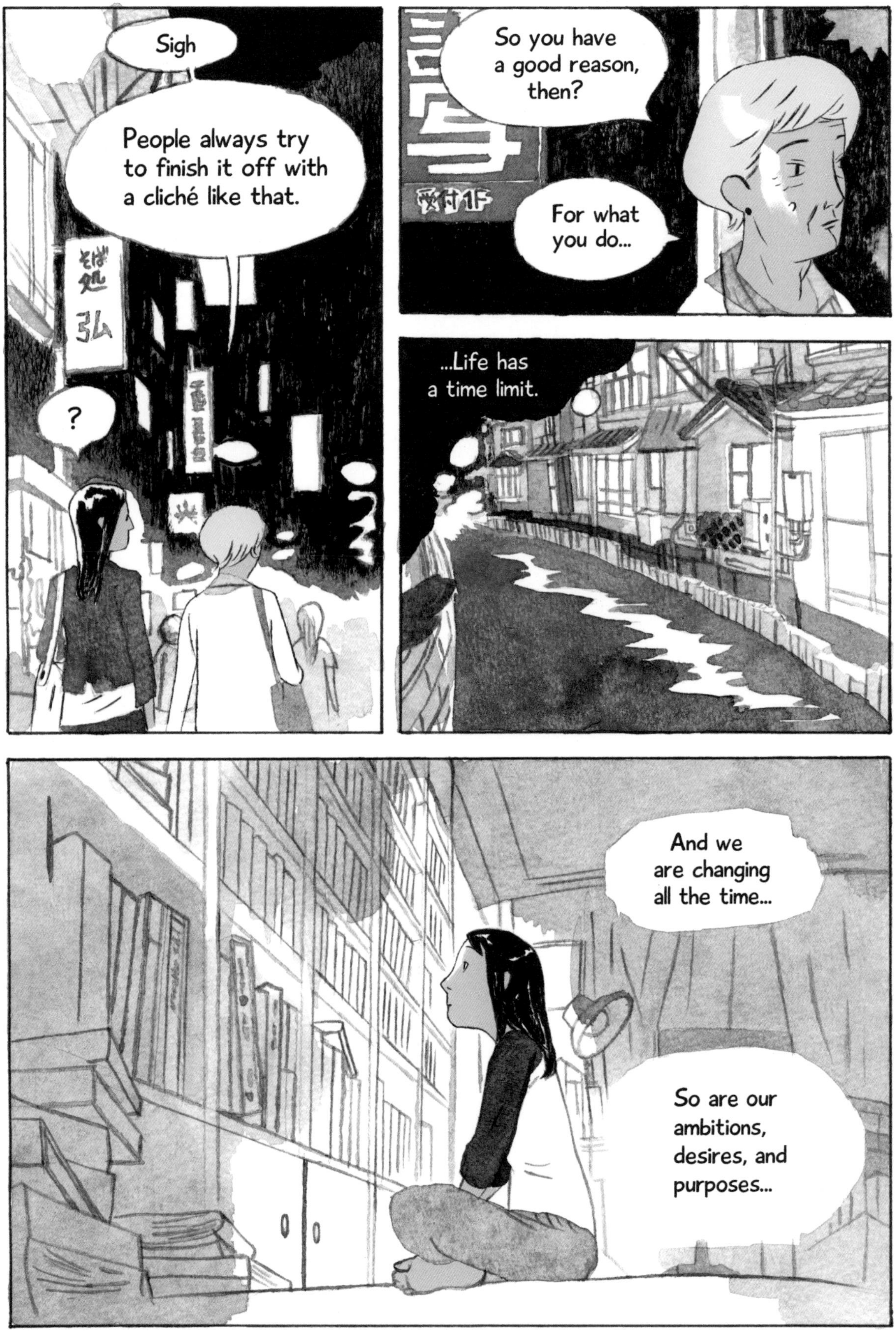
Sigh
People always try to finish it off with a cliché like that.
?
So you have a good reason, then?
For what you do...
...Life has a time limit.
And we are changing all the time...
So are our ambitions, desires, and purposes...

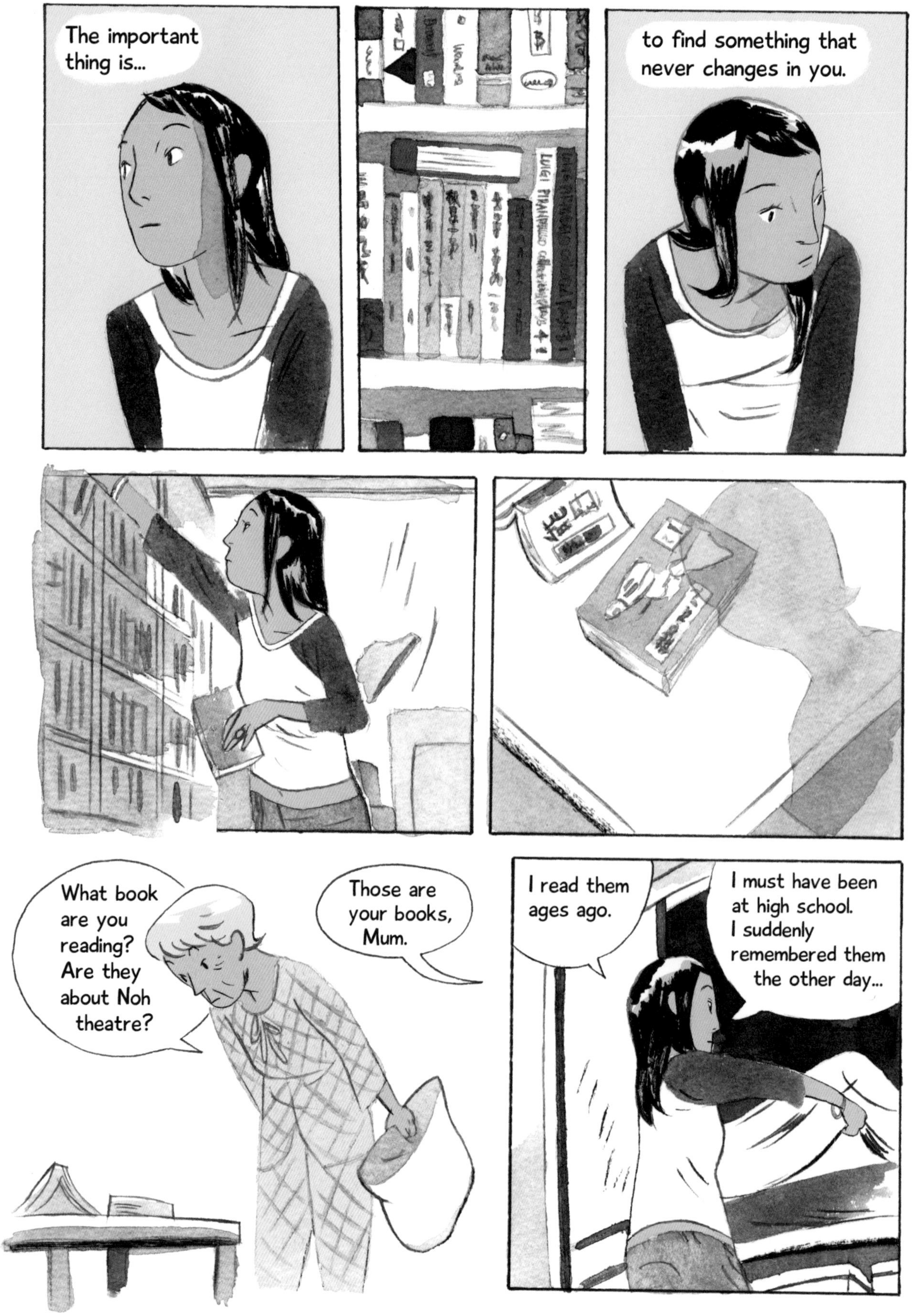
The important thing is...
to find something that never changes in you.
What book are you reading? Are they about Noh theatre?
Those are your books, Mum.
I read them ages ago.
I must have been at high school. I suddenly remembered them the other day...

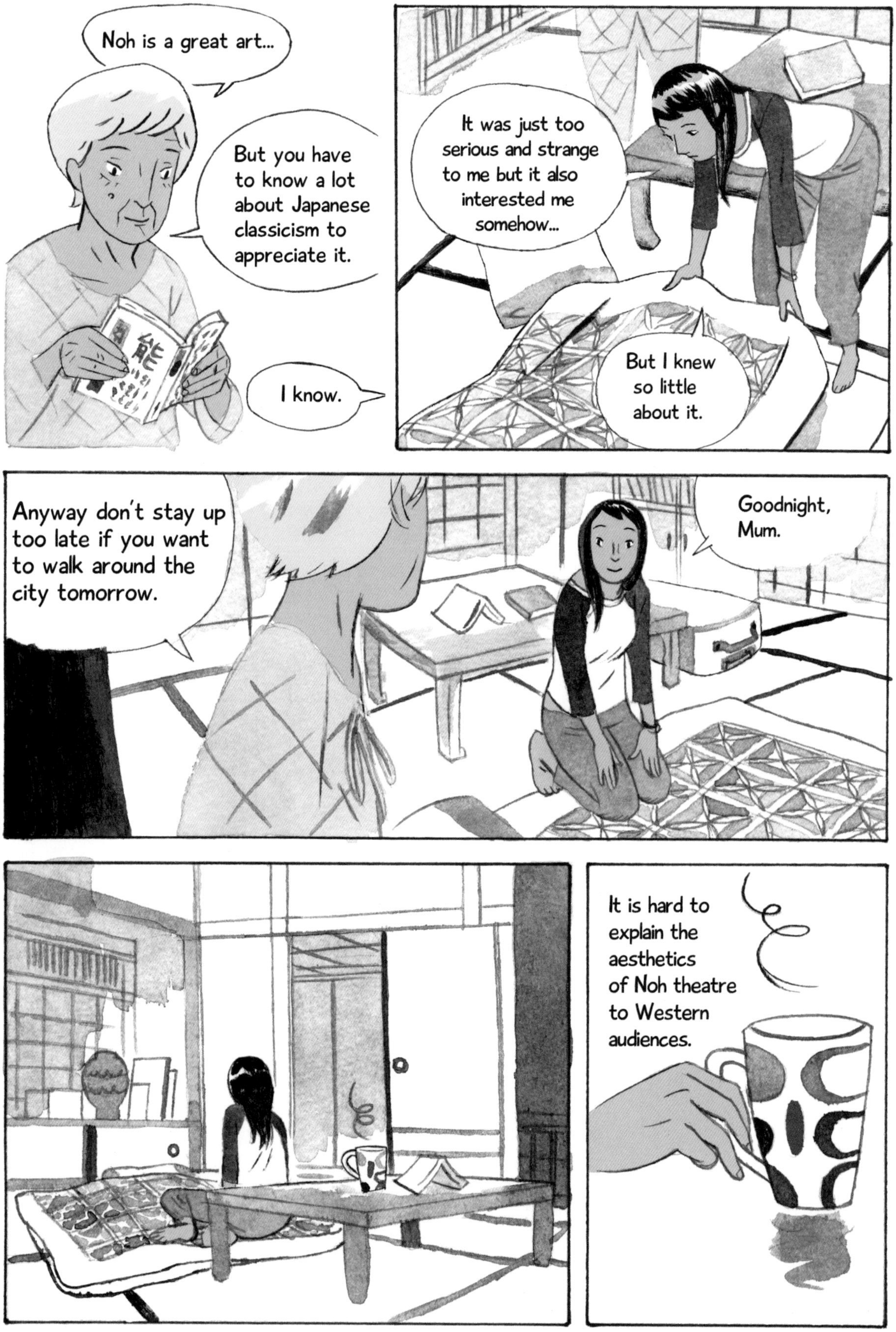
Noh is a great art...
But you have to know a lot about Japanese classicism to appreciate it.
I know.
It was just too serious and strange to me but it also interested me somehow...
But I knew so little about it.
Anyway don't stay up too late if you want to walk around the city tomorrow.
Goodnight, Mum.
It is hard to explain the aesthetics of Noh theatre to Western audiences.

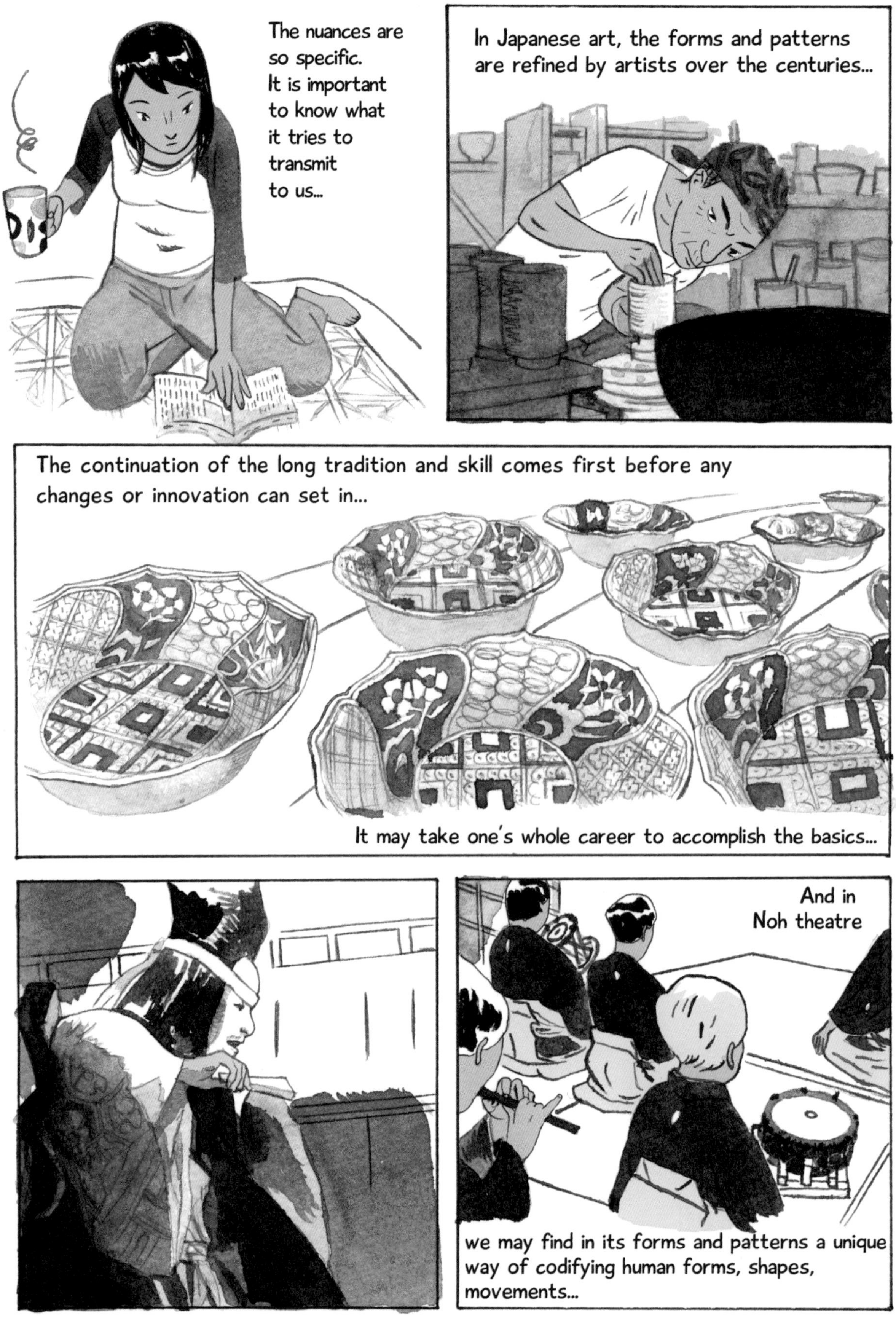
The nuances are
so specific.
It is important
to know what
it tries to
transmit
to us...
In Japanese art, the forms and patterns
are refined by artists over the centuries...
The continuation of the long tradition and skill comes first before any
changes or innovation can set in...
It may take one's whole career to accomplish the basics...
And in
Noh theatre
we may find in its forms and patterns a unique
way of codifying human forms, shapes,
movements...

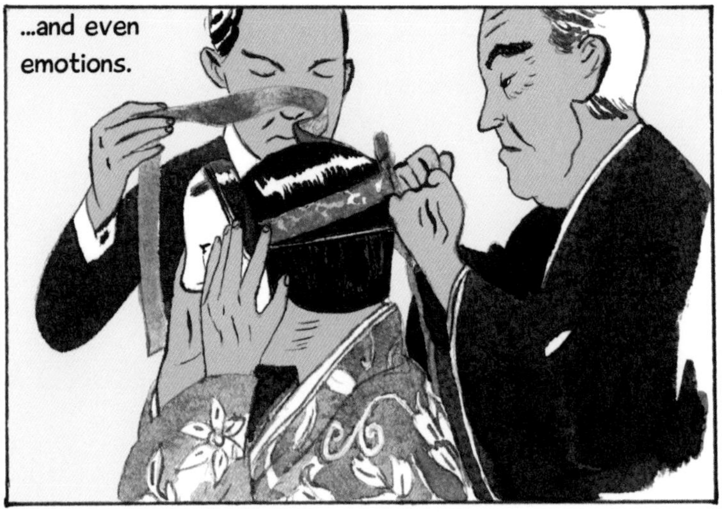
...and even
emotions.

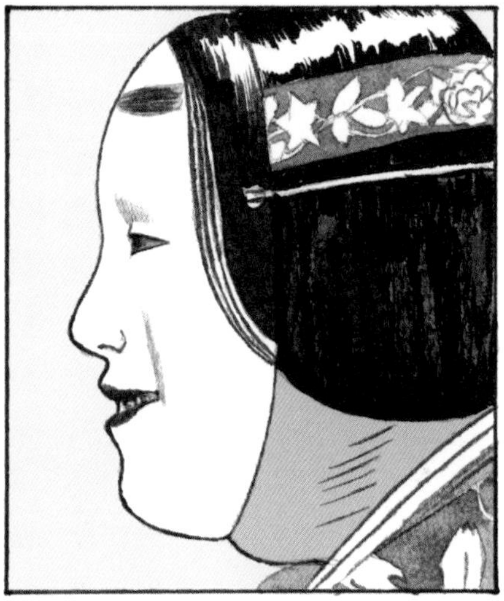

This is a transformation in a ritual sense,
to be totally possessed by the theatre, or to be subject to it.

In order to express its idea of a transcendental world,
one must put the heart and mind in total resonance
with the theatrical role.

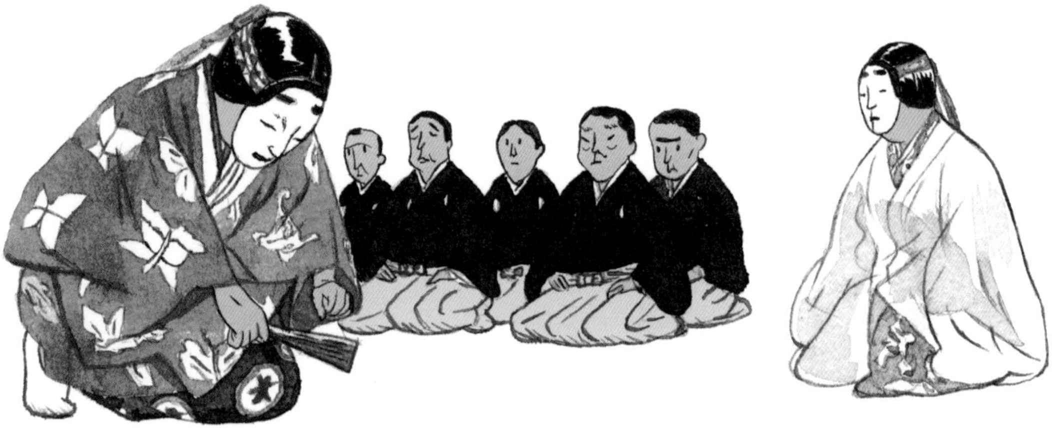

And during the process all the natural traits are simplifed.

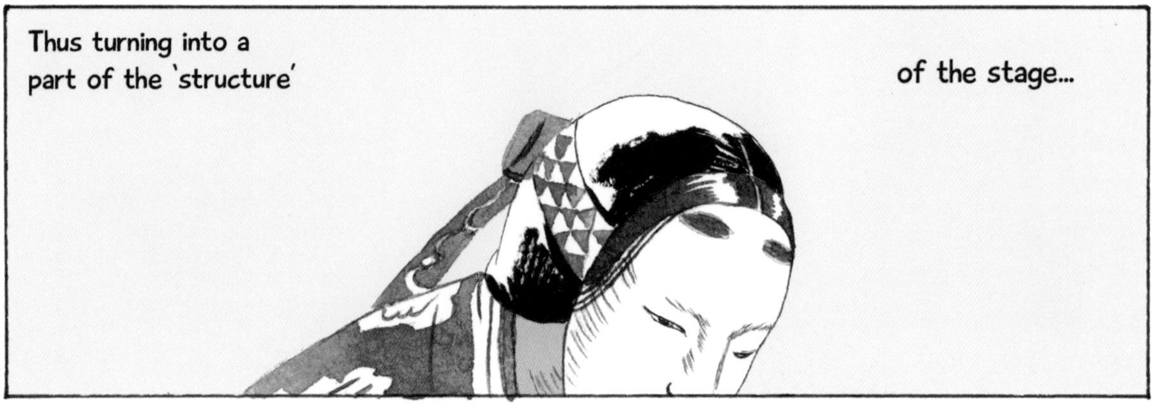
Thus turning into a
part of the 'structure'
of the stage...

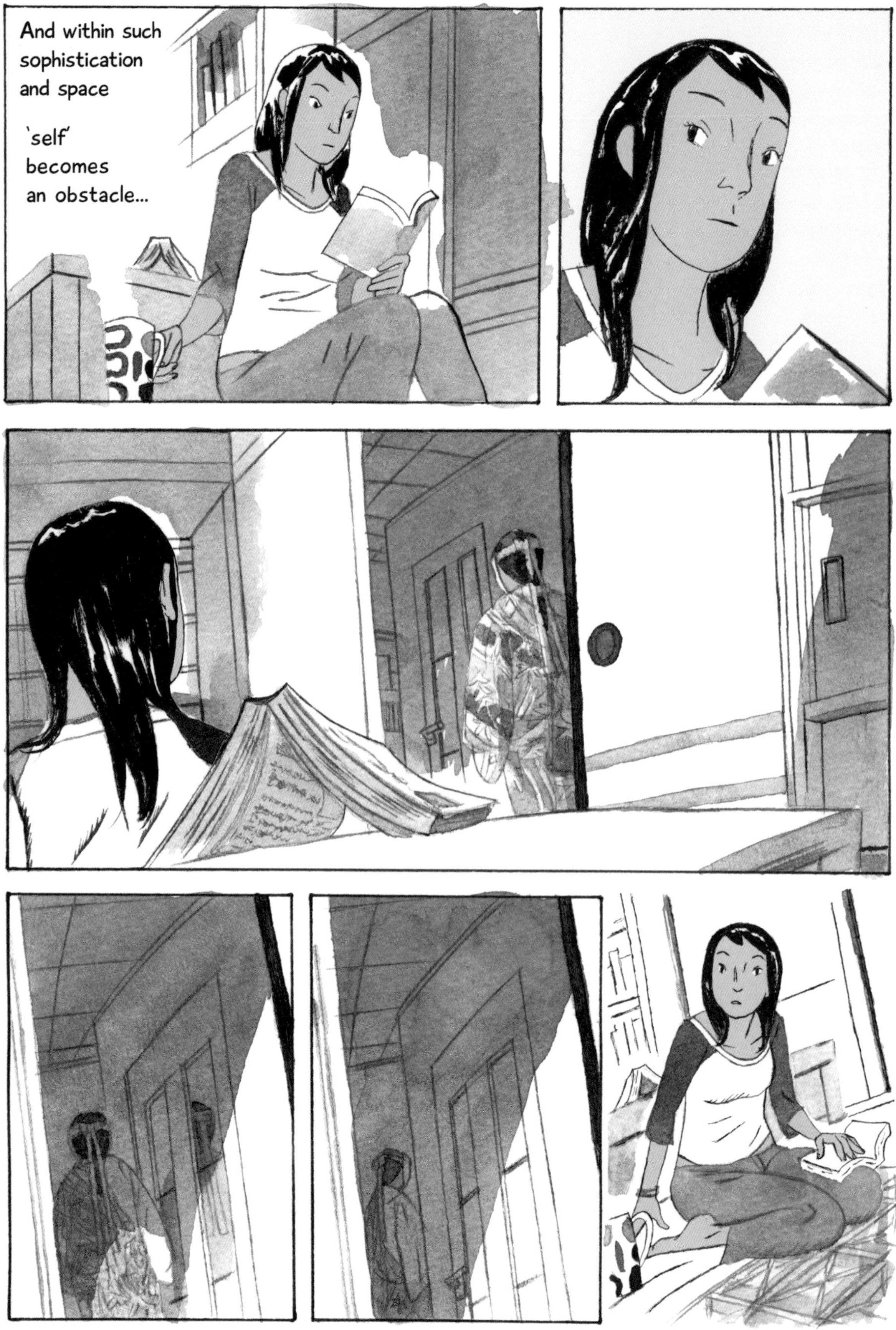
And within such sophistication and space
'self' becomes an obstacle...

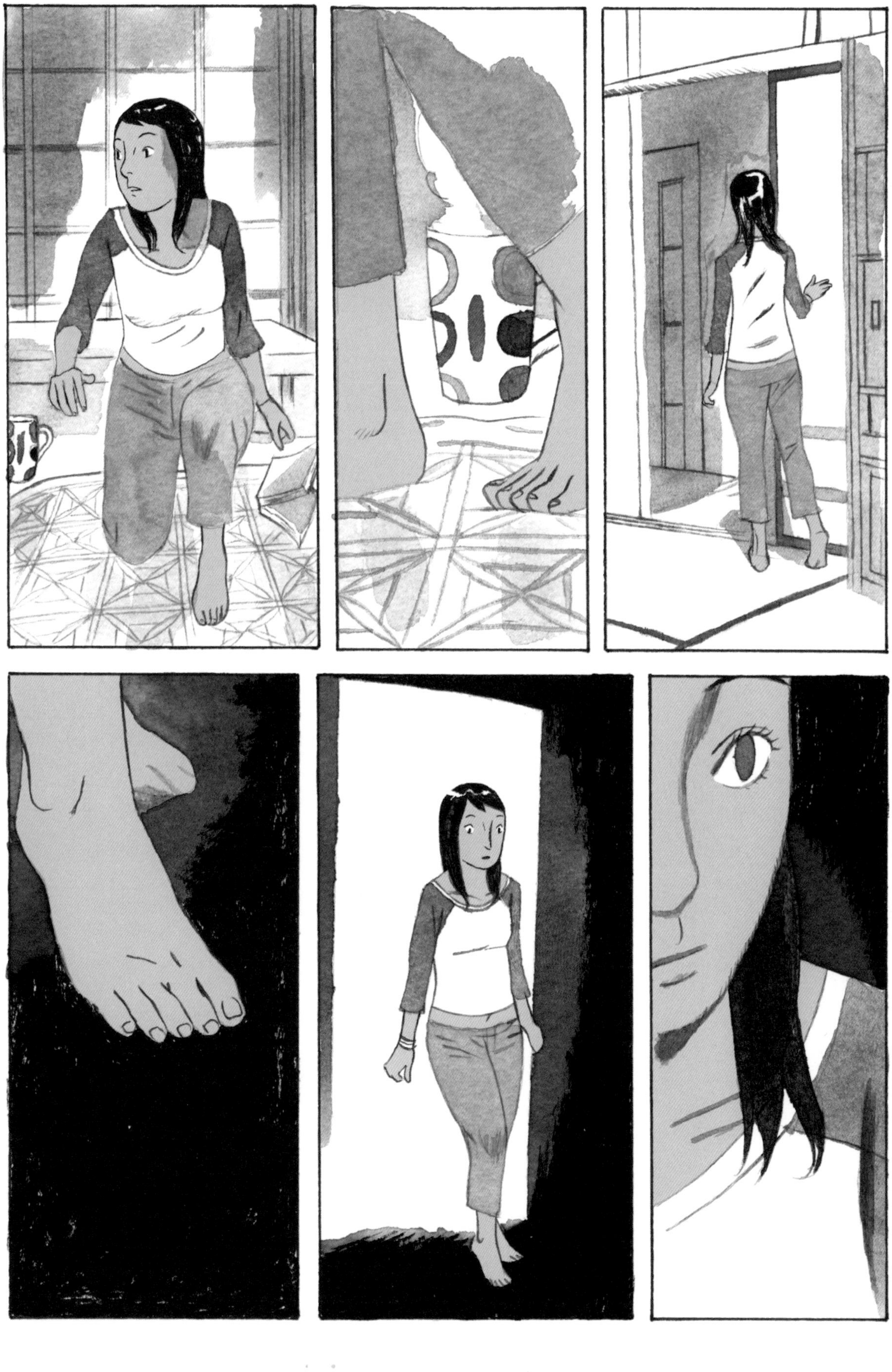

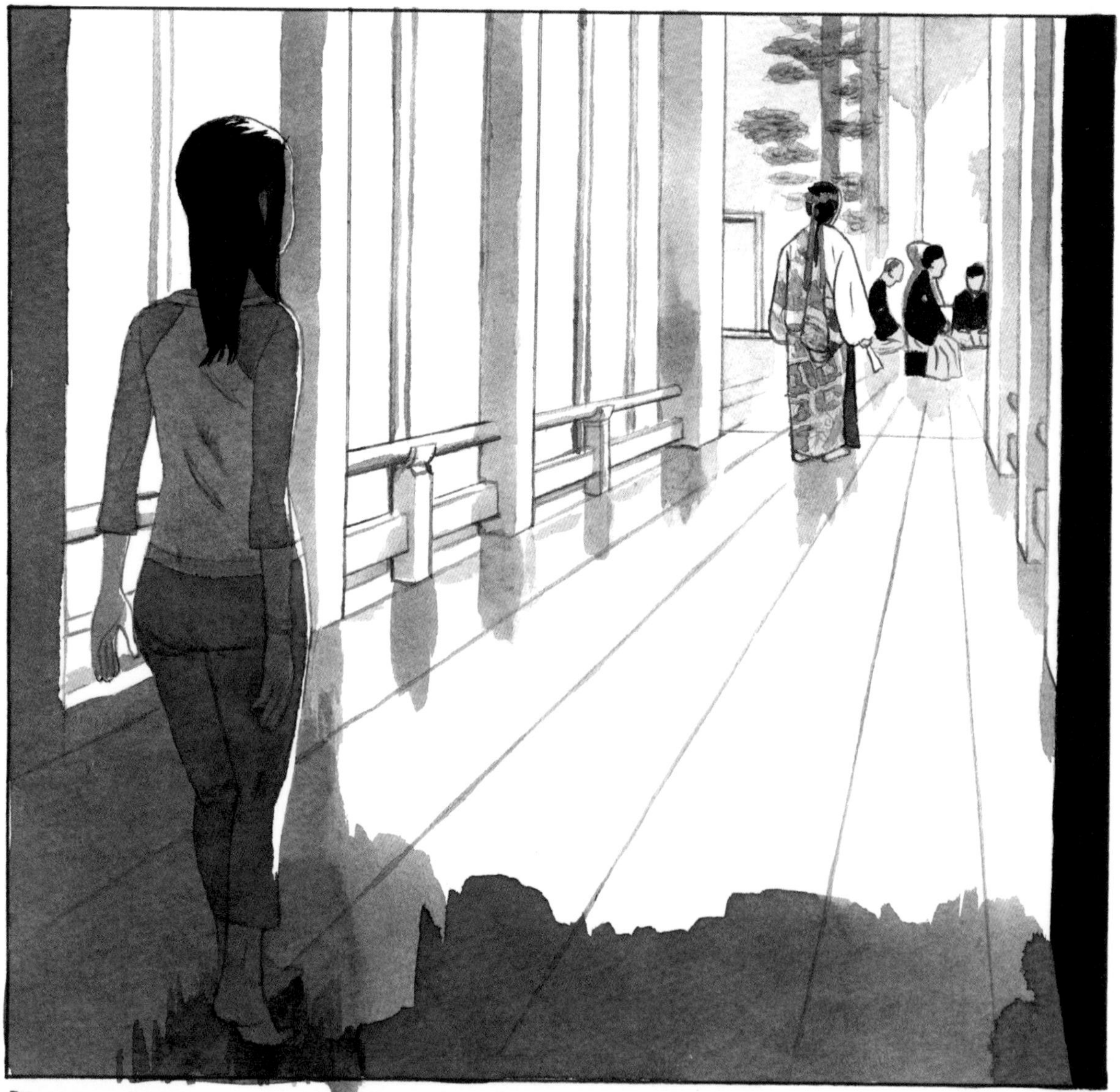

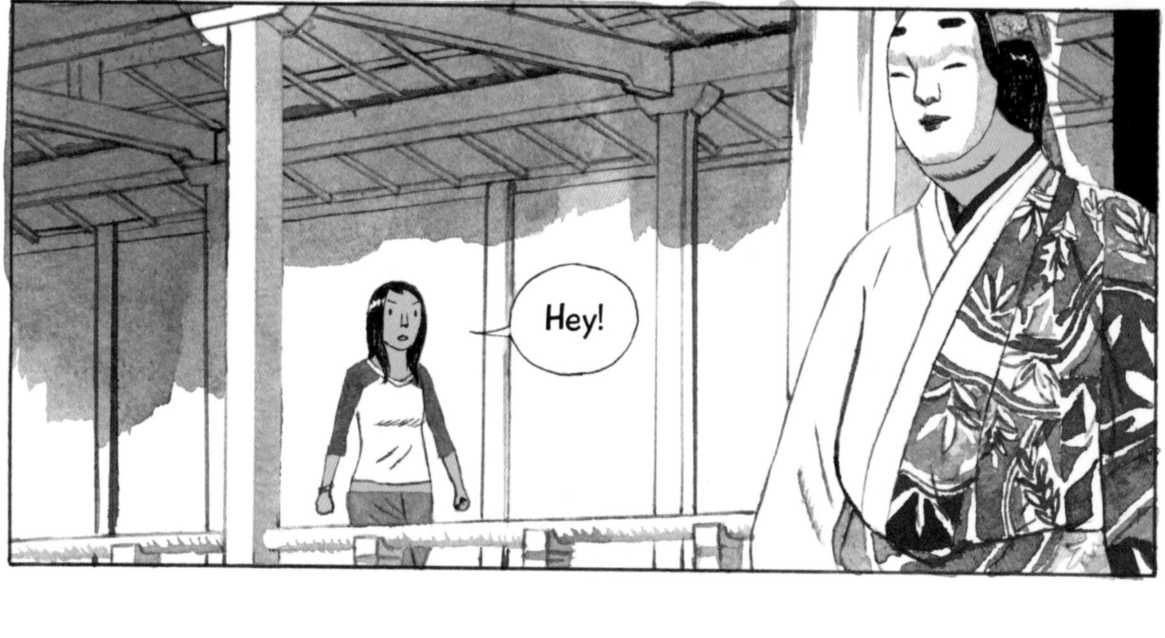
Hey!

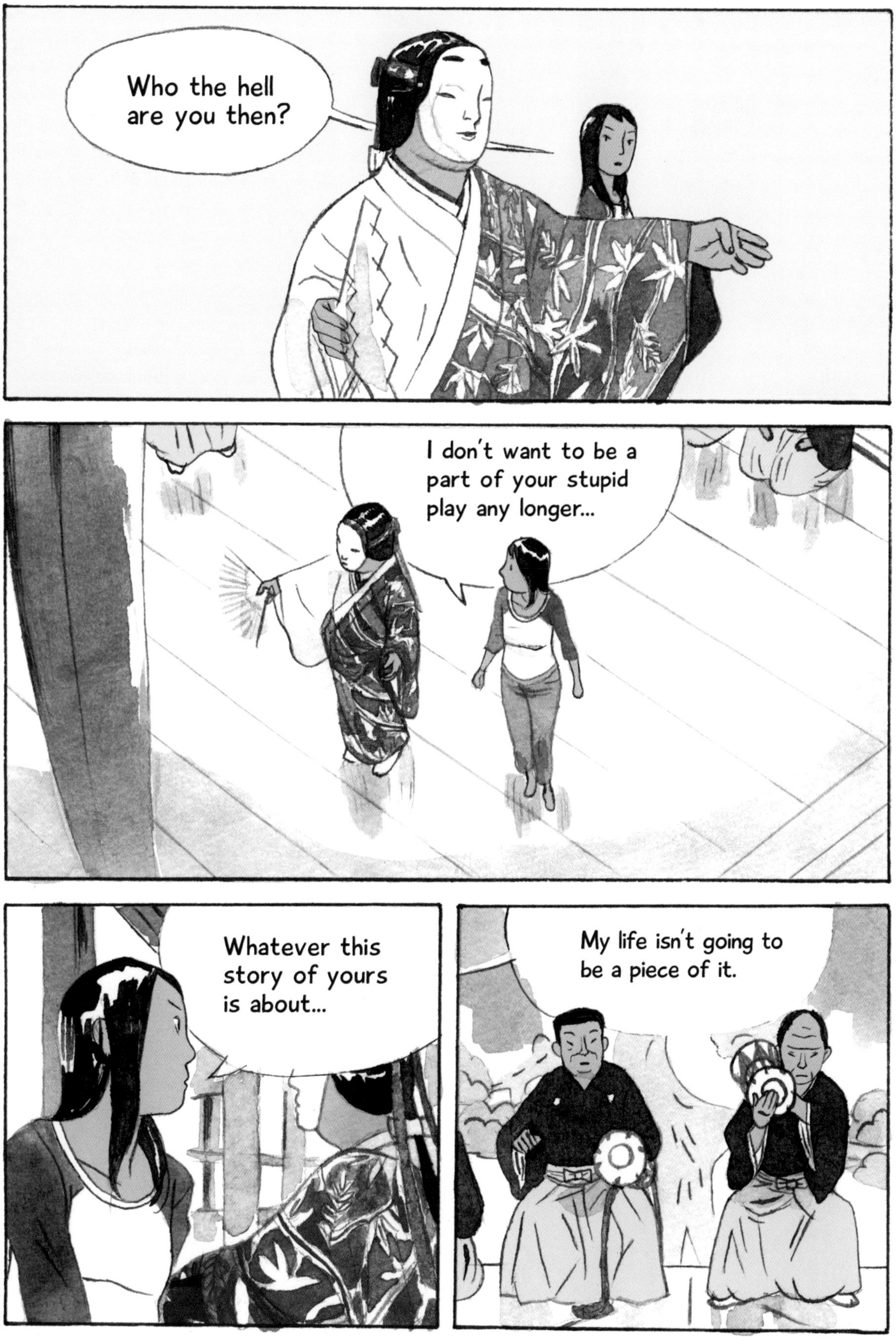
Who the hell are you then?
I don't want to be a part of your stupid play any longer...
Whatever this story of yours is about...
My life isn't going to be a piece of it.

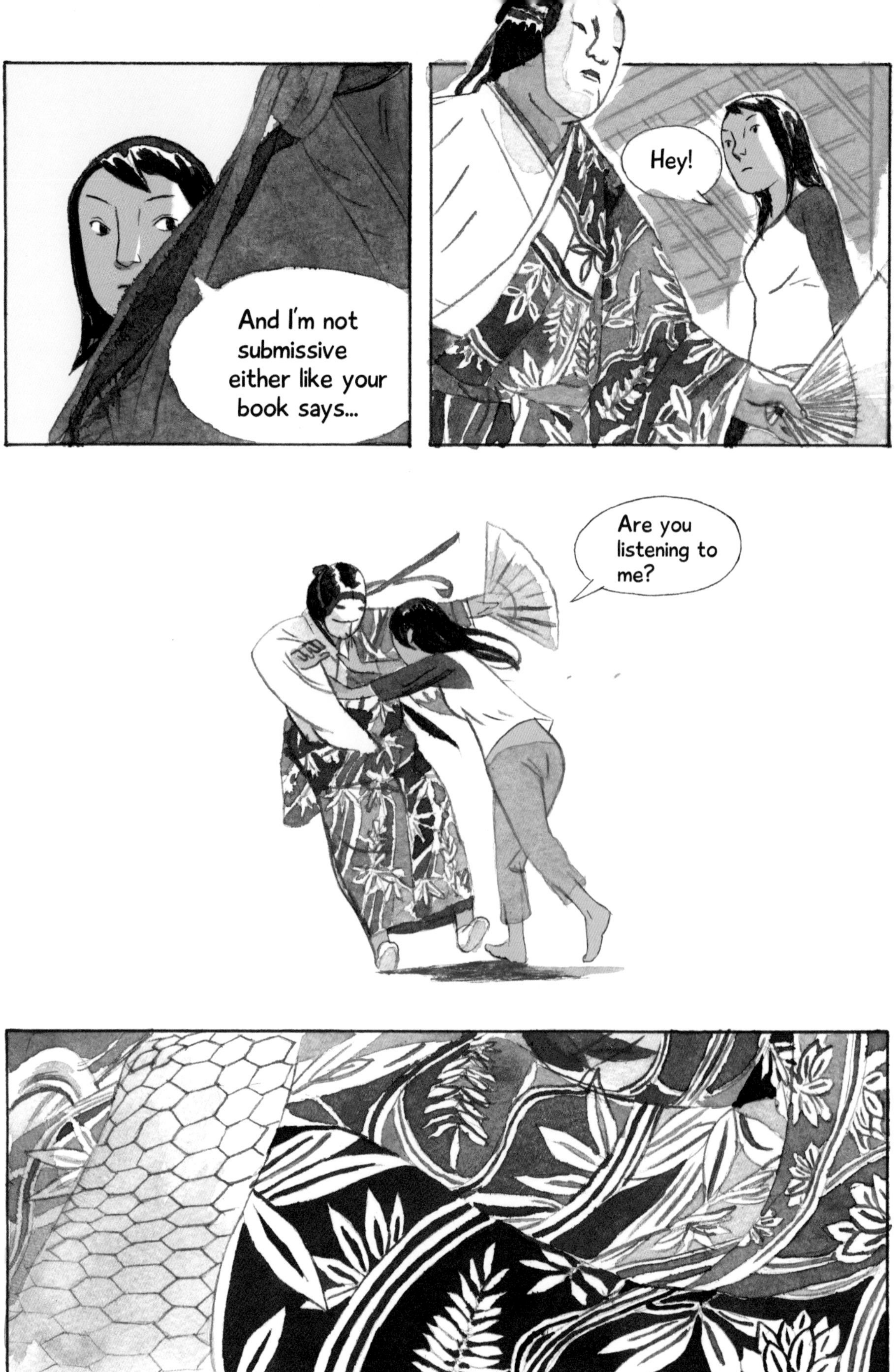
And I'm not submissive either like your book says...
Hey!
Are you listening to me?

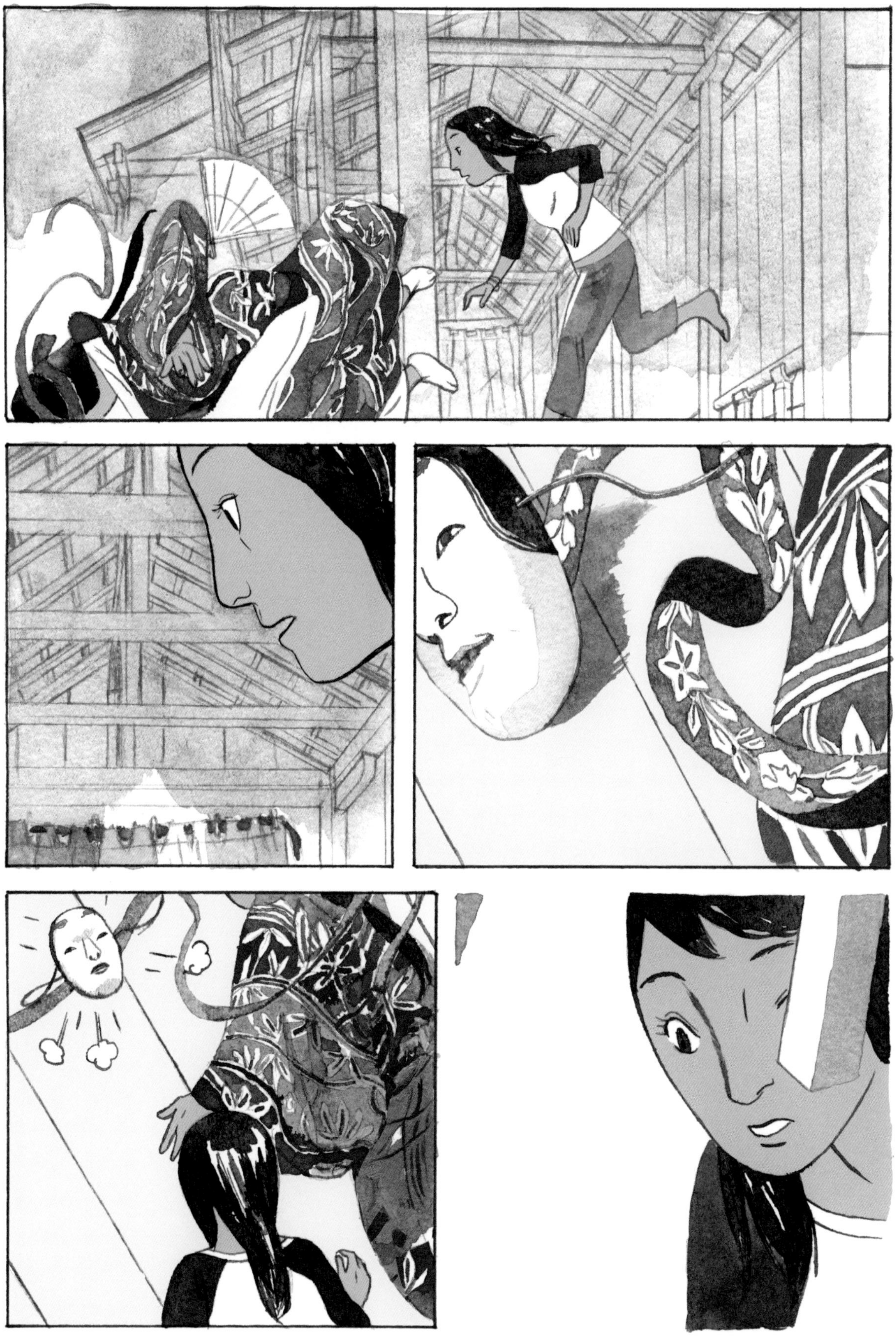

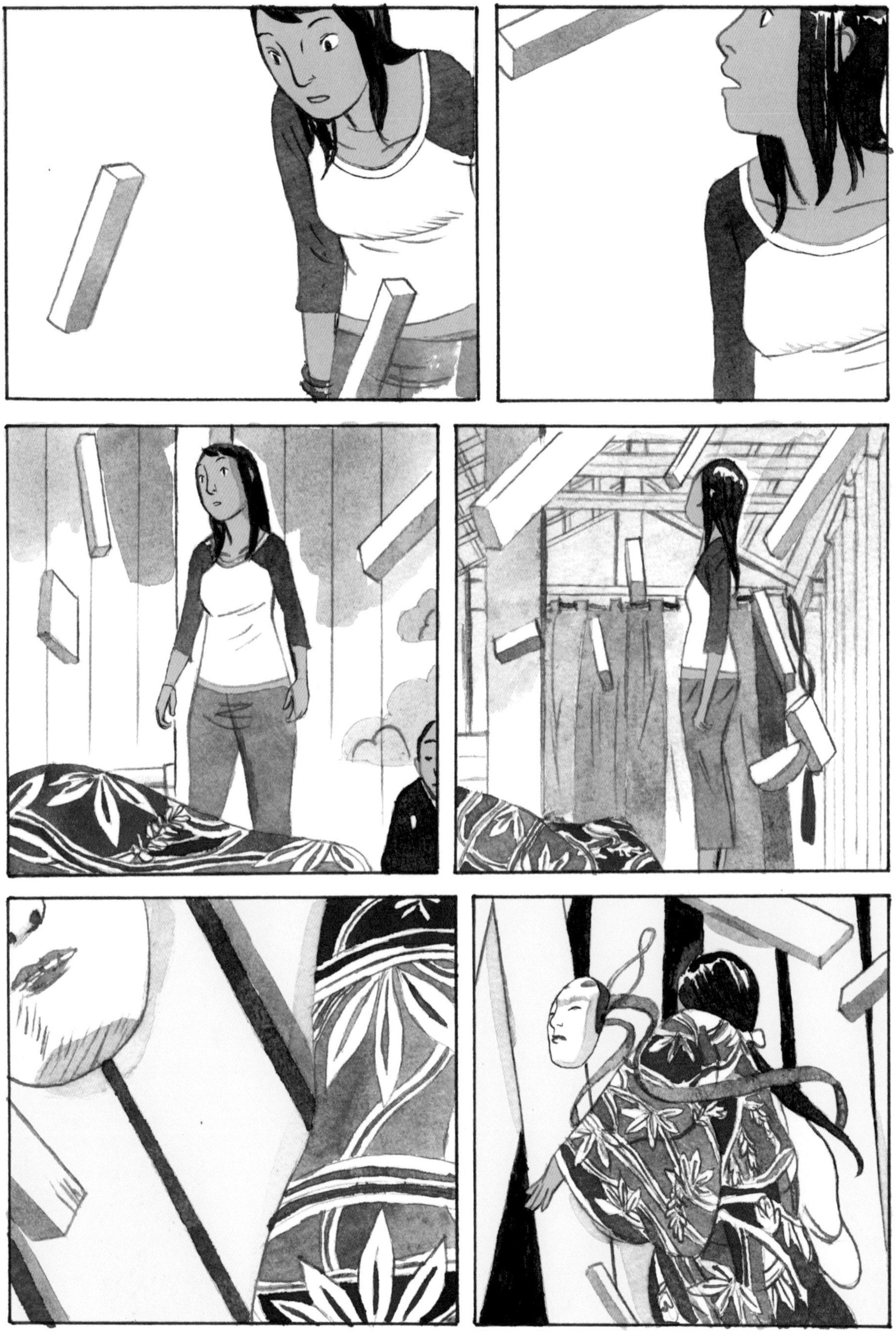

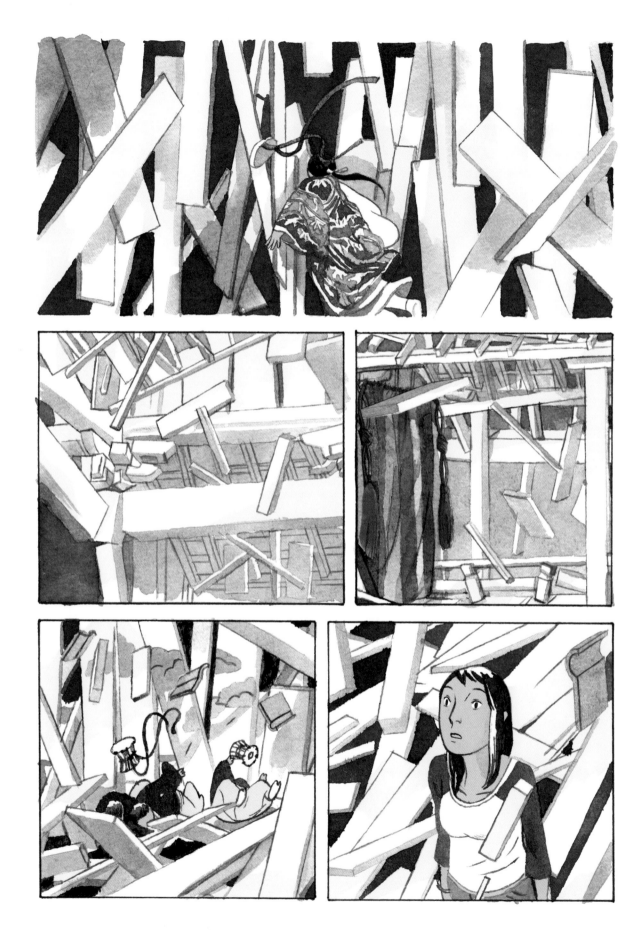

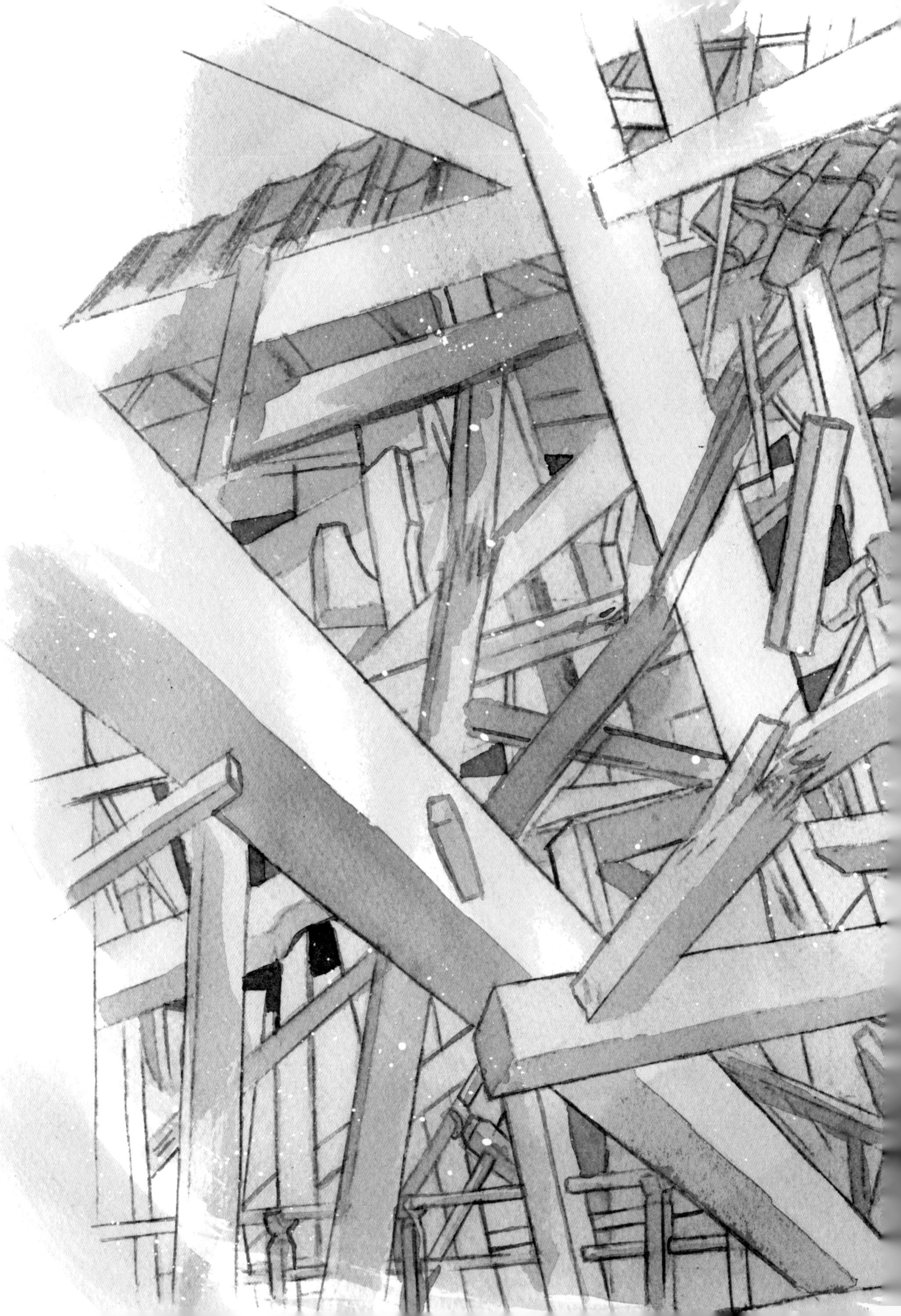

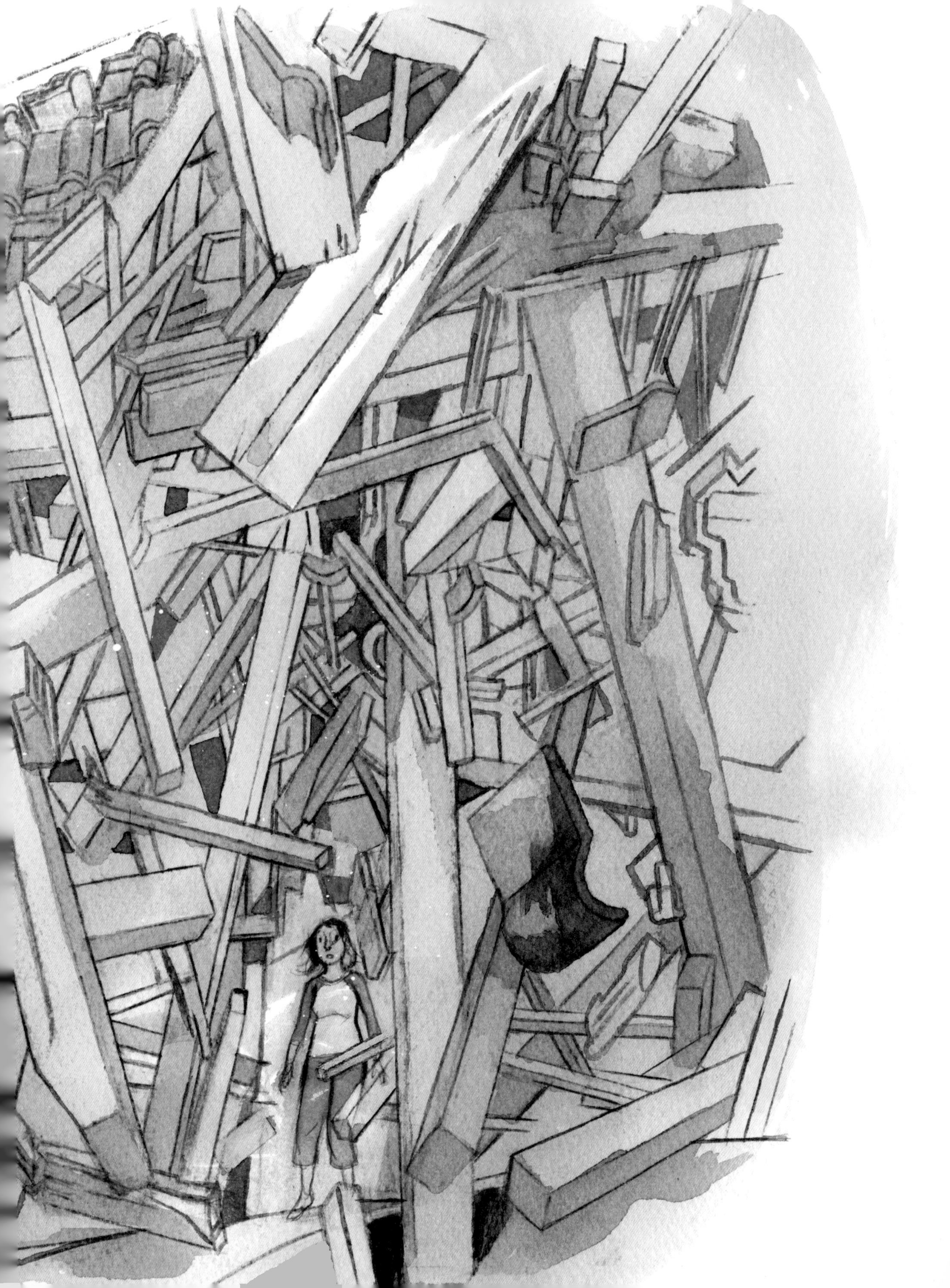

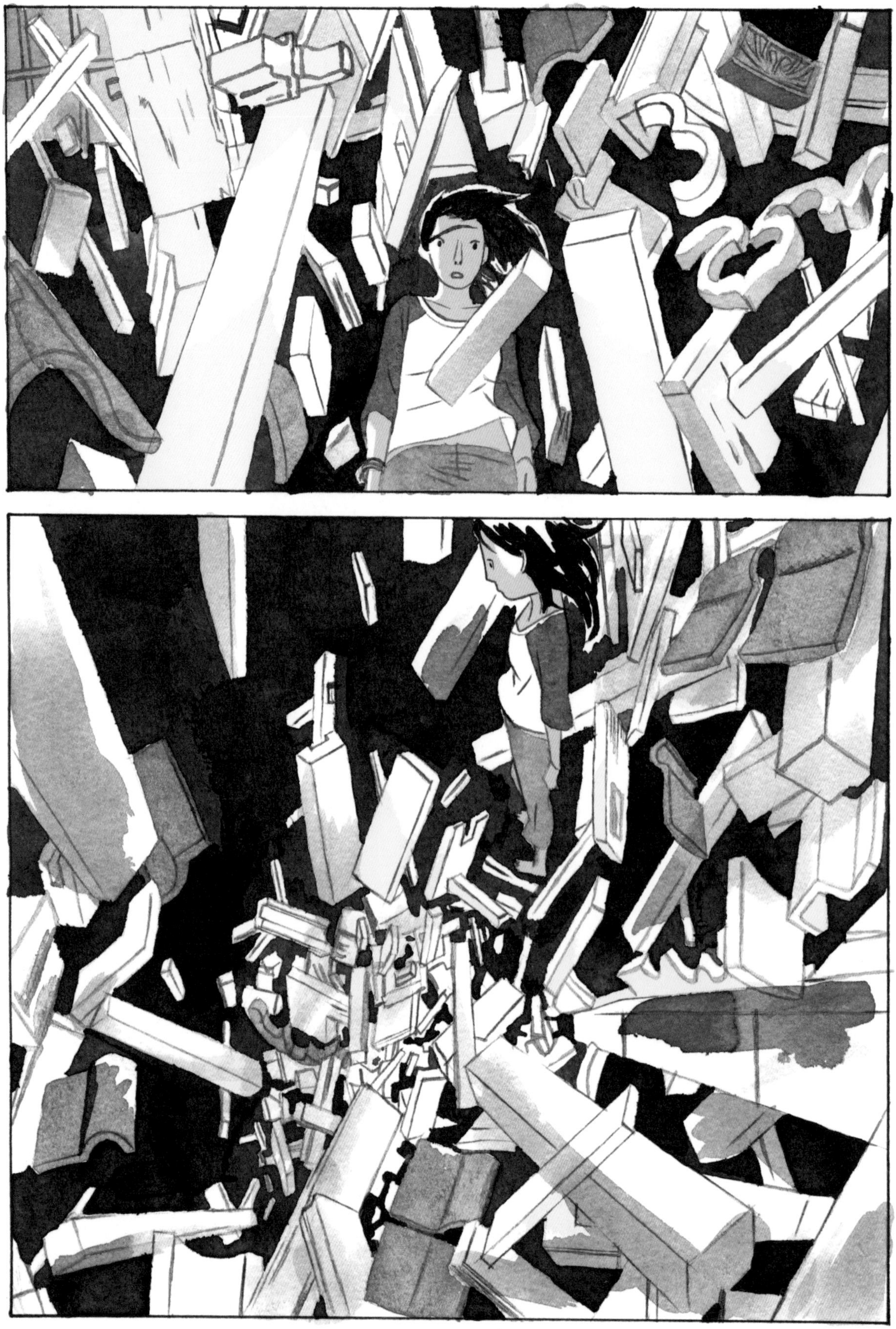

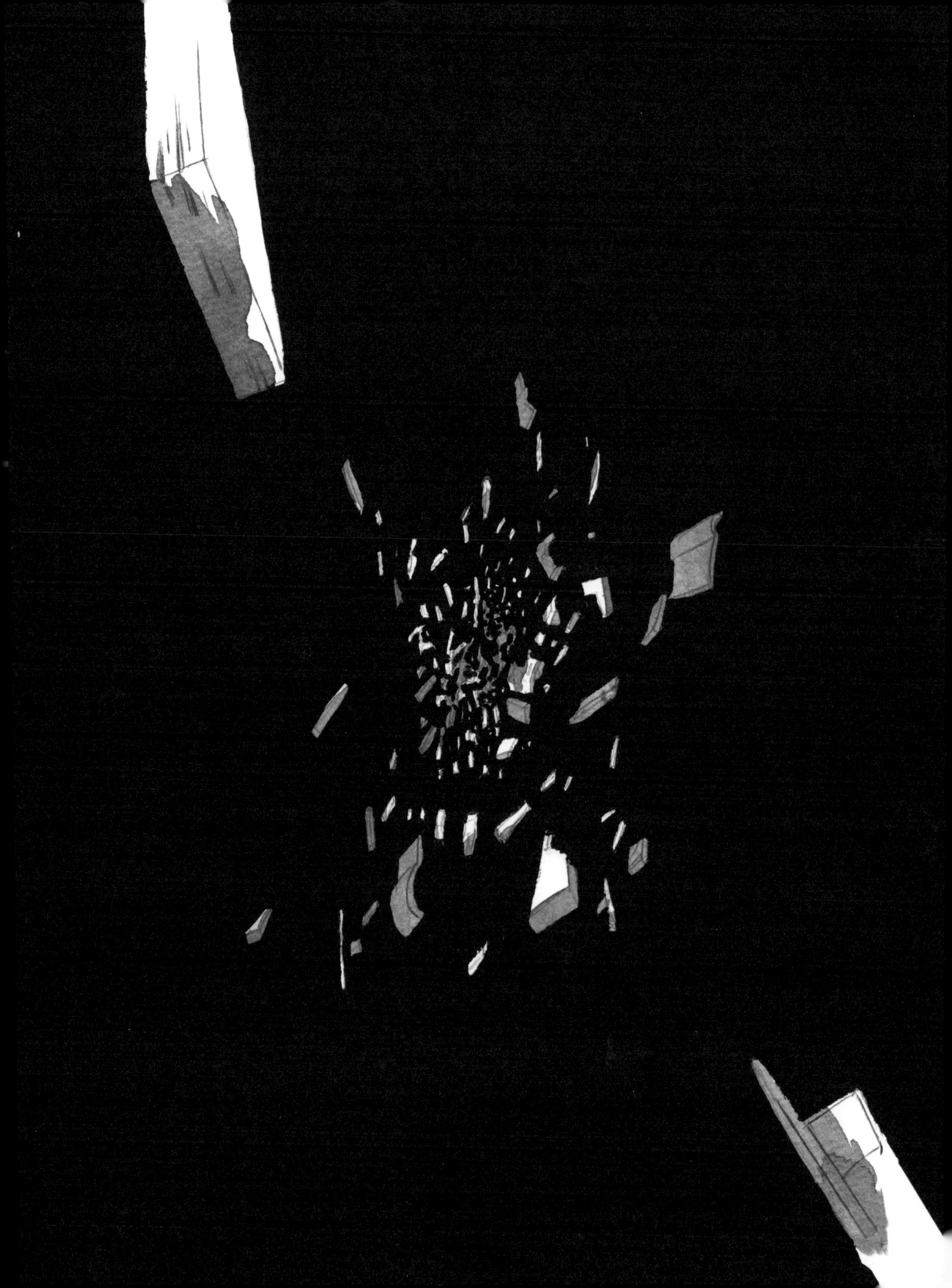

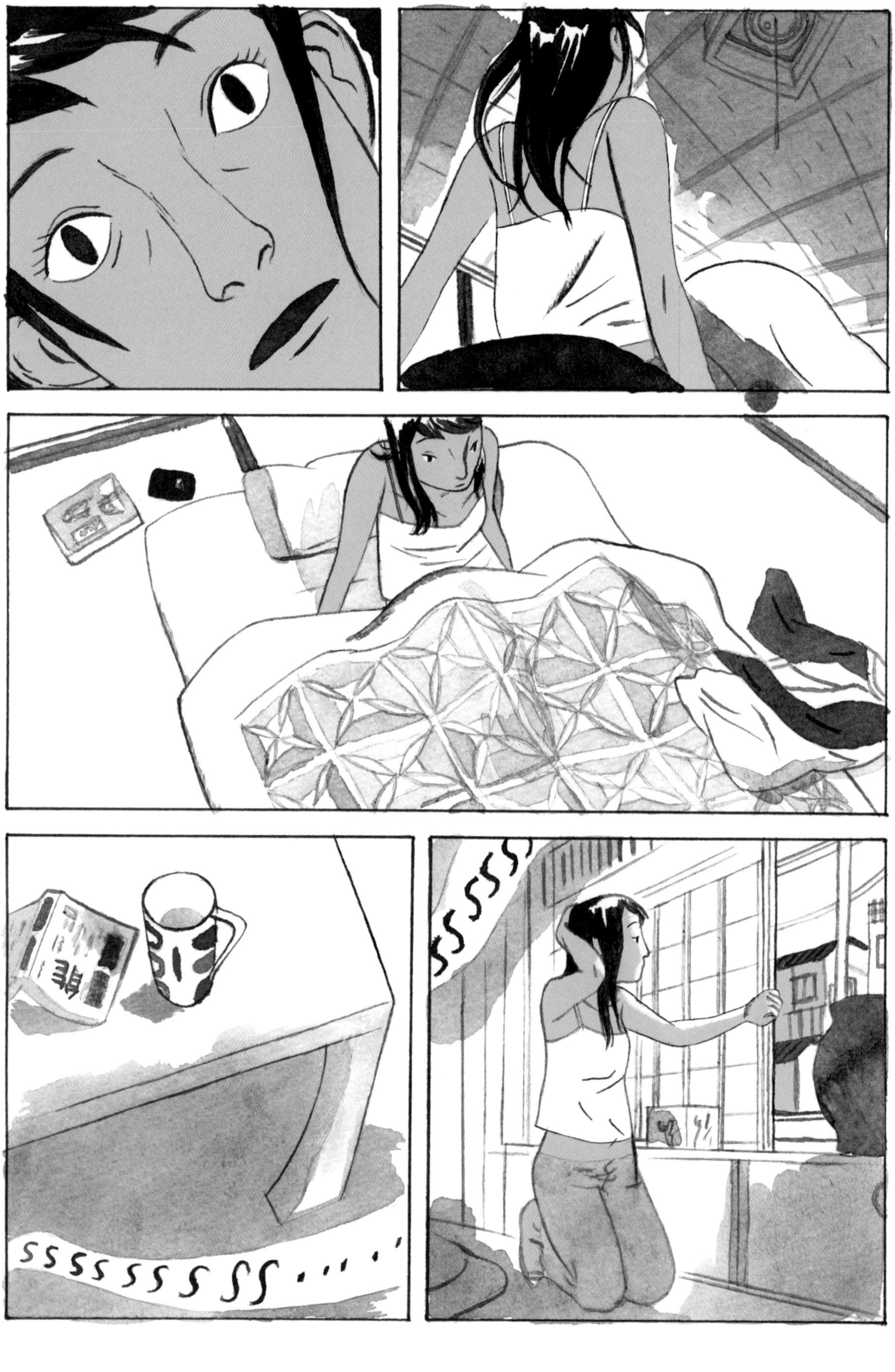
SSSSSSSSS.....

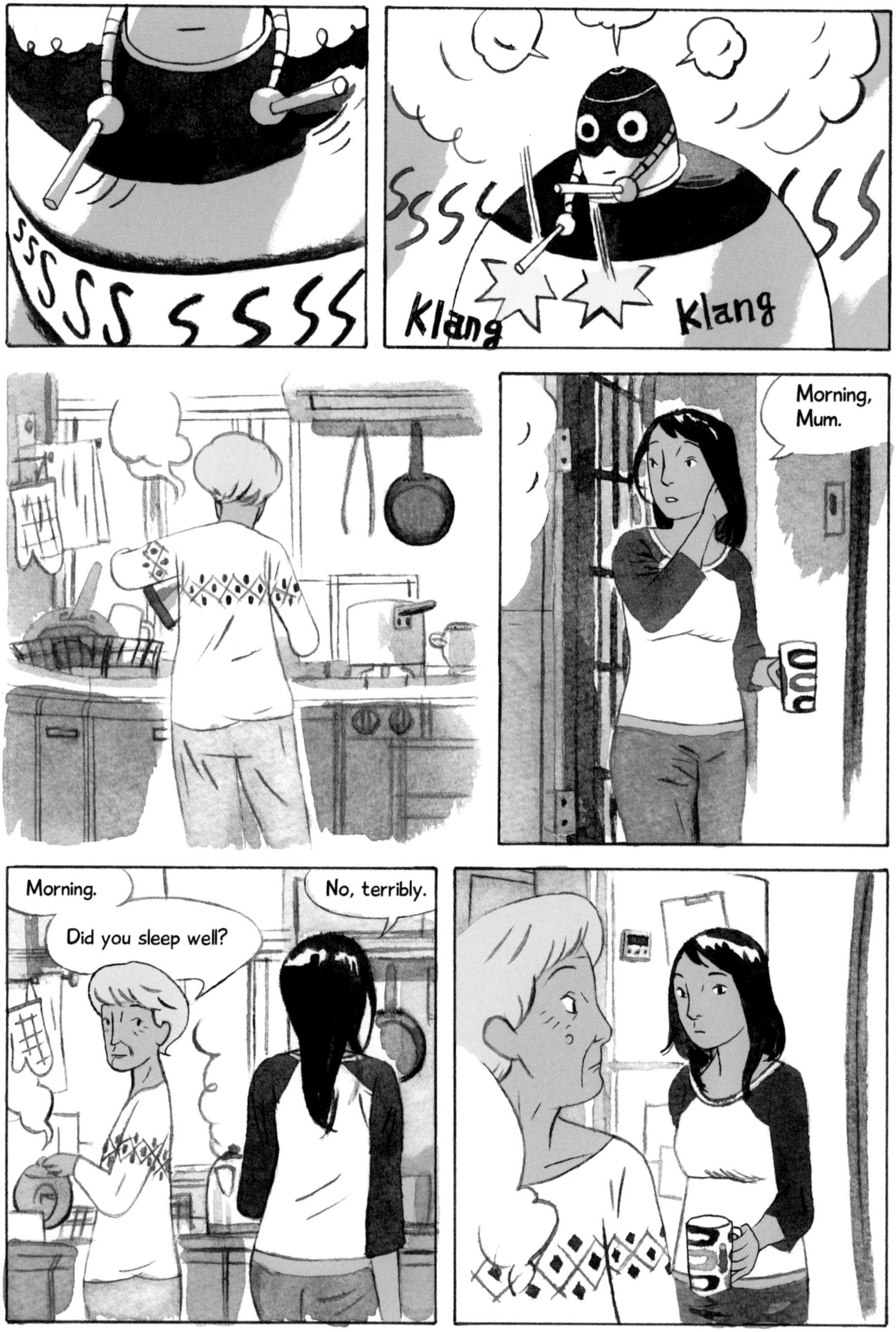
SSSSSSSSS
SSSS
SSS
Klang
Klang
Morning, Mum.
Morning.
Did you sleep well?
No, terribly.

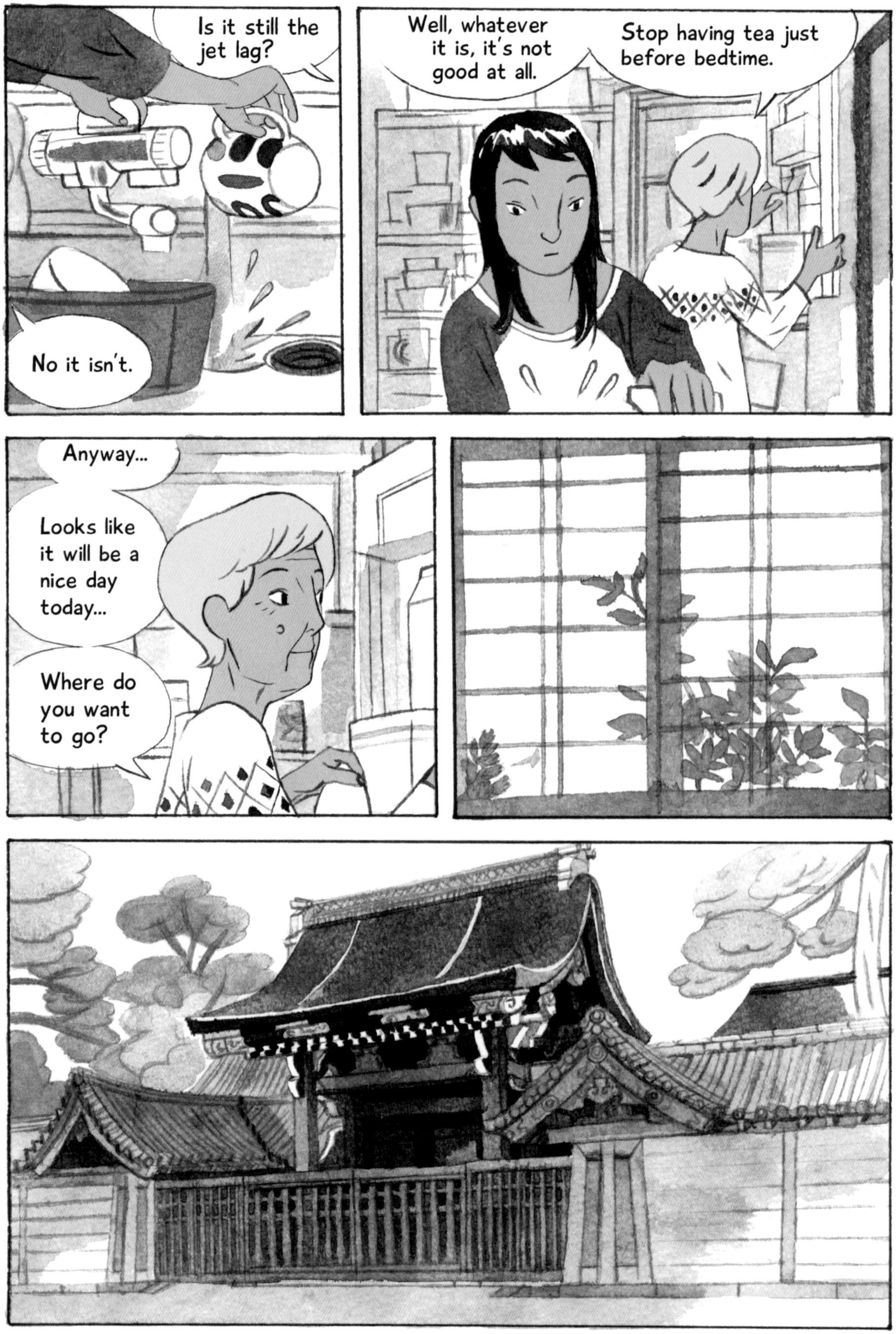
Is it still the jet lag?
No it isn't.
Well, whatever it is, it's not good at all.
Stop having tea just before bedtime.
Anyway...
Looks like it will be a nice day today...
Where do you want to go?

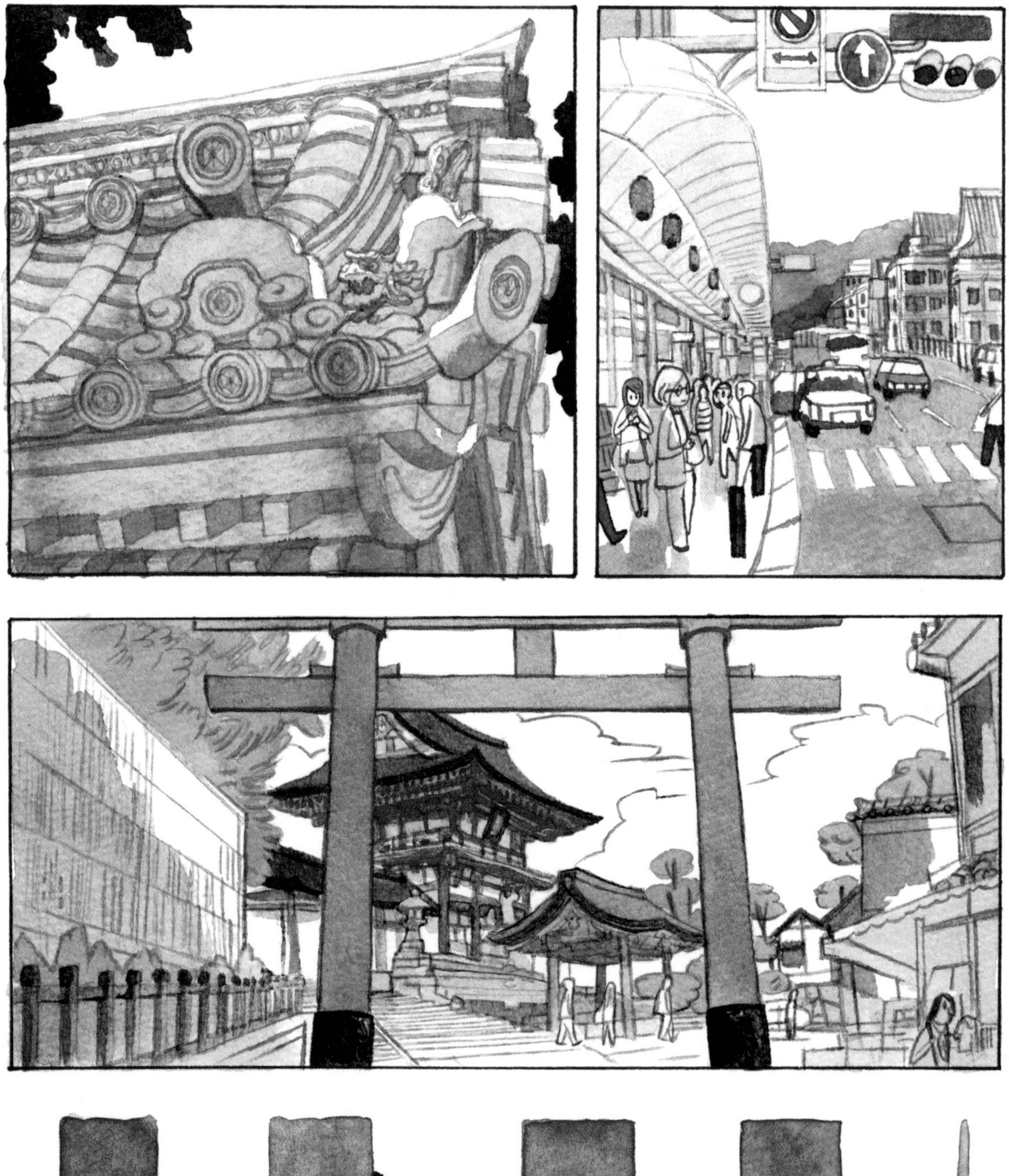

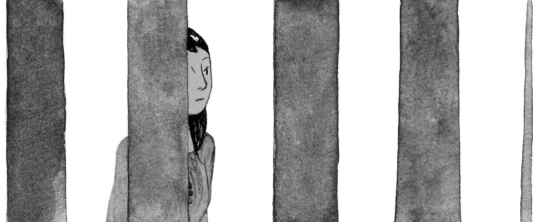

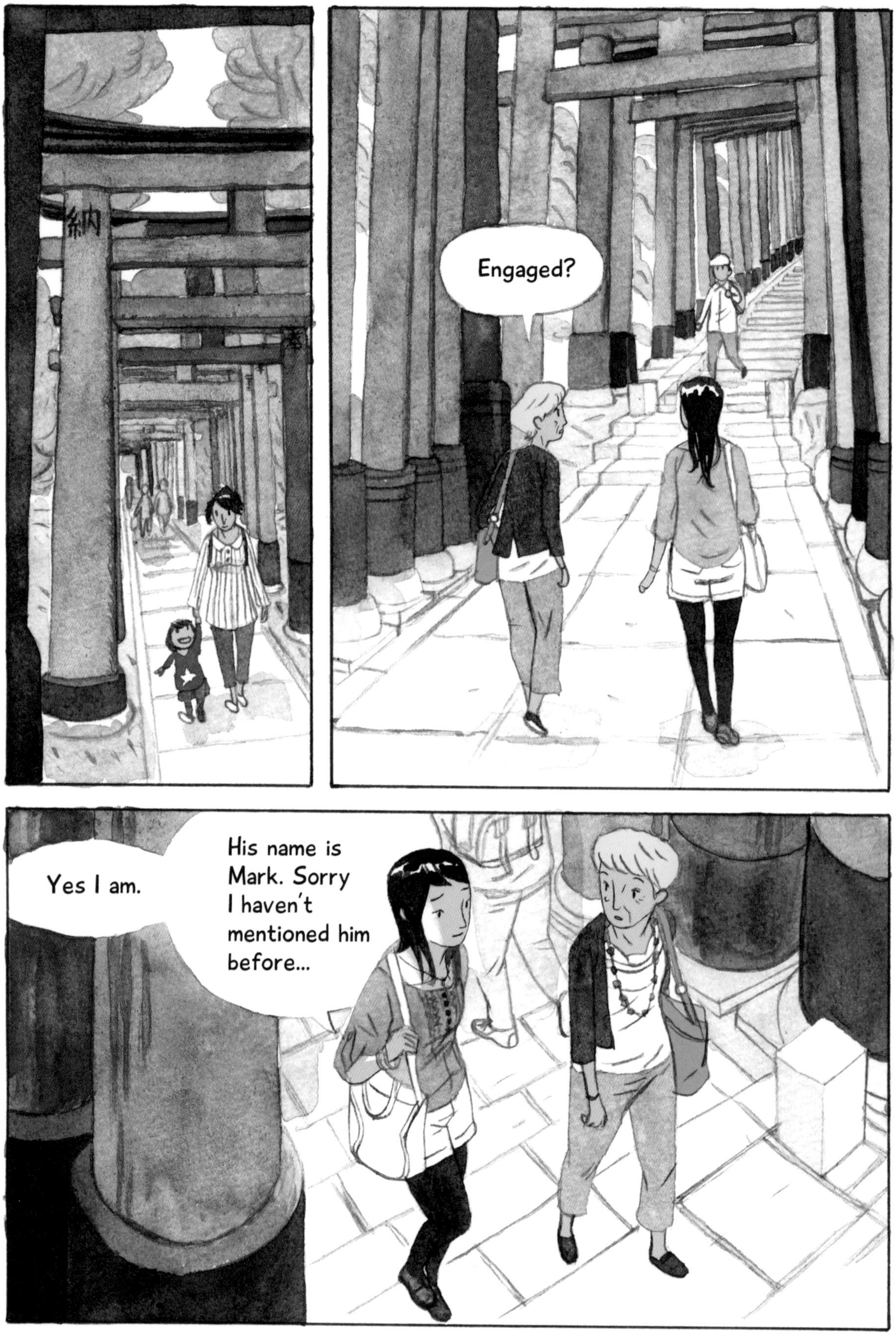
納
Engaged?
Yes I am.
His name is Mark. Sorry I haven't mentioned him before...

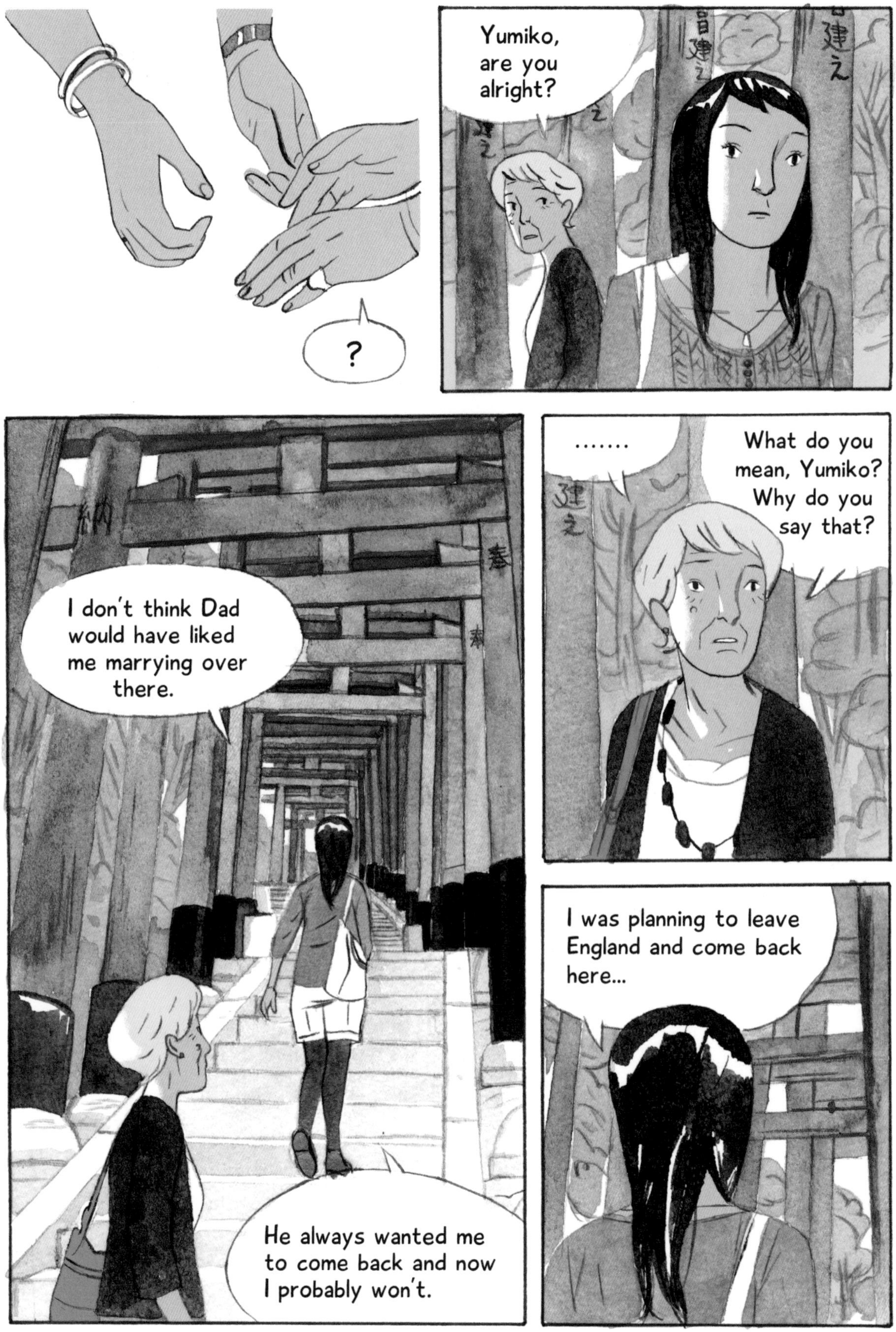
?
Yumiko, are you alright?
I don't think Dad would have liked me marrying over there.
He always wanted me to come back and now I probably won't.
....
What do you mean, Yumiko? Why do you say that?
I was planning to leave England and come back here...

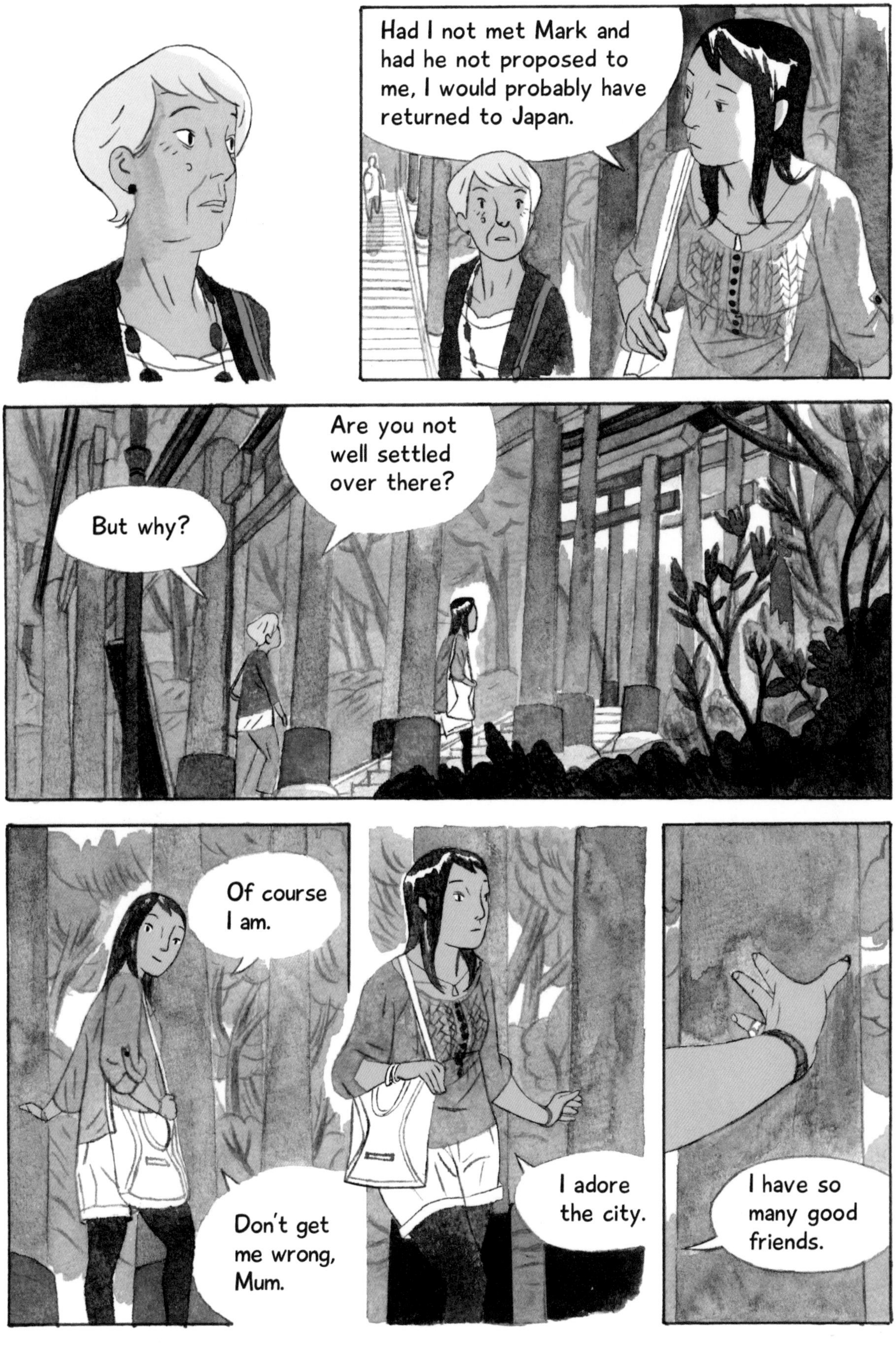
Had I not met Mark and had he not proposed to me, I would probably have returned to Japan.
But why?
Are you not well settled over there?
Of course I am.
Don't get me wrong, Mum.
I adore the city.
I have so many good friends.

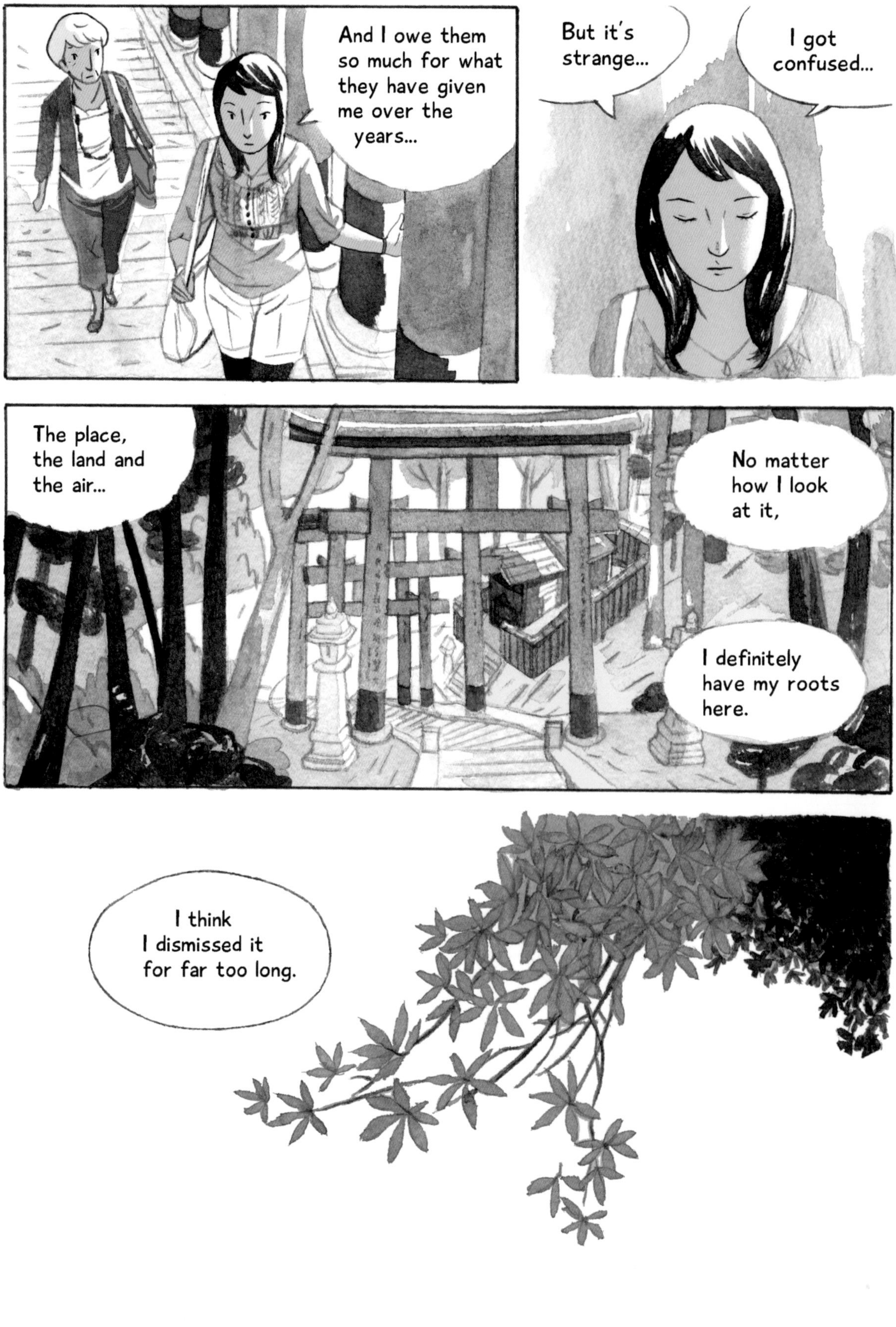
And I owe them so much for what they have given me over the years...
But it's strange...
I got confused...
The place, the land and the air...
No matter how I look at it,
I definitely have my roots here.
I think I dismissed it for far too long.

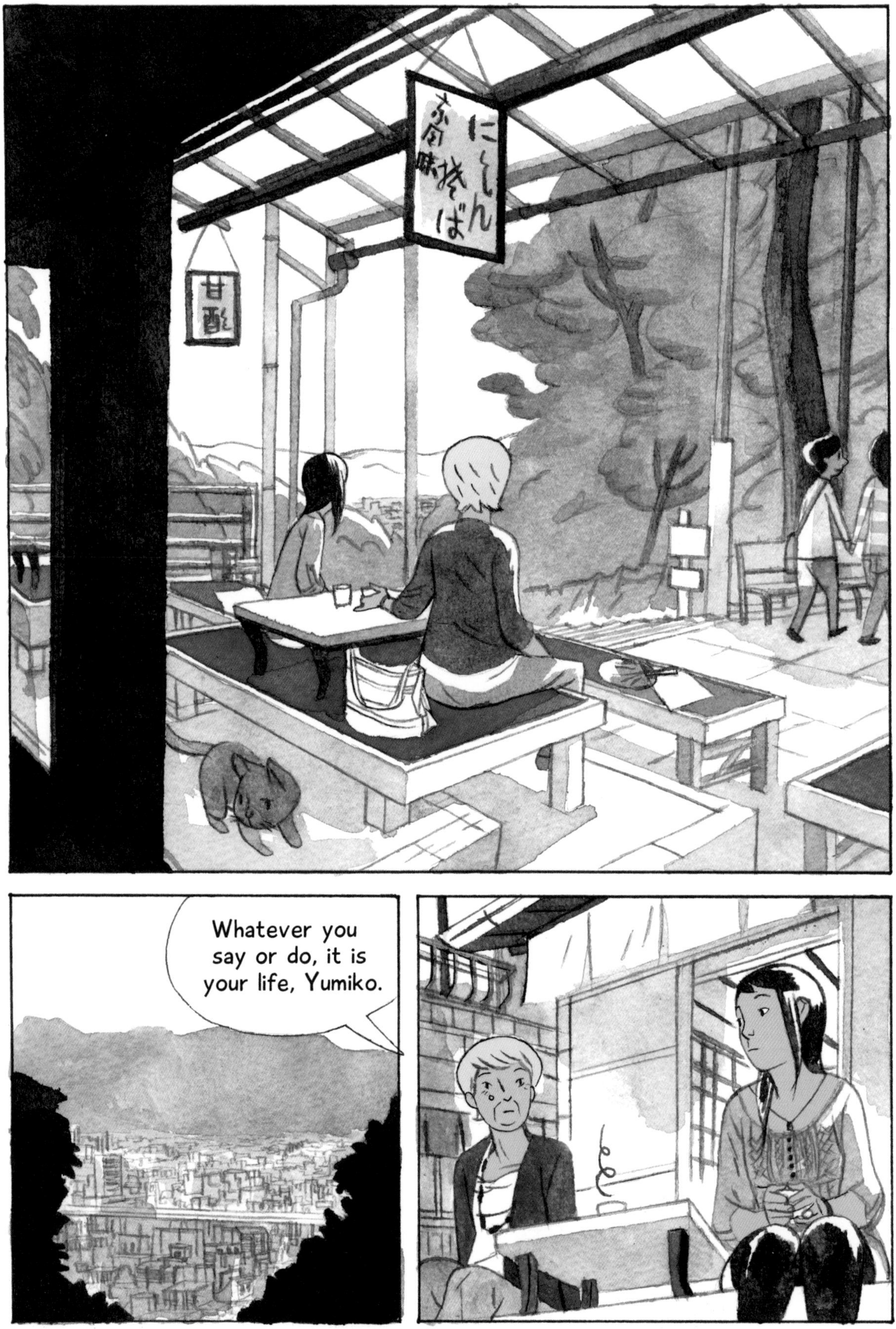
Whatever you say or do, it is your life, Yumiko.

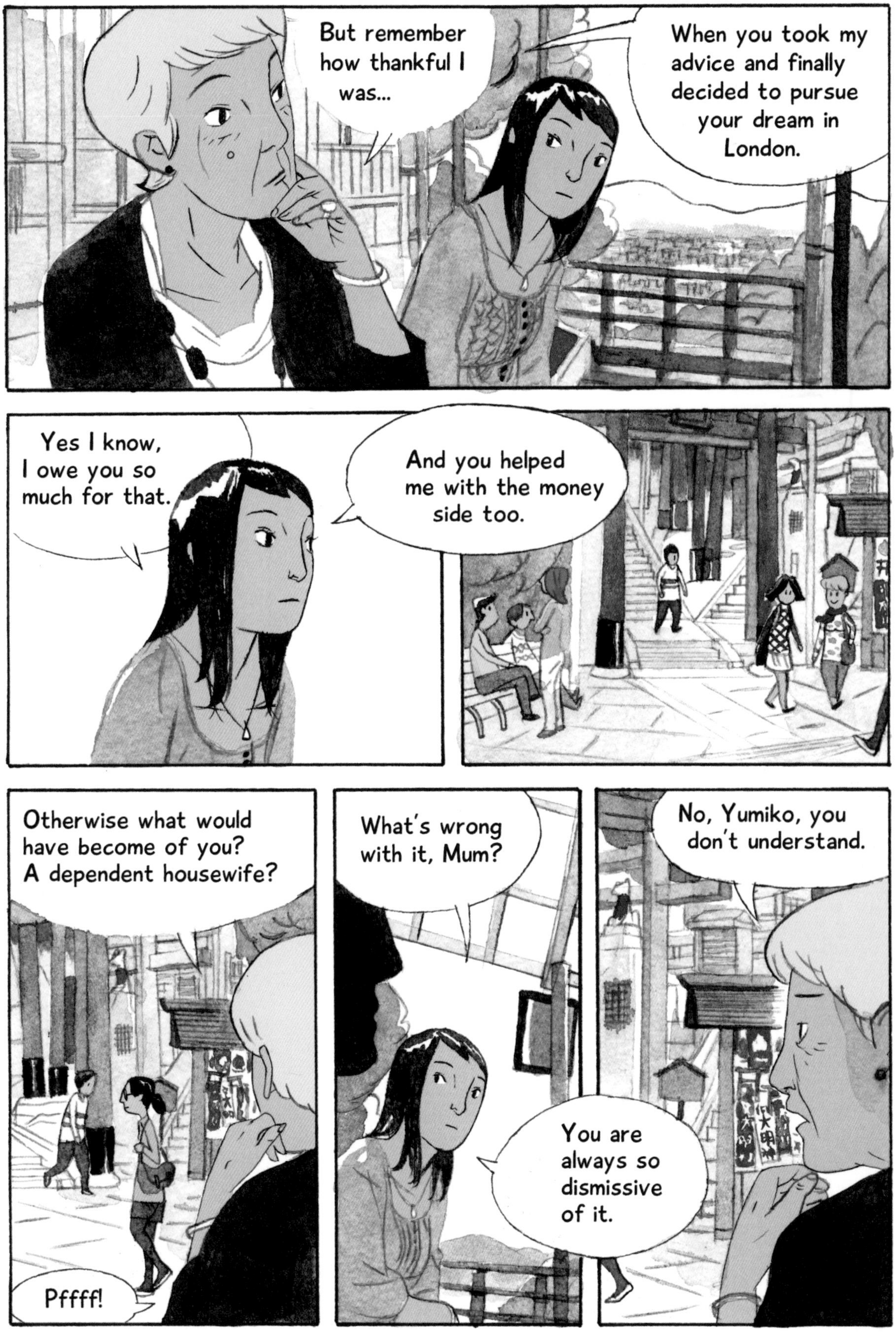
But remember how thankful I was...
When you took my advice and finally decided to pursue your dream in London.
Yes I know, I owe you so much for that.
And you helped me with the money side too.
Otherwise what would have become of you? A dependent housewife?
Pffff!
What's wrong with it, Mum?
You are always so dismissive of it.
No, Yumiko, you don't understand.

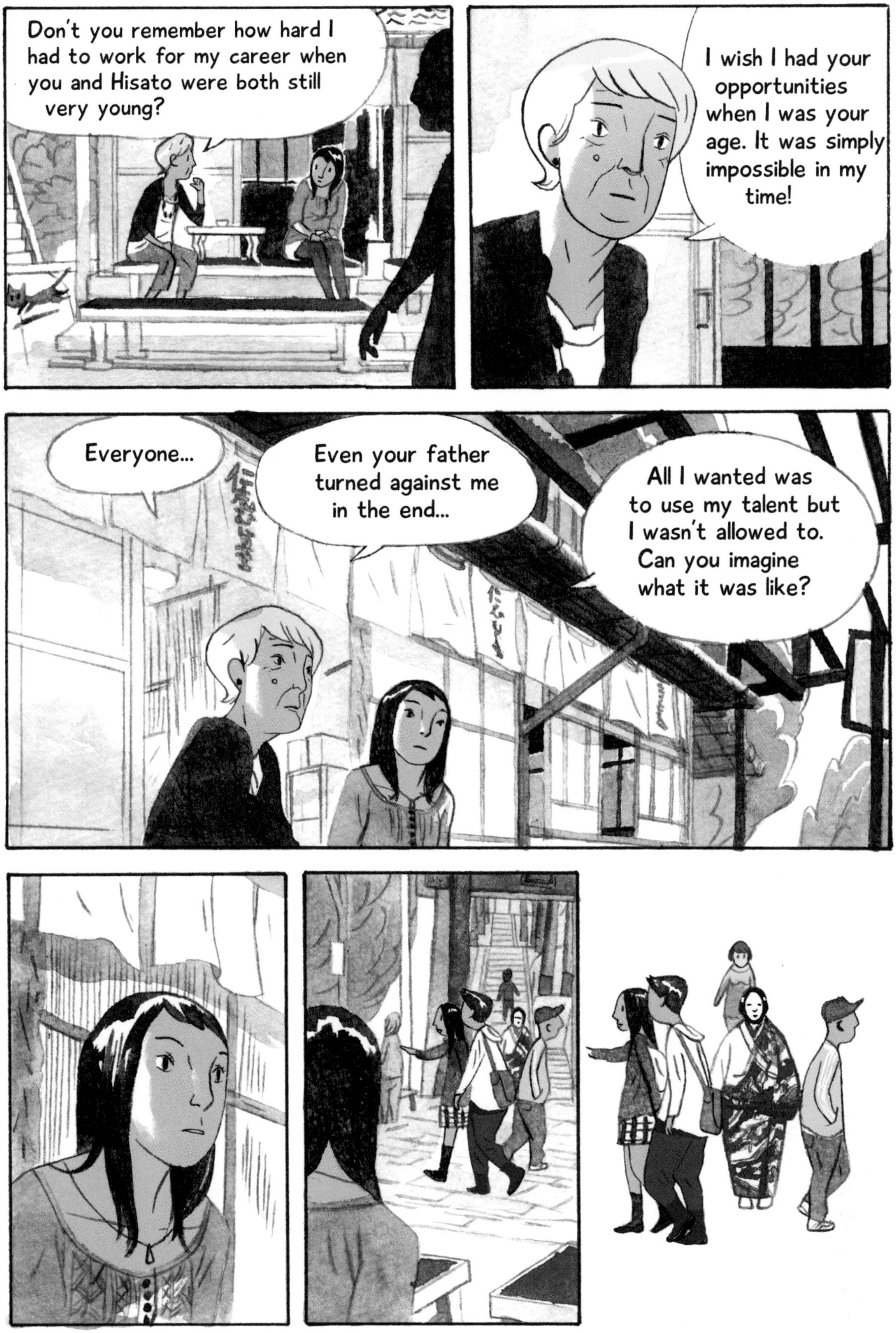
Don't you remember how hard I had to work for my career when you and Hisato were both still very young?
I wish I had your opportunities when I was your age. It was simply impossible in my time!
Everyone...
Even your father turned against me in the end...
All I wanted was to use my talent but I wasn't allowed to. Can you imagine what it was like?

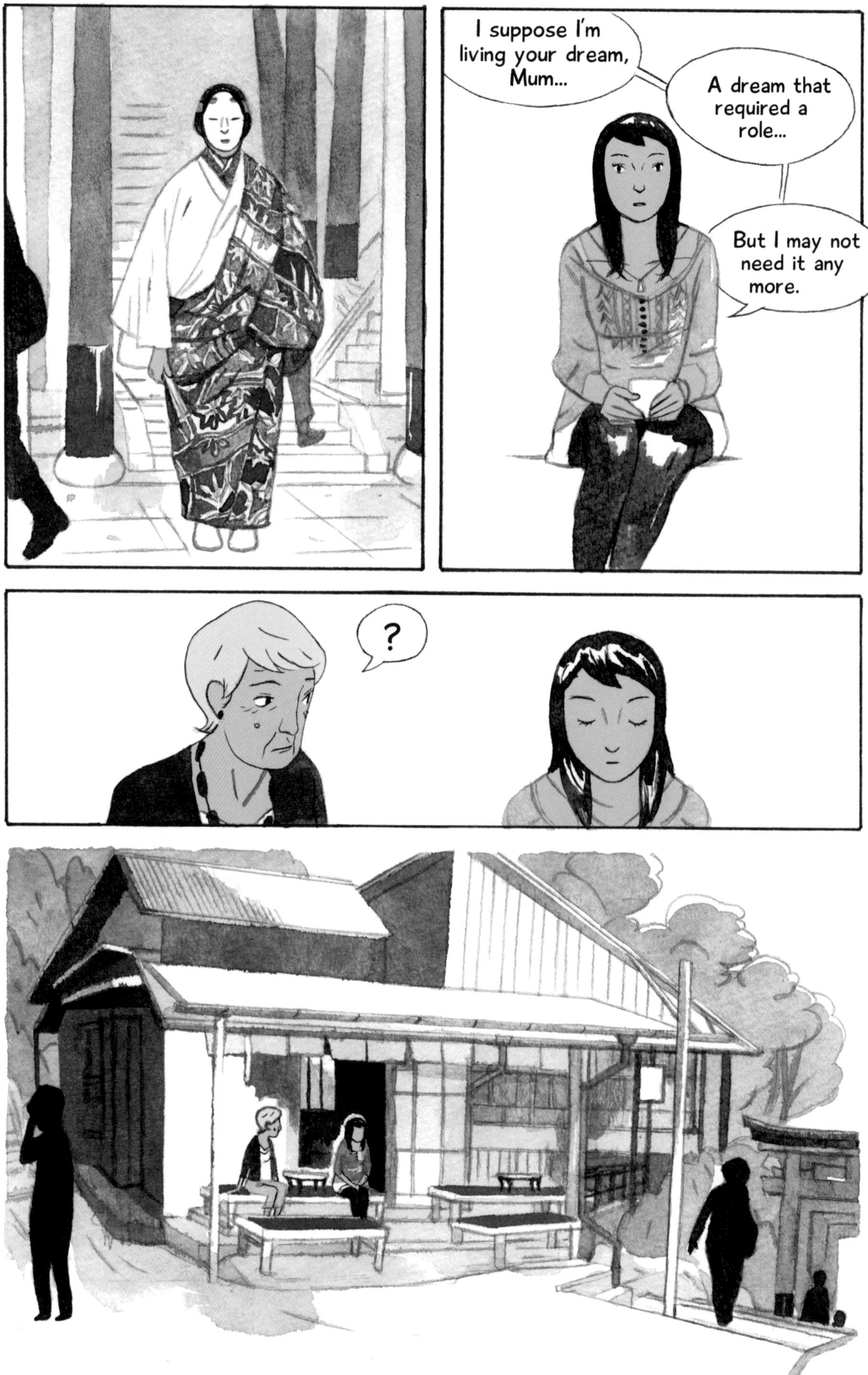
I suppose I'm living your dream, Mum...
A dream that required a role...
But I may not need it any more.
?

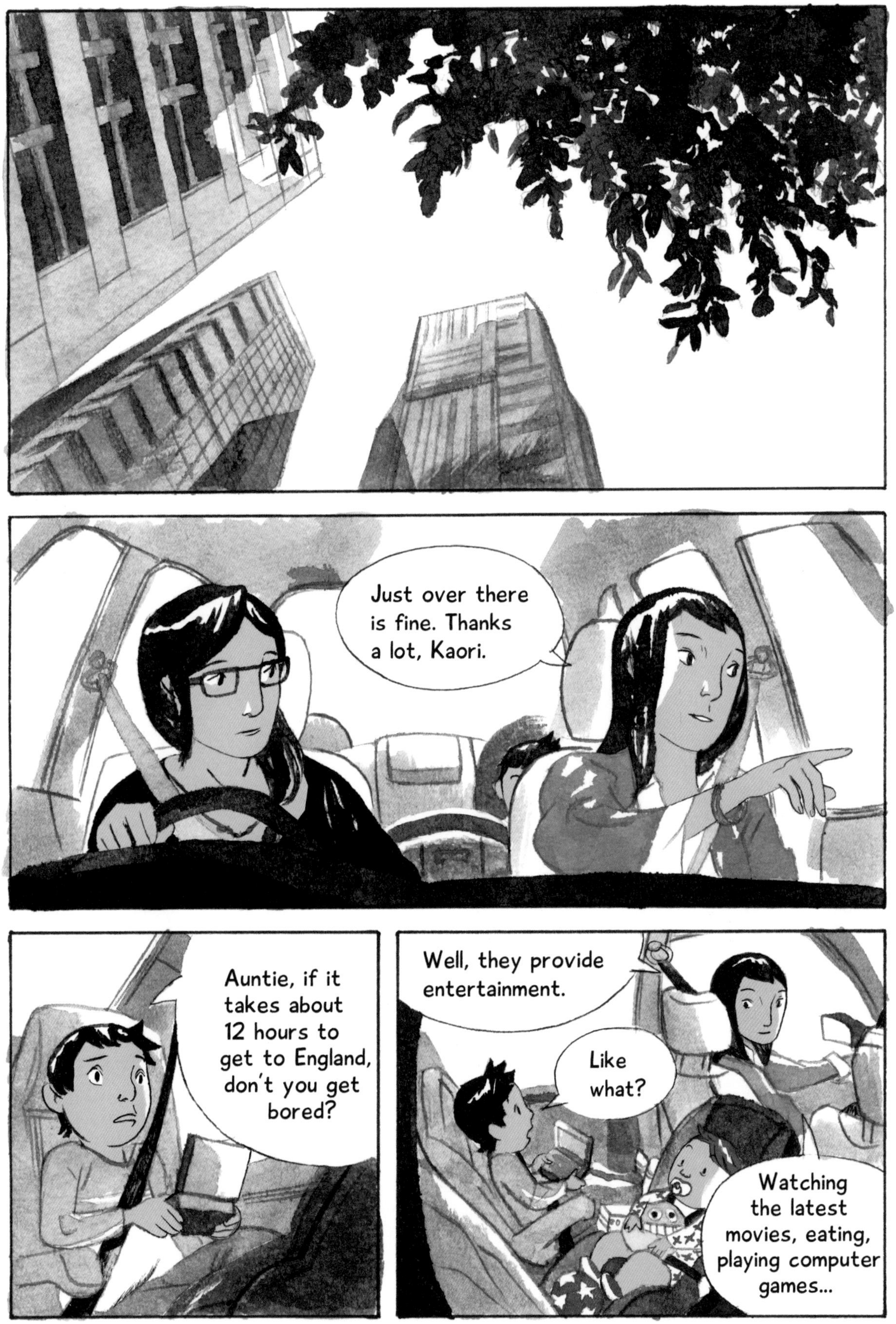
Just over there is fine. Thanks a lot, Kaori.
Auntie, if it takes about 12 hours to get to England, don't you get bored?
Well, they provide entertainment.
Like what?
Watching the latest movies, eating, playing computer games...

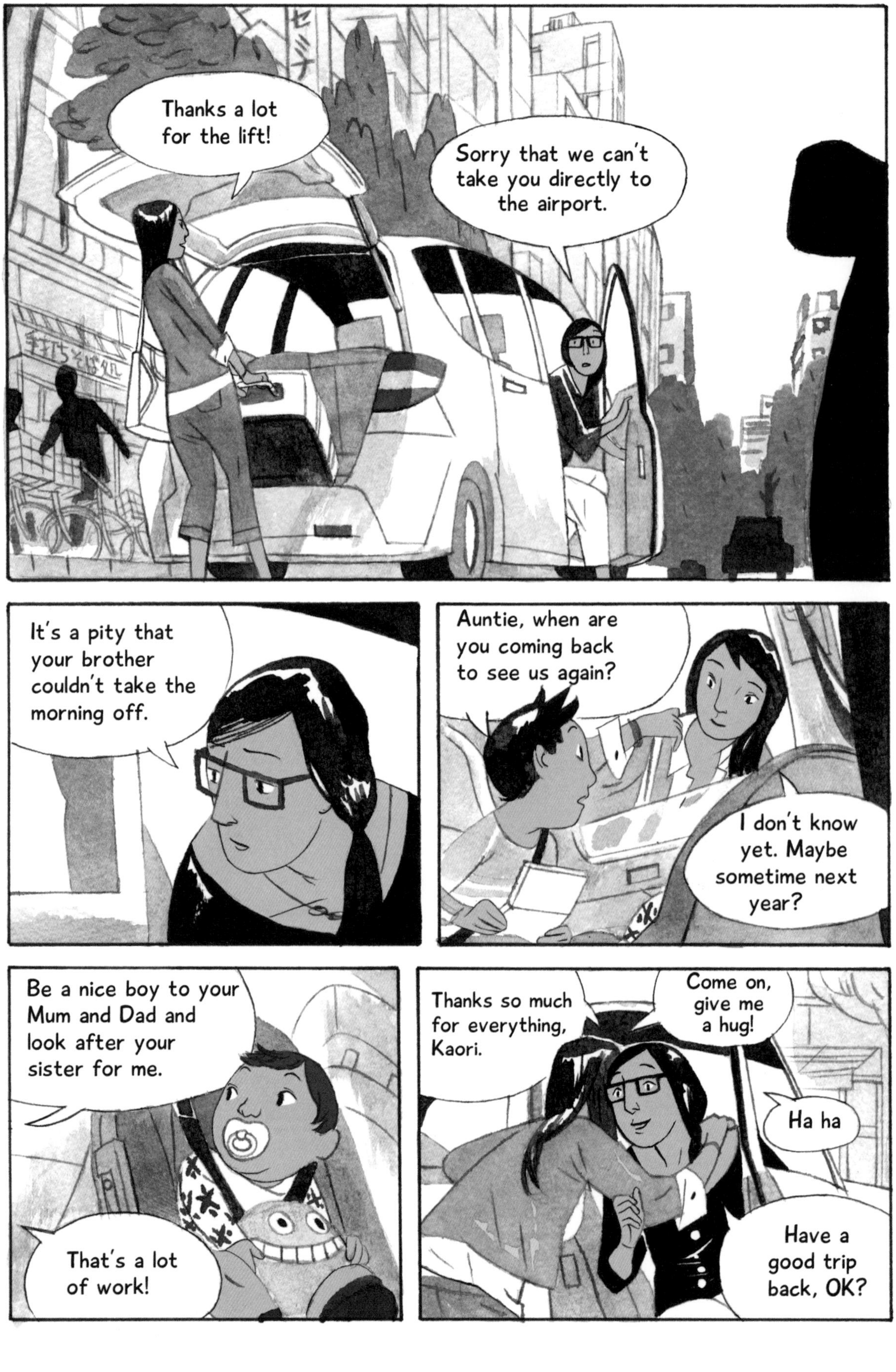
Thanks a lot for the lift!
Sorry that we can't take you directly to the airport.
It's a pity that your brother couldn't take the morning off.
Auntie, when are you coming back to see us again?
I don't know yet. Maybe sometime next year?
Be a nice boy to your Mum and Dad and look after your sister for me.
That's a lot of work!
Thanks so much for everything, Kaori.
Come on, give me a hug!
Ha ha
Have a good trip back, OK?

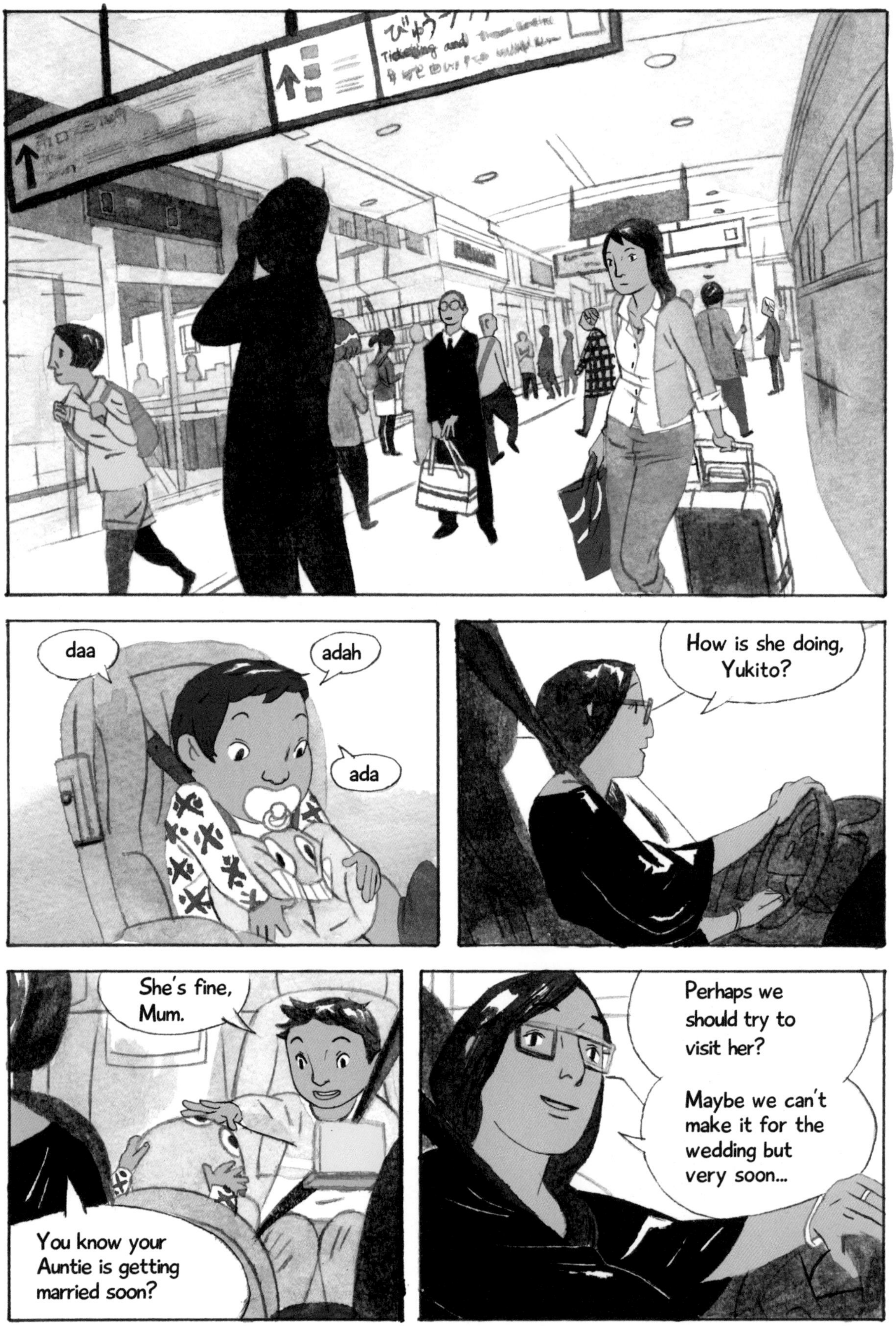
daa
adah
ada
How is she doing, Yukito?
She's fine, Mum.
You know your Auntie is getting married soon?
Perhaps we should try to visit her?
Maybe we can't make it for the wedding but very soon...

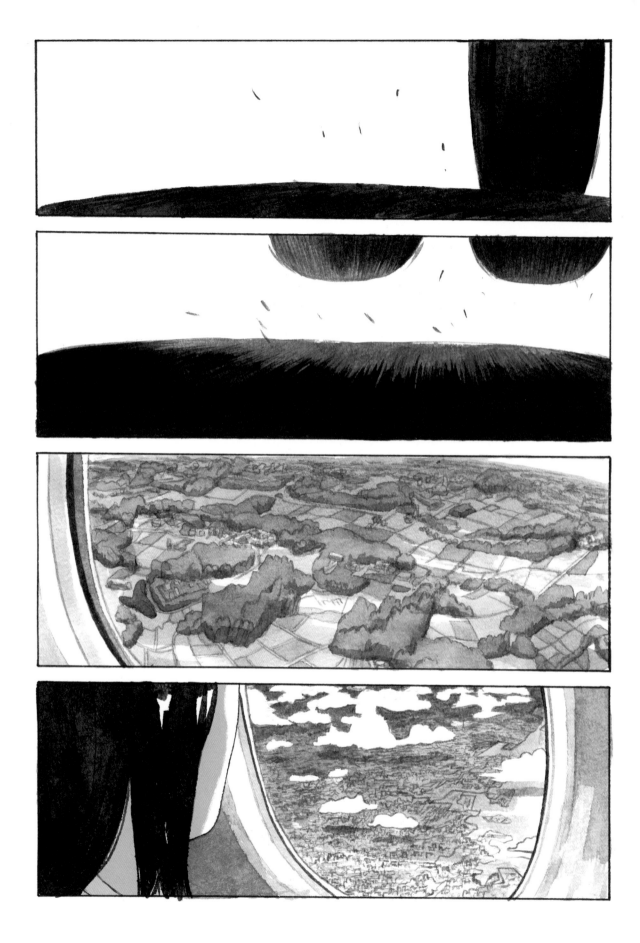

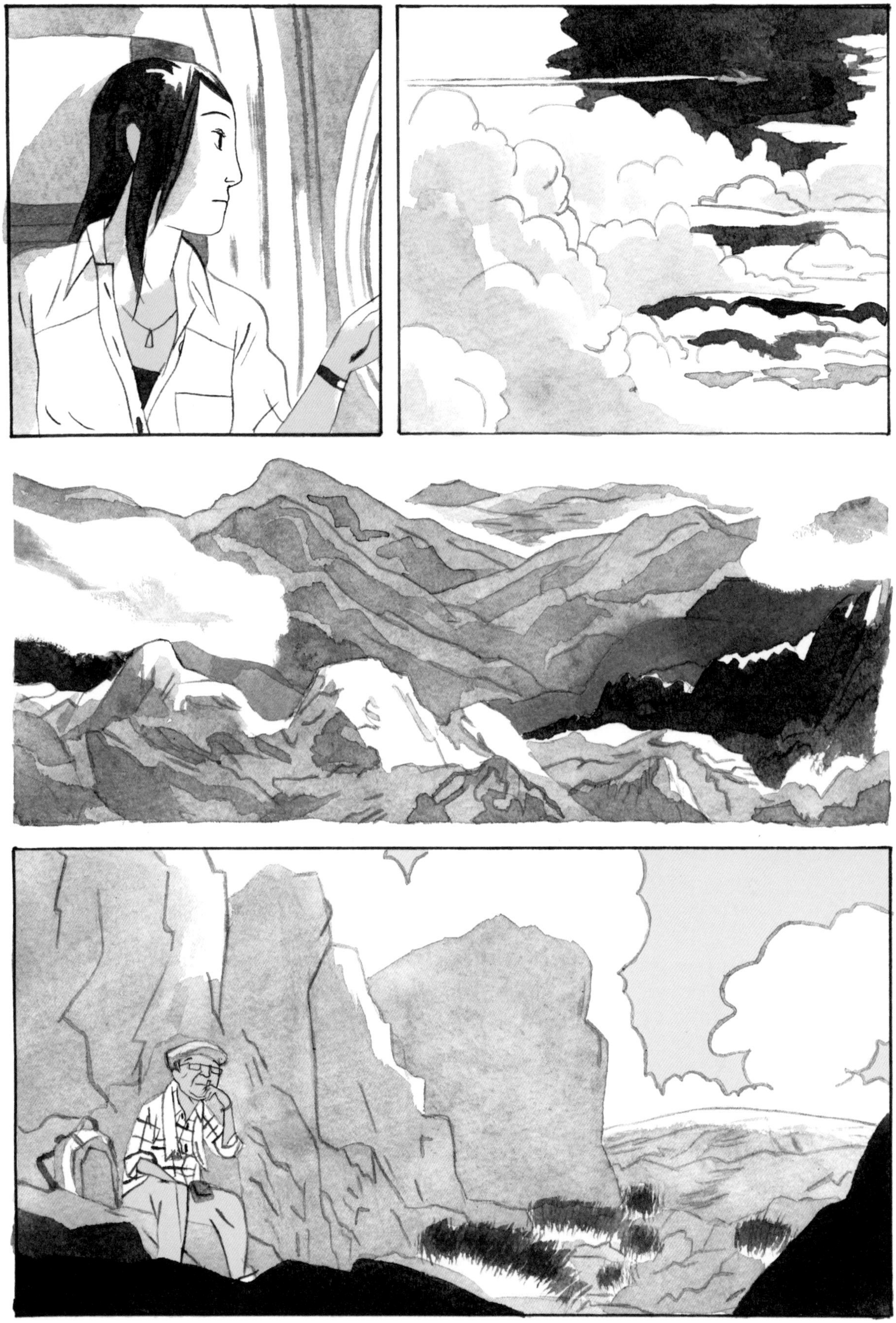

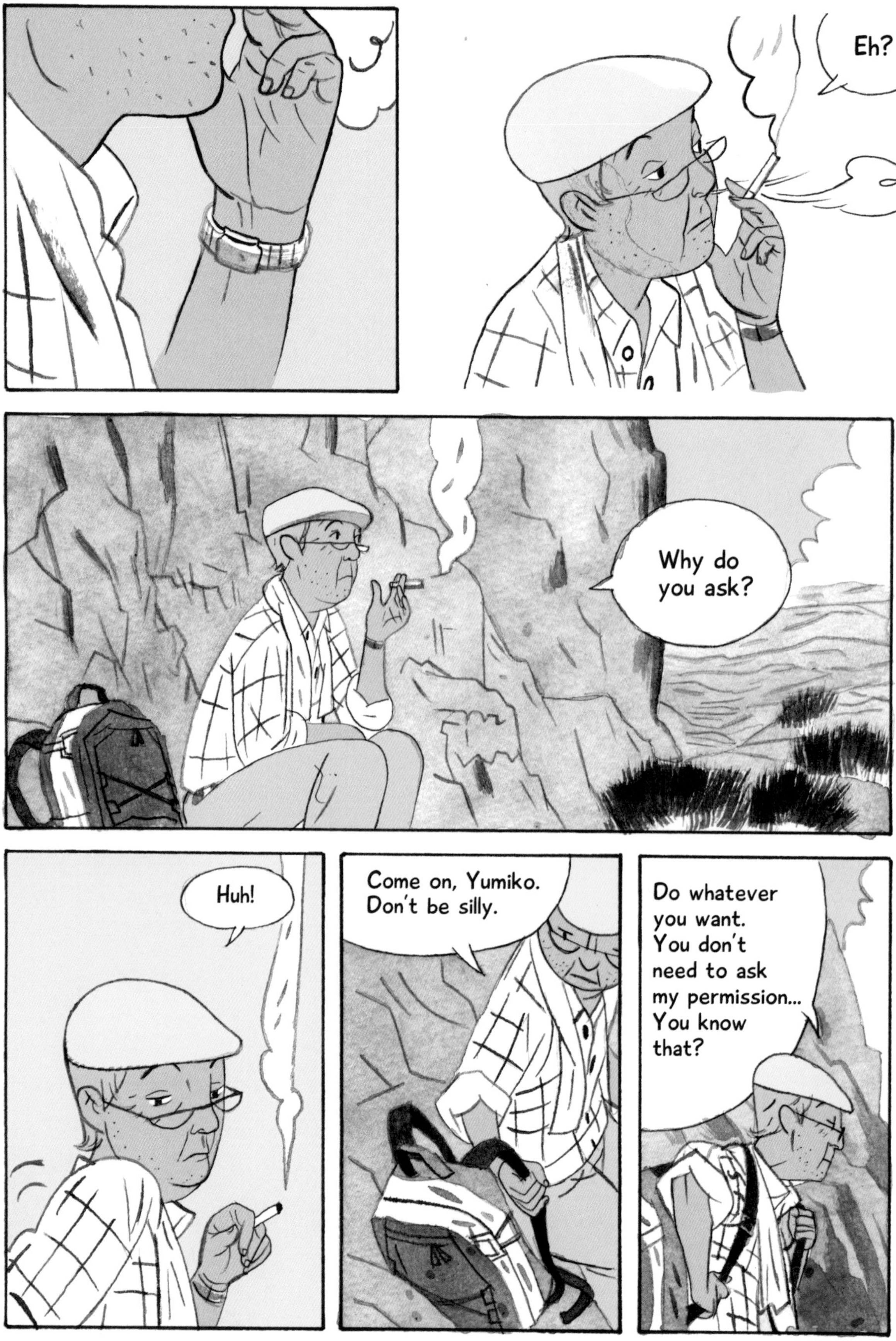
Eh?
Why do you ask?
Huh!
Come on, Yumiko. Don't be silly.
Do whatever you want. You don't need to ask my permission... You know that?

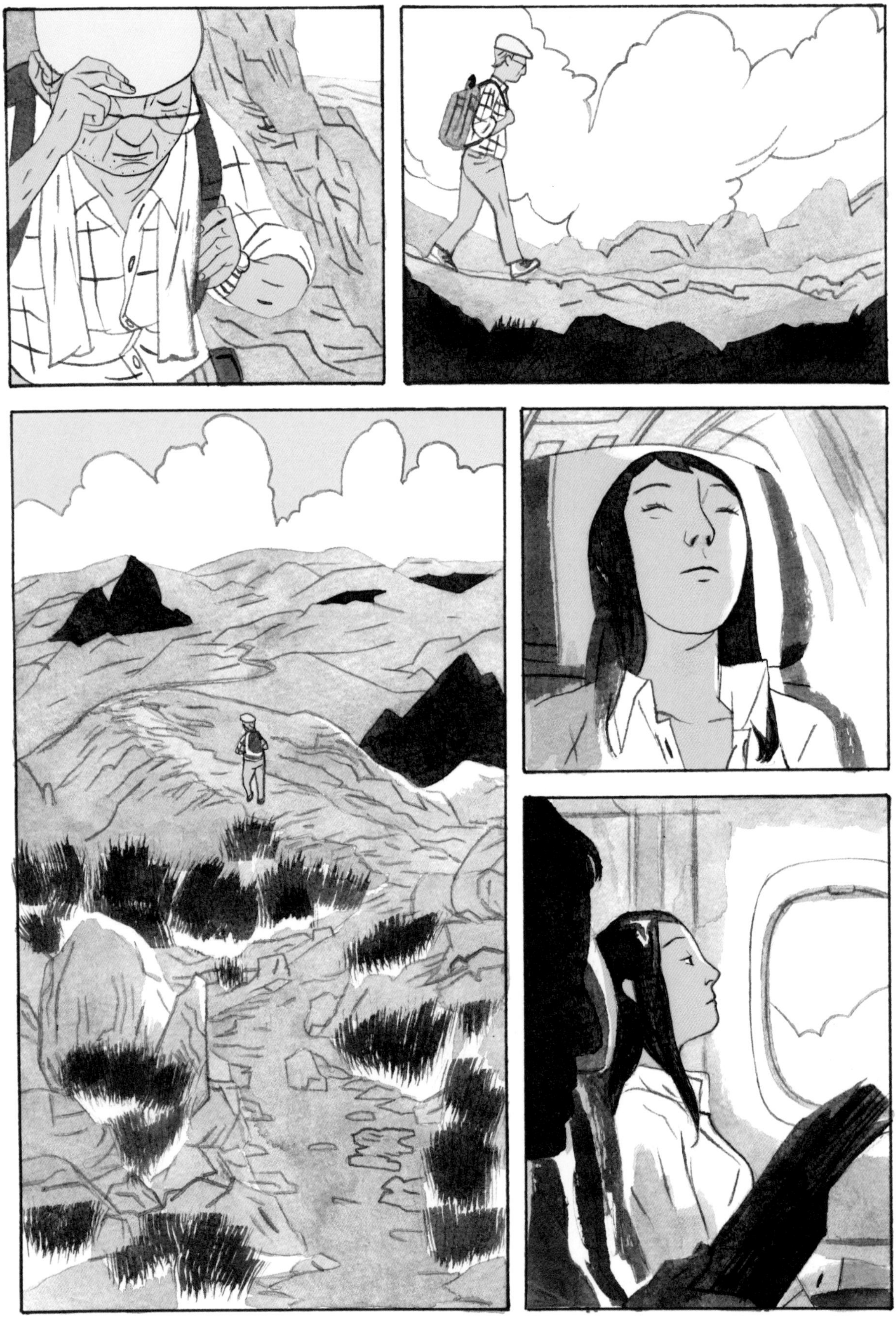

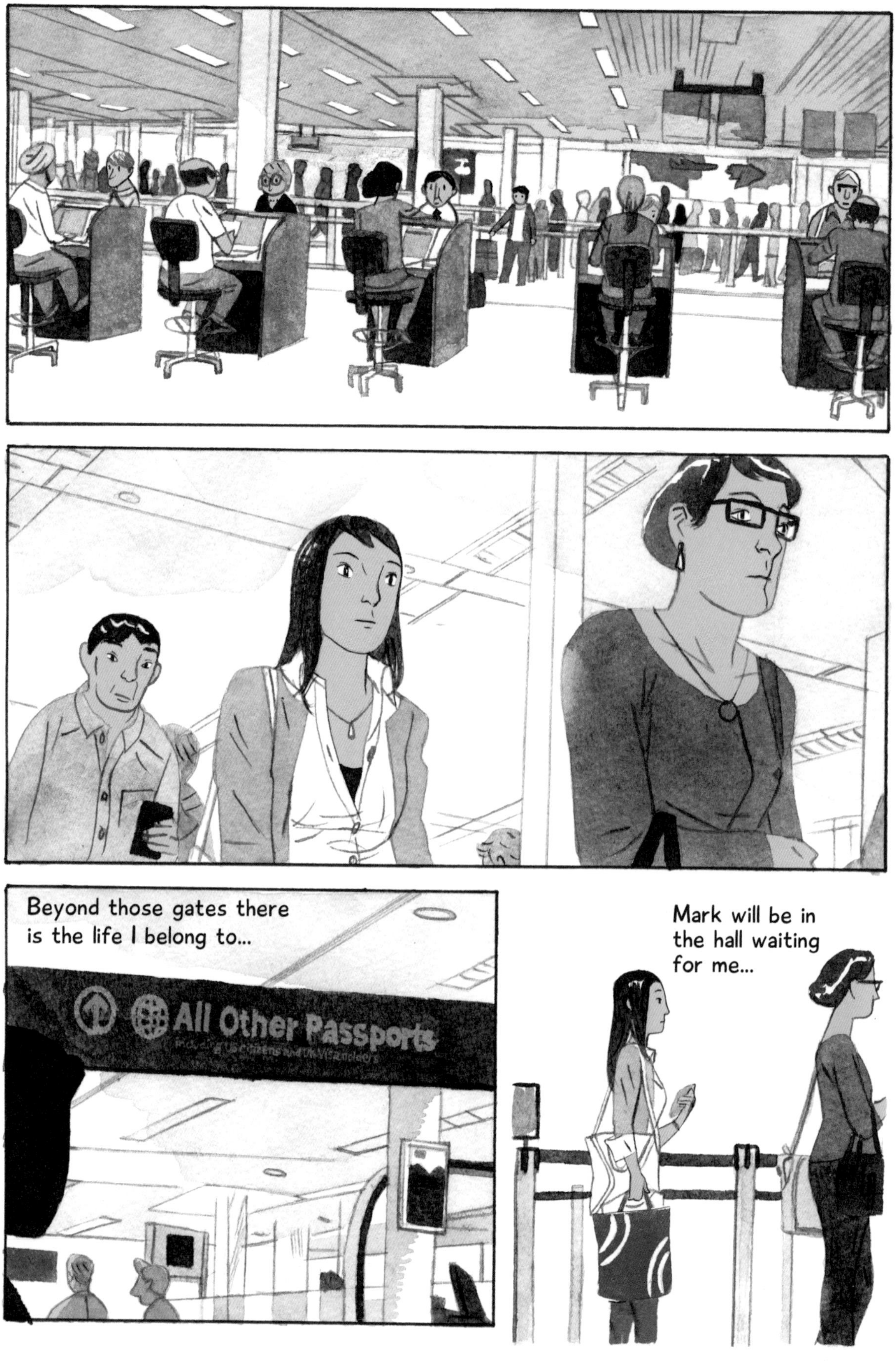
Beyond those gates there is the life I belong to...
All Other Passports
Mark will be in the hall waiting for me...

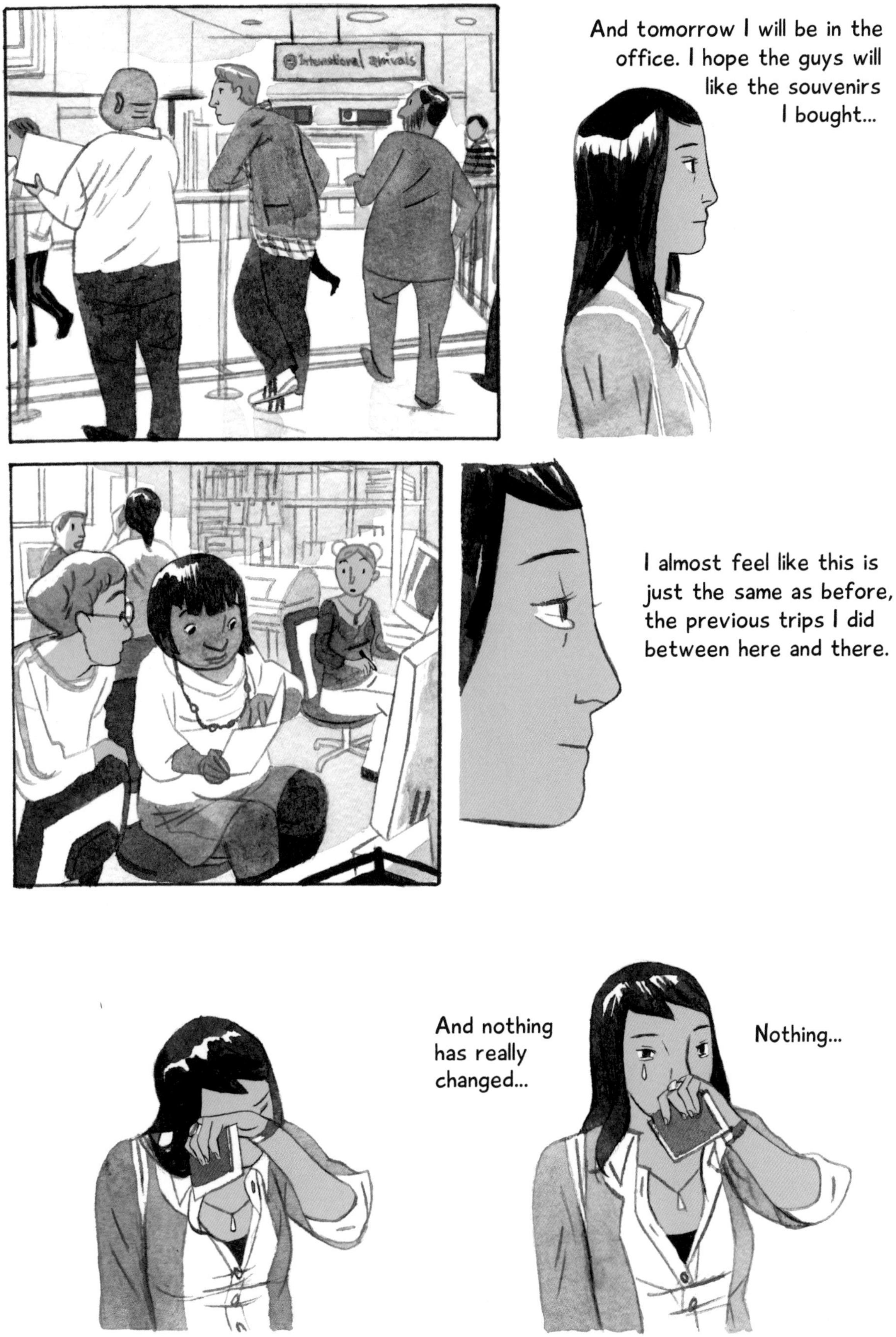
International arrivals
And tomorrow I will be in the office. I hope the guys will like the souvenirs I bought...
I almost feel like this is just the same as before, the previous trips I did between here and there.
And nothing has really changed...
Nothing...

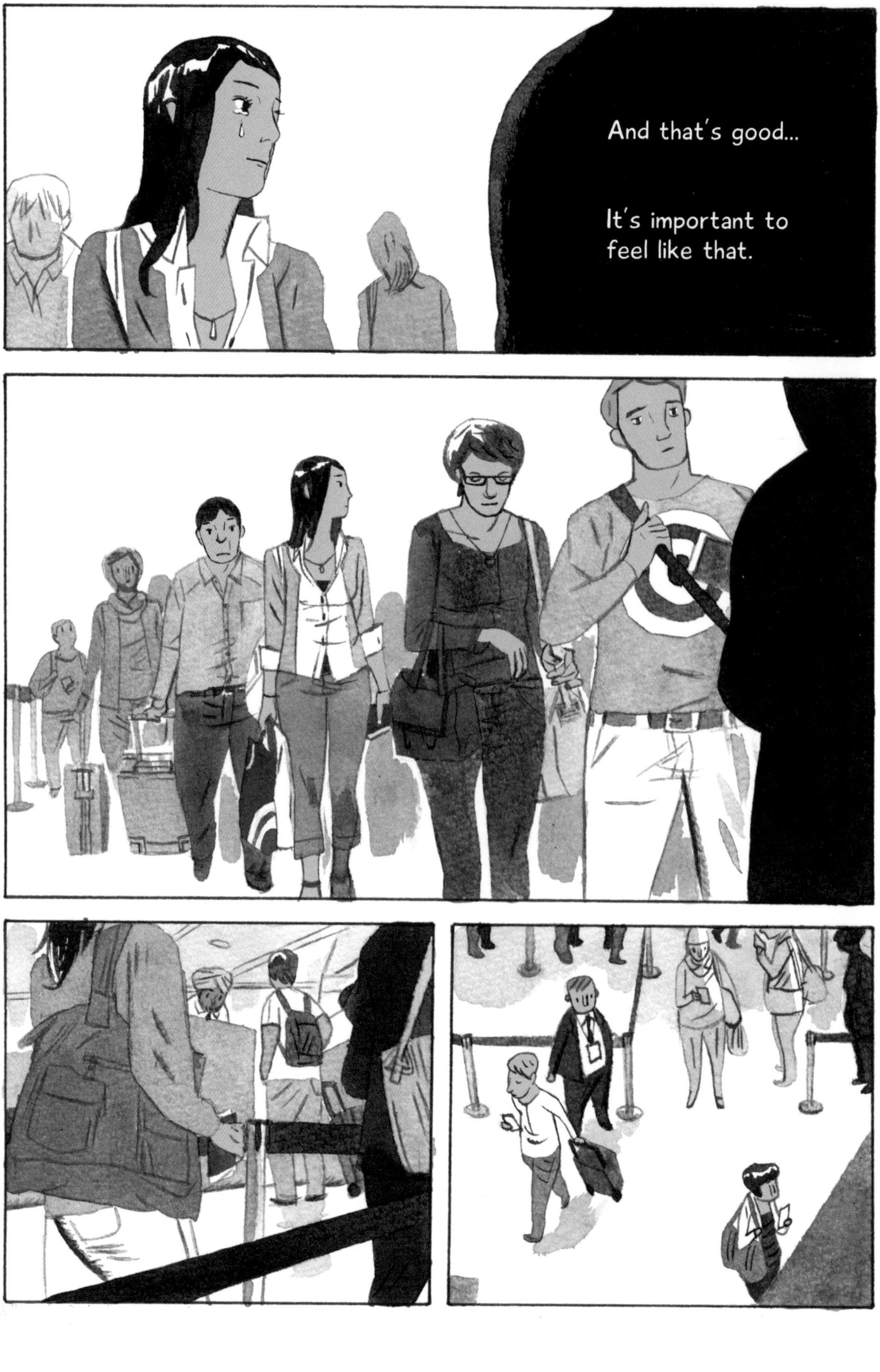
And that's good...
It's important to feel like that.

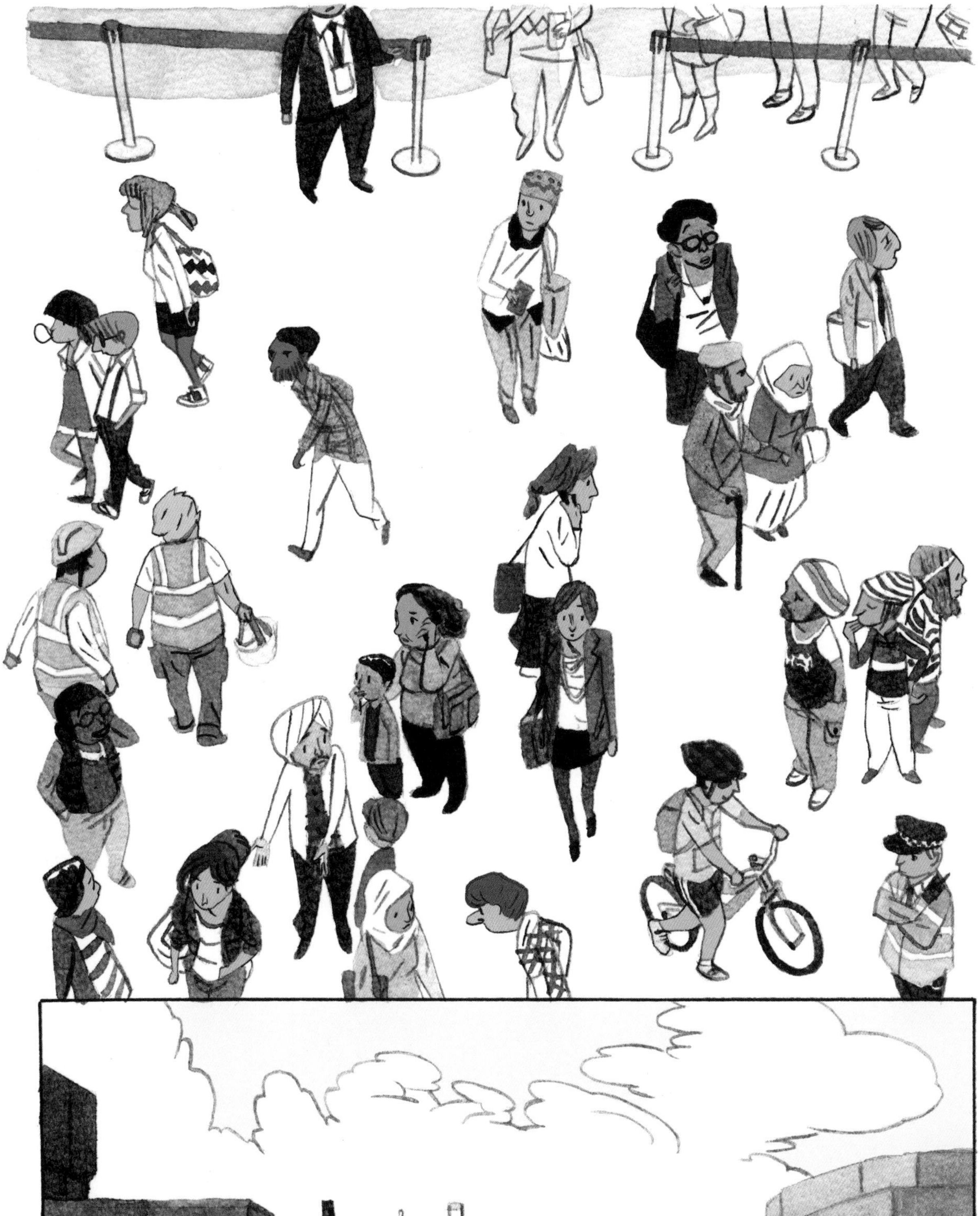

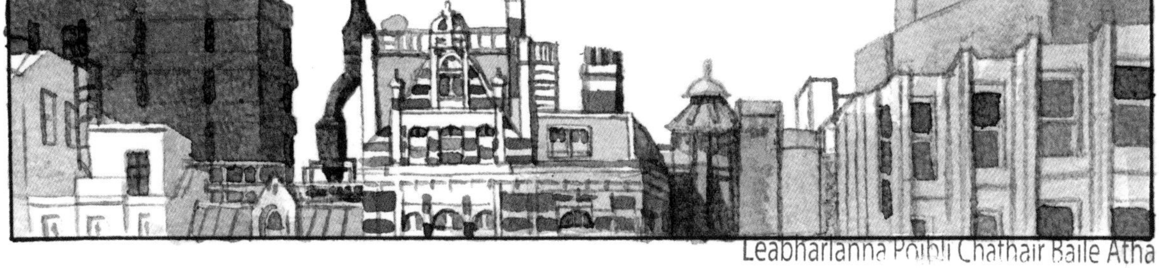

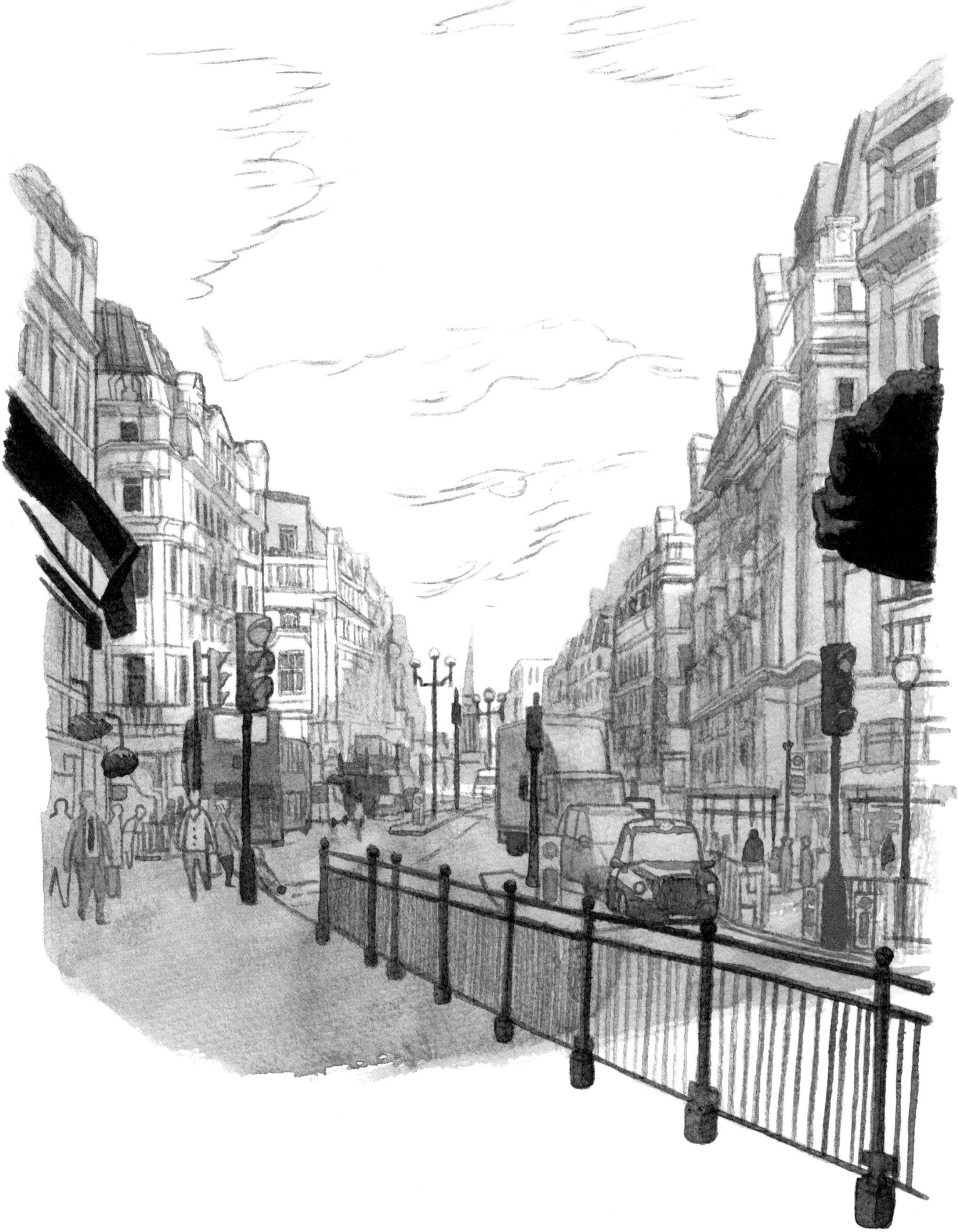

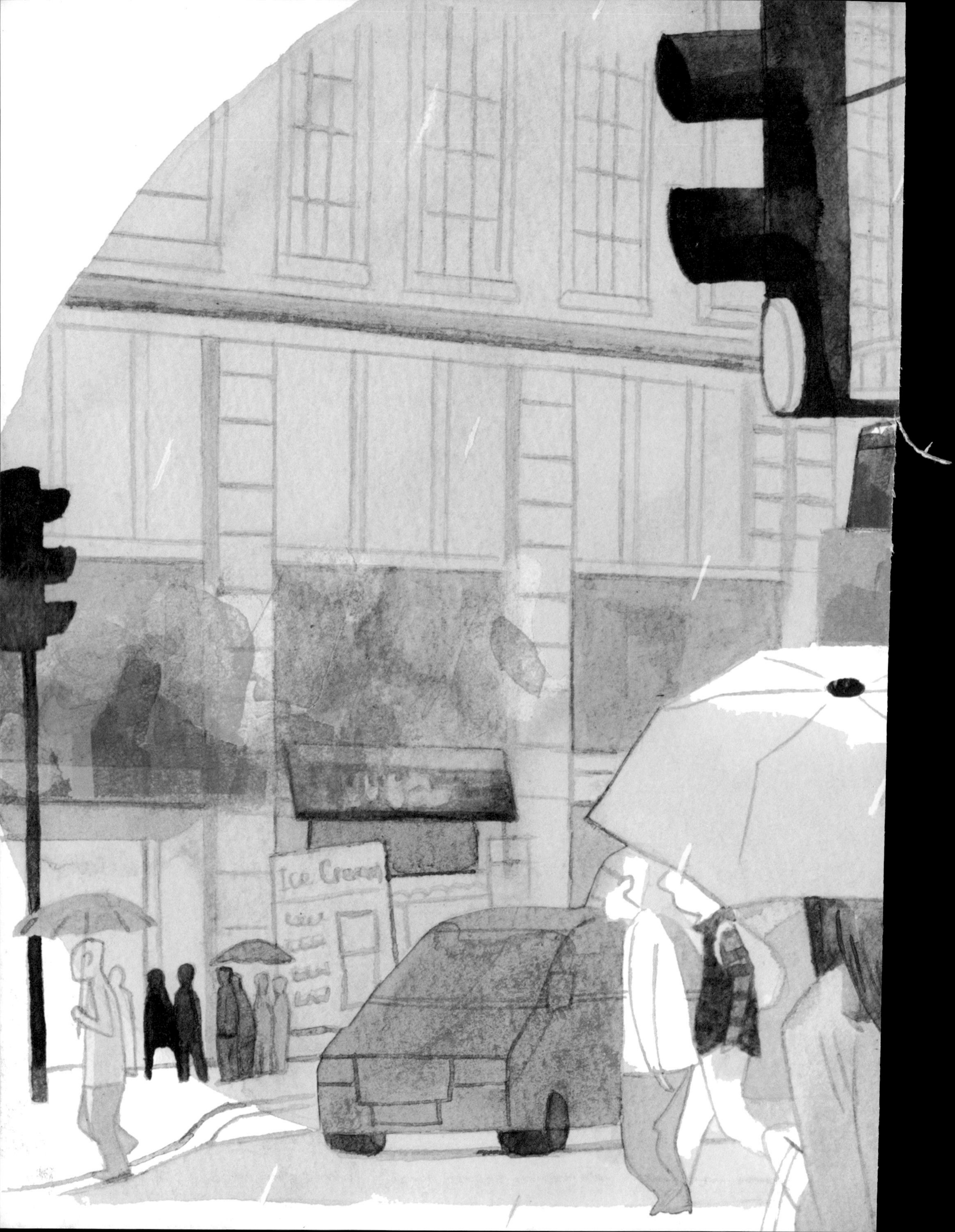
Ice Cream